REPUBLICANISM AND THE AMERICAN GOTHIC

Series Preface

Gothic Literary Studies is dedicated to publishing groundbreaking scholarship on Gothic in literature and film. The Gothic, which has been subjected to a variety of critical and theoretical approaches, is a form which plays an important role in our understanding of literary, intellectual and cultural histories. The series seeks to promote challenging and innovative approaches to Gothic which question any aspect of the Gothic tradition or perceived critical orthodoxy.

Volumes in the series explore how issues such as gender, religion, nation and sexuality have shaped our view of the Gothic tradition. Both academically rigorous and informed by the latest developments in critical theory, the series provides an important focus for scholastic developments in Gothic studies, literary studies, cultural studies and critical theory. The series will be of interest to students of all levels and to scholars and teachers of the Gothic and literary and cultural histories.

Series Editors

Andrew Smith, University of Glamorgan
Benjamin F. Fisher, University of Mississippi

Editorial Board

Kent Ljungquist, Worcester Polytechnic Institute Massachusetts
Richard Fusco, St Joseph's University, Philadelphia
David Punter, University of Bristol
Chris Baldick, University of London
Angela Wright, University of Sheffield
Jerrold E. Hogle, University of Arizona

Republicanism and the American Gothic

Marilyn Michaud

UNIVERSITY OF WALES PRESS
CARDIFF
2009

© Marilyn Michaud, 2009

All rights reserved. No part of this book may be reproduced in any material form (including photocopying or storing it in any medium by electronic means and whether or not transiently or incidentally to some other use of this publication) without the written permission of the copyright owner except in accordance with the provisions of the Copyright, Designs and Patents Act 1988 or under the terms of a licence issued by the Copyright Licensing Agency Ltd, Saffron House, 6–10 Kirby Street, London, EC1N 8TS. Applications for the copyright owner's written permission to reproduce any part of this publication should be addressed to the University of Wales Press, 10 Columbus Walk, Brigantine Place, Cardiff, CF10 4UP.

www.uwp.co.uk

British Library Cataloguing-in-Publication Data
A catalogue record for this book is available from the British Library.

ISBN 978-0-7083-2146-1
e-ISBN 978-0-7083-2233-8

The right of Marilyn Michaud to be identified as author of this work has been asserted by her in accordance with sections 77, 78 and 79 of the Copyright, Designs and Patents Act 1988.

Printed in Great Britain by CPI Antony Rowe, Chippenham, Wiltshire

Contents

Introduction		1
1	Republican Historiography	30
2	Vampires and the Cyclical Theory of History	52
3	The Double and Republican Masculinity	80
4	Conspiracy and Hypocrisy in *Rosemary's Baby*	107
5	Virtue and Corruption in Truman Capote's *In Cold Blood*	142
Afterword		174
Bibliography		177
Index		191

Introduction

> To penetrate fully into a work of literature is finally to make a serious effort to develop the historical imagination, to view the world ... through another culture, another time, another nationality.
>
> Joseph Anthony Mazzeo[1]

The initial task of scholarship devoted to the Gothic is often an attempt at definition: what is Gothic? Typically, the discussion will begin with an exploration of the relationship between the nascent British form and its various progenitors followed by the inevitable conclusion that the term is 'fluid', 'troublesome' and 'mutable'. The solution, Fred Botting suggests, is more criticism: 'Elusive, phantom-like, if not phantasmatic, floating across generic and historical boundaries, Gothic (re) appearances demand and disappoint, and demand again, further critical scrutiny to account for their continued mutation.'[2] In an effort to illuminate the genre, analysis has splintered into a host of thematic, temporal and regional sub-specialities each functioning to demarcate the multiplicity of approaches and the changing interpretative needs orbiting the term 'Gothic'. Yet, while these new readings challenge some durable myths surrounding the production, circulation and interpretation of texts, they too tend to be fragments, telling only part of the story of the Gothic's origin and meaning. The result is that significant explanatory relations often go unrecognized and, in particular, the relationship between the term's literary meaning and its prevalent historical and ideological usages.[3] This is particularly true in relation to the American Gothic which for many critics represents a troublesome contradiction. As Teresa Goddu argues, when modified by the word American, the Gothic loses all its 'usual referents'; not only does it lack the 'self-evident validity of its British counterpart', it is essentially antagonistic to American identity.[4] American Gothic, Robert Miles asserts, is an 'oxymoron signalling its own uncanniness': 'The Gothic ought to have undergone ideological erasure, for its meaning was essentially anti-American: it spelled entrapment, enclosure, the inescapable, parasitic power of the past, the inglorious triumph of class, feudalism, vestigial institutions, and even nature itself.'[5]

While it is no longer contentious to claim that American culture is 'drenched in Gothic sensibility', for many critics, its presence in the land of 'light and affirmation' remains an unremitting paradox.[6] The popularity of American Gothic fiction indicates how ardently critics feel the need to explain the persistence of the form in a political and cultural environment seemingly divorced from traditional Gothic impulses. To account for a Gothic imagination in American culture, analysis has centred on psychology. Seen as a reflection of colonial anxieties, Puritan repression and pathological guilt resulting from the nation's encounter with slavery and Indian massacre, the parameters of the American Gothic are marked primarily by 'psychological, internalised, and predominately racial concerns'.[7] In *Love and Death in the American Novel*, arguably the first work to focus exclusively on American Gothic writing, Leslie Fielder's reading of early American texts exemplifies this approach: 'European Gothic identified blackness with the super-ego and was therefore revolutionary in its implications; the American gothic ... identified evil with the id and was conservative at its deepest level of implications, whatever the intent of its authors.'[8] Unlike their British counterparts, American writers are always in a state of 'beginning, saying for the first time ... what it is like to stand alone before nature, or in a city as appallingly lonely as any virgin forest'. For Fiedler, the Gothic is juvenile and repetitive because it deals primarily with a world of limited experience: a world American authors return to time and again due to their inability 'to deal with adult heterosexual love and [their] consequent obsession with death, incest, and innocent homosexuality'. Contemporary writers, he claims, are doomed to repeat these patterns because they share a similar consciousness and the inescapable conditions of American life. Therefore, for Fiedler, the Gothic must be '*symbolically* understood, its machinery and décor translated into metaphors for a terror psychological, social and metaphysical'.[9]

Fiedler's analysis has had enormous influence on contemporary readings of American Gothic fiction. Propelled by his unequivocal announcement that the American novel is 'pre-eminently a novel of terror', subsequent critics constructed their analysis of the Gothic around the assumption that 'the psyche is more important than society'.[10] As an explanation for why the Gothic is 'so at home on such inhospitable ground', Eric Savoy contends that Gothic narratives express 'a profound anxiety about historical crimes and perverse human desires that cast their shadow over what many would like to be the sunny American republic'. Like Fielder, Savoy views the American Gothic as 'a pathological symptom rather than a proper literary movement'.[11] In *American Gothic: New Interventions in a National Narrative*, Martin and Savoy claim their project is 'indebted and in many way supplementary' to Fiedler's 'pioneering conjunction of historicism and psychoanalysis'. For these critics, Fiedler's analysis has lost none of its 'freshness' and provides 'the cultural frame for subsequent inquiry'.[12] Yet, however valuable Fiedler's work has been to our understanding of American Gothic, it is useful to remember that his interpretative framework arises out of a political culture that eschewed social and ideological conflict in favour of an all-pervading liberal consensus. It was, as Daniel Bell declared, the 'end of ideology', a period in which academics were less interested in political history than in wresting the fiction of the 'American renaissance' away from the Marxist intellectuals of the 1920s and 1930s and replacing it with a pluralist, consensus model free of the anti-capitalism of the Progressives and the formulism of the New Critics. The intellectual movement from Progressive to new liberal ideology was also contemporaneous with the development of the American studies curriculum in the 1950s and a new-found interest in the study of culture. Crystallizing this change was Lionel Trilling's *The Liberal Imagination*, a work that would come to dominate cultural theory in the mid twentieth century. While conservatives called for 'a life-drive in literature, for immersion in the American past, for recognition of progress and the goodness of man', Trilling emphasized 'the disenchantment of our culture with culture'.[13] If the Progressive school interpreted American history as edging ever closer toward a form of democracy that would expose the material roots of conflict in class struggle, post-war liberals were suspicious of a linear model of progress and substituted a model of history characterized by ambiguity, paradox and irony.[14] Trilling's novel, *The Middle of the Journey* (1947), exposes this interest in the new dialectic, a belief in the self finding a middle way through a confrontation with reality and experience. Although Trilling shared the Progressive desire to reveal the underlying forces of history, his goal was synthesis, not opposition: it was a model that posited, as his novel's title suggests, a 'middle landscape' rejecting the materialistic emphasis on economics or extremism in politics in favour of the internal human psyche. As Russell Reising observes, Trilling's work 'presaged a general shift in aesthetic evaluation, an elevation of works which tended to see reality as an ambiguous fabric and a denigration of those which dealt frankly with social, political, and economic matters'. In this new evaluation of 'realism', '[p]rotest was out, equipoise was in'. The result was an 'obsession with the search for symbols, allegories and mythic patterns' in American literature.[15]

Coetaneous to this intellectual movement was the political determination to redefine liberalism. As Marxism and the Communist party faded from the American intellectual scene, the nineteenth-century concept of liberalism went into decline. The shift began with the outbreak of the Second World War and the federal government's decade-long curbing of individual liberties. The Alien Registration Act (1940), the Selective Service Act (1940), the conferring of permanent status on the Un-American Activities Committee (1945), federal loyalty programmes and the passage of the McCarran Internal Security Act (1950) outlawing Communism, all resulted in what many liberals viewed as a garrison state using police state methods. The effect was 'to pose a conflict between national security and individual liberty'. In this climate, the optimism and nostalgia of the liberal imagination weakened and '[f]ear settled upon large segments of the citizenry; silence followed; and dissent seemed almost dead'. Individual liberty, the mainstay of traditional liberalism, was suddenly under threat by the growth of the centralized state:

Introduction

The growth of the corporation in an industrialized and interdependent society also promised economic security to those who fitted into the corporate structure. But such people, the faceless organization men, stood to lose their freedom and their identity. The liberal's faith in progress and science as avenues which would liberate the individual had brought him to the bleak possibility that these avenues would instead eliminate the individual.

What emerged in its place is what Eisinger termed the 'new liberalism'; 'chastened' and 'modified', it projected an ambiguous and tortured vision which recognized the limitations and problems it had previously been unable to identify.[16] This revised liberalism originated from a sense of betrayal and disillusionment after the Moscow show trials and Stalin's nonaggression pact with Hitler. In 'Our country and our culture', Philip Rahv, editor of the *Partisan Review*, summarized the prevalent view: 'Among the factors entering into the change, the principal one, to my mind, is the exposure of the Soviet myth and the consequent resolve (shared by nearly all but the few remaining fellow travellers) to be done with Utopian illusions and heady expectations.'[17] From the perspective of new liberalism, the Progressive conception of reality was naive and extreme; instead, in both politics and culture, the centre was the place to be. 'The thrust of the democratic faith', declared Arthur Schlesinger, Jr., 'is away from fanaticism; it is towards compromise, persuasion, and consent in politics, towards tolerance and diversity in society.'[18]

Liberal consensus politics had enormous influence on readings of American Gothic fiction. When Richard Chase set out to define the American novel, he found it to be 'shaped by the contradictions and not by the unities and harmonies of our culture', and founds his tradition on the thesis that Americans do not write social fiction.[19] In *The American Novel and its Tradition*, he conceives of an isolated hero on a quest through a symbolic universe unfettered by the pressure of social limits. Stirred by the 'aesthetic possibilities of radical forms of alienation, contradiction, and disorder', the American novel is essentially romantic. 'In a romance', Chase explained, '"experience" has less to do with human beings as "social creatures" than as individuals. Heroes, villains, victims, legendary types, confronting other individuals or confronting mysterious or other dire forces – this is what we meet in romances.'[20] One of the central assumptions of pluralism was that American writers adopted a variety of literary strategies as a way of compensating for their impoverished social existence. Paradoxically, in their attempt to canonize the writers of the American renaissance, critics avoided association with the Gothic while acknowledging its prevalence in American literature. As Goddu notes, the term 'Gothic' and its popular connotations are substituted with a literary vocabulary more amenable to a clean or, we might say, liberal canon.[21] Chase, for example, subsumes Gothic under the heading of melodrama:

> The term [Gothic] has taken on a general meaning beyond the Mrs. Radcliffe kind of thing and is often used rather loosely to suggest violence, mysteries, improbabilities, morbid passions, inflated and complex language of any sort. It is a useful word but since, in its general reference, it becomes confused with 'melodrama', it seems sensible to use 'melodrama' for the general category and reserve 'Gothic' for its more limited meaning.[22]

For Chase, the Gothic's 'limited meaning' is characterized by the romances of Radcliffe, Lewis and Godwin and their 'ill-conceived sensational happenings and absurd posturings of character and rhetoric'. Brockden Brown's work departs from the Gothic because he inaugurates 'that particular vision of things that might be described as a heightened and mysteriously portentous representation of abstract symbols and ideas on the one hand and the involution of the private psyche' on the other. Chase elevates Brown's work from its social and political referents to the realm of psycho-symbolic realism. *Edgar Huntly*, for example, is Gothic only in tone, in its 'highly wrought effect of horror, surprise, victimization, and the striving for abnormal psychological states'; only in its irony, symbolism and psychological interiority does Brown's novel rise above the Gothic to become Romance.[23]

Critics who focused primarily on twentieth-century Gothic fiction equally ignored the genre's historical or political contours in favour of terrors psychological. In *New American Gothic*, Irving Malin locates the distinction between contemporary Gothic writers and their nineteenth-century predecessors in their lack of interest in political tensions and their engagement with the 'disorder of the buried life'. In Malin's analysis, 'the writers of the new American Gothic are aware of tensions between ego and super-ego, self and society; they study the field of psychological conflict'. Organized around the theme of narcissism, for Malin the typical Gothic hero is crippled by self-love. Contrasted with those heroes found in Hawthorne and Melville, who are 'great' and 'Faustian' in their narcissism, the characters of the new American Gothic are weaklings who cannot demonstrate their self-love in strong ways: 'Love for him is an attempt to create order out of chaos, strength out of weakness; however, it simply creates monsters.'[24] A similar theme drives Ihab Hassan's *Radical Innocence*. In his examination of works by Truman Capote, Flannery O'Connor and Carson McCullers, Hassan finds only 'the self in recoil': anti-heroes, rebel-victims and innocent narcissists all on a quest for existential fulfilment.[25]

Despite pronunciations of cultural disenchantment and disaffection, it is now widely acknowledged that the post-war search for an essential Americanism in the nation's fiction was more reaffirming than adversarial, leading to what David Suchoff calls a 'safe modernist subversion', which valued a literature of 'fragmentation and instability'.[26] Liberalism creates, in Irving Howe's phrase, 'an atmosphere of blur in the realm of ideas'. To be free of conflicting ideologies, to call yourself a liberal, Howe argued, meant that you did not have to believe in anything; the new aesthetic merely sustained the period's cultural nationalism and intellectual abdication to the right.[27] It was, as Sacvan Bercovitch described it, the 'cultural secret of academia', the development of a new discipline 'designed not to explore its subject':

> If America was not literally a poem in these scholar's eyes, it was a literary canon that embodied the national promise ... What followed was a series of investigations of the country's 'exceptional' nature that was as rich, as complex, as interdisciplinary as America herself—a pluralist enterprise armed with the instruments both of aesthetic and of cognitive analysis, all bent on the appreciation of a unique cultural artefact.[28]

While the current movement of criticism towards historicism offers renewed relevance to the continuing inquiry into the Gothic's meaning, the analytic and conceptual identity of American fiction is heir to the liberal model of interpretation forged in the post-war era, a mode in which history is 'internalized as second nature and so forgotten as history'.[29] The consequence is that both historians and literary critics have, to borrow Joyce Appleby's phrase, 'burned their bridges not to the past—but rather to past ways of looking at [the] past'.[30] The central task of this book, therefore, is to approach the Gothic through a different historical lens. *Republicanism and the American Gothic* argues that the persistence of the Gothic imagination in the United States is more readily understood from a republican than a liberal paradigm, and that a recognition of the transatlantic exchange of ideas is crucial to an understanding of how Americans viewed their past, present and future generally, and specifically what made them distinct from their British counterparts. The importance of revolution in the development of the Gothic cannot be overstated; however, this is not solely in relation to the French Revolution as critics suggest, but to the widespread reforming impulse that characterized the late seventeenth and early eighteenth centuries. The English Revolution of 1688 and the American War of Independence, in other words, cannot be isolated from discussion of the revolutionary dimensions of the Gothic. The first aim, therefore, is to examine the central intellectual ideas influencing the revolutionary generation and, in particular, the concept of republicanism as both a political theory and as a form of discourse translated and filtered through seventeenth- and eighteenth-century radical and anti-authoritarian thinkers. While it is true that the words of the revolutionary generation remain strange to us, it is nonetheless useful to perceive events, as much as possible, as the participants themselves saw them in an attempt to rediscover the forgotten dynamism of eighteenth-century language and culture. The Gothic emerged in a period that, next to the English revolutionary decades of the seventeenth century, is the most productive era in the history of Western political thought; this historical context has not been sufficiently explored in terms of its overarching effect on eighteenth-century European and American Gothic fiction. Any attempt to interpret the Gothic outside the context of its originating Enlightenment discourse or, to explain its continuing persistence in American culture, is to ignore one of the essential organizing principles of American politics, culture and manners. 'The Enlightenment', Fred Botting reminds us, 'invented the Gothic' and this is no less true in the case of American Gothic.³¹ This approach does not negate the influence of Puritanism on American culture; however, the focus of this study is on the secular expressions of republican ideology primarily because religion was largely removed from political discourse in the late eighteenth century due to the rapid rise of commercialism, the doctrine of separation of church and state and secular explanations for human behaviour which were formulated in the new disciplines of science, psychology, economics and law.³² While Puritanism and the concept of liberty were and remain in constant tension, it is equally true that in the process of national formation, the attempt at institutionalizing religious doctrine failed; it was secular republican ideals which not only persisted, but continued to embarrass the progress of liberal values in America. It is with these ideals that this book is primarily concerned.

The second aim is to examine the relevance of the republican tradition in cold war America. While I begin with a focus on the founding era and on the many ways republicanism preoccupied the revolutionary generation, I will also explore how republican ideals continued to shape national consciousness in the twentieth century. The central argument is that the moral and political imperatives that characterized republicanism in the late eighteenth century do not disappear with the rise of modern industrialization, but continue to equip twentieth-century liberal culture with a mode of self-criticism. Accordingly, this book will juxtapose the last decades of the eighteenth century with the early post-war decades of the twentieth century. The first reason for selecting these two periods is that the years 1780 to 1800, and 1950 to 1970 are both post-war cultures and represent moments in American history when questions of national identity and social stability were most pressing. Equally, while both periods are characterized as prosperous, optimistic and progressive, they were also periods of perceived crisis and reactionary zeal. In the early national and antebellum scene, the survival of the new republic was by no means certain. Escalating self-interest did not result in the perfection of society, but to perversions of the self and the corruption of civilization.³³ In the wake of the Second World War, Americans were once again accessing the security of the republic and the value of liberalism in the face of totalitarianism, conformity and mass culture. This comparative approach advances a number of propositions. First, when viewed historically through the prism of ideas and the active transmission of these ideas from Europe to America, the distinction between British and American Gothic fiction is less precise. Whether British or American, the Gothic is nourished by the eighteenth century's often-violent encounter with democracy (whether glorious or terrifying), with the Enlightenment's quest for knowledge regarding the nature of man's will and by the search for ideological myths of national origin. Secondly, in the wake of an emerging liberal individuality, the Gothic expresses a profound fear of modernity. As Cathy Davidson notes, in the Gothic, the individual's propensity for benevolence and self-sacrifice is undercut by the discovery of man's potential for corruption, deception and self-interest: 'The American Gothic often provided a perturbing vision of self-made men maintaining their new found power by resorting to the same kinds of treachery that evil aristocrats of Europe used to support their own corrupt authority.'[34] These fears are particularly forceful in the American context because, as Moses Coit Tyler observed, what was significant about the American experience was that fear was directed 'not against tyranny inflicted, but only against tyranny anticipated'.[35] It was this sense of vulnerability, this fear of the future, which animated political, social and cultural anxiety in the early American republic. Gleaned from an understanding of classical and British history, the perceived threat of encroaching tyranny, corruption and national degeneration bred potent fears in revolutionary America which, despite the rise of liberal capitalism, are still some of the overriding obsessions in contemporary American culture, repeatedly represented in fiction, film and other modes of discourse. As Eric Savoy notes, the odd centrality of Gothic cultural production in the United States is that 'the past constantly inhabits the present, [and] progress generates an almost unbearable anxiety about its cost'.[36]

Approaching American Gothic from a republican perspective also requires an examination of the central themes and assumptions pervading contemporary criticism. The first is the belief that America has no past or history therefore its literature is free of ancestral ghosts. It was Fielder who first posited the view that in the 'sunlit, neo-classical world' of Thomas Jefferson, the Gothic was improbable and unconvincing. While writers may have borrowed elements from British tales of terror, the nation's possession of neither a past nor a history made it difficult to adapt.[37] Fiedler's characterization of the early republic as bathed in Jeffersonian optimism functions to collapse eighteenth-century American culture into an all-pervading consensus devoid of political conflict and dissension. Such analysis is in itself an act of containment, an example of the liberal project of turning history into myth. Undoubtedly, for many republicans, a period of giddy exhilaration followed independence, but this was by no means consensual and more importantly, its moment of optimism was short lived. As a culture on the cusp of industrialization, post-revolutionary America experienced wide-scale political and social unrest, and therefore is more accurately characterized by both promise and peril. Fiedler's related observation that the nation has no past or history has also proven remarkably tenacious in the criticism of American Gothic fiction. David Punter, for example, claims that where British Gothic has a past to deal with, America's conception is represented only by 'a vague historical "Europe"'. Generally defined against, or as a mere refraction of the British form, early American Gothic is thought to draw upon European examples while ultimately failing to replicate the Gothic's basic impulse of historical tyranny.[38] The tendency to bifurcate British and American historical traditions can be traced, in part, to the ideological manipulation of history by post-war academics who largely ignored eighteenth-century culture in their revision of the American renaissance. In 1948, *The Literary History of the United States* proposed 'to draw a new and truer picture' of American literature. In contrast to Moses Coit Tyler's nineteenth-century concept of joint ownership of America's literary tradition, the post-war editors of the *Literary History* rejected a European influence on American writing and instead presented their readers with a vastly different image:

> The literary history of this nation began when the first settler from abroad of sensitive mind paused in his adventure long enough to feel that he was under a different sky, breathing new air, and that a New World was all before him with only his strength and Providence for guides. With him began a different emphasis upon an old theme in literature, the theme of cutting loose and faring forth, renewed under the powerful influence of a fresh continent for civilized man. It has provided, ever since those first days, an element in our native literature,

whose other theme has come from a nostalgia for the rich culture of Europe, so much of which was perforce left behind.[39]

Invoking Henry James's famous list of the 'absent things in American life', the new approach abandoned references to the Old World in favour of a wholly American environment: the new frontier. Like Fiedler's analysis, the liberal contention that Old World social tensions did not exist in the new republic performs two functions: it brackets ideology out of the frame and once again substitutes history for myth. 'It is notorious', wrote J. G. A. Pocock, 'that American culture is haunted by myths, many of which arise out of the attempt to escape history and then regenerate it.'[40] Examining eighteenth-century culture from a republican paradigm allows for a reassessment of this interpretation. It reveals that early Americans' sense of history was in many ways indistinguishable from the British Whig interpretation, particularly one that advanced an anti-authoritarian or republican tradition in Europe. Republican historiography argues that American history, through the colonial and revolutionary periods, is an episode in British history, 'the history of one of those cultures carried to the point where it left the British orbit and began to shape a history of its own'.[41] Moreover, while the best of Britain's constitution with its themes of liberty and equality provided the model for American republicanism, British history's darker themes of tyranny, corruption and degeneration also reached across the Atlantic to haunt Americans within their own borders.

The second, closely related, assumption is that because revolutionary America had no past or concept of historical tyranny, traditional Gothic figures had no place in American culture. 'With what native classes or groups', Fiedler asks, 'could [hero-villains] be identified? Traditionally aristocrats, monks, servants of the Inquisition, members of secret societies like the Illuminati, how could they be convincingly introduced on the American scene?'[42] Contemporary critics echo this view: 'the malevolent aristocrats, ruined castles and abbeys and chivalric codes dominating a gloomy and Gothic European tradition were highly inappropriate to the new world of North America. They were too far removed to have the same significance or effects of terror.'[43] Yet, the writings of the revolutionary generation reveal that Americans possessed a profound understanding and fear of aristocratic tyranny. Nourished by the anti-establishment tradition that helped define British consciousness, early Americans viewed the rise of power and corruption as the predominant threat to republican institutions and manners. The profusion of sermons, speeches and orations on the rising influence of the aristocratic class, on the canker of corruption, the spectre of treason and the insidious infiltration of America by the Illuminati, all expose the generation's fear of tyranny, degeneracy and conspiracy. Not only did staunch monarchists, fledgling aristocrats and radical subversives stalk the American scene, each functioned as the republic's first gothicized villains. Therefore, while the physical manifestations of crumbling castles and abbeys may have been absent, the ideas inherent in these conventions, transmitted through the flow of expatriates to America and from the revolutionaries' own experiences and readings of history provided a wellspring of terror deep enough to support an American Gothic tradition.

The third assumption is that as the revolutionary generation forged a new national identity, the Gothic departed from its initial impulse of terror and took on uniquely American characteristics. It is now axiomatic to cite Brockden Brown's preface to *Edgar Huntly* (1799) as the principal example of how early American authors were abandoning the traditions of the Old World to initiate a literary aesthetic of their own. Brown's repudiation of the 'puerile superstition and exploded manners; Gothic castles and chimeras' of European authors in favour of writing that is 'peculiar to ourselves' is repeatedly offered as evidence of the uniqueness of American Gothic writing.[44] Undoubtedly, many young republicans were keen to establish their nation's literary fame: it was, after all, an age of experiments and authors understood that new initiatives applied not only to politics or culture generally, but to the shaping of imaginative works. However, to accept an a priori national distinctiveness in the reading of early American Gothic is to ignore one of the fundamental concerns of the age. As Clinton Rossiter observes, from Washington onwards, 'the American people were engaged in an industrious search for *self-identity*' and in the late eighteenth century, they were only beginning to establish what form this identity would assume:

> [w]hile Americans saw and identified themselves as a new people on the face of the earth, two fateful questions remained to be answered:

First, were they different and better enough to rejoice confidently in the fact and, if they were, in what ways? Second, was the fate of America to be a country, that is, one sovereign nation like Britain and France, or a 'country', that is, a parcel of related yet basically sovereign half-nations, city-states, and provinces like Germany and Italy?[45]

It was a French national who posed the all important question: '[w]hat then is the American, this new man?' For Crèvecoeur, the American is a man who 'acts upon new principles', entertains 'new ideas', and forms 'new opinions'.[46] Yet, exactly what these new principles, ideas and opinions actually were was only in the process of being clarified. Phrases such as 'the condition of our country', 'American character' and 'American peculiarities' in revolutionary writing do not point to a fully formulated national identity; rather they were exercises in the creation of a national discourse voiced everywhere by Americans, English expatriates, French émigrés and anyone else who supported the republican cause. As William Hedges observes, 'the magic of *e pluribus anum* should not blind us. The literature is indeed that of a people who did not know themselves to a much greater extent than we have acknowledged.'[47]

If the contours of American identity remained unfixed in the 1780s and 1790s, the notion that Americans sought to create an independent culture free from colonial imitation of English models is equally problematical. While there was much talk of printing specifically American books, this had less to do with aesthetics than with commercial national rhetoric. As Michael Warner argues,

> when advertisements and subscription proposals tell readers than an author is American, they do not necessarily point to a link between traits of nationality and those of aesthetics; they merely solicit patrons' encouragement of the domestic trade, much as they might for the making of shoes.[48]

Brockden Brown's call to excite the passions and sympathy of his readers through the inclusion of 'new ingredients' could also be read as the attempt by an author to promote his novel in America's burgeoning print culture, a culture that identified literature with the public and commercial spheres. As Brown's friend Samuel Miller declared, 'In this century, for the first time AUTHORSHIP BECAME A TRADE. Multitudes of writers toiled, not for the promotion of science, nor even with a governing view to advance their own reputation, but for the market.'[49] The tendency to privilege authorial or private subjectivity rather than republican didacticism in eighteenth-century American fiction creates what Warner calls 'a space between the novel and the public sphere', which, he argues, in the 1790s was not clearly formed. To define cultural goods as indigenous or 'American' required a set of cultural assumptions that did not exist before the nineteenth century when 'a national imaginary and a liberal ideology of literature arose together, because both divorced the public value of printed commodities from the public discourse'.[50] That American Gothic is characterized as paradoxical is largely down to the persistence of these assumptions. Influenced by liberal aesthetics and ideology, criticism has largely ignored eighteenth-century discourse in favour of psychological interiority and myth analysis. Therefore, in order to uncover the ideological contours of American Gothic fiction, it is necessary to employ a method of historical inquiry that examines the vocabulary and rhetorical strategies of another generation; to recapture, as much as is possible, the fears of those who participated in events.

To begin historicizing the Gothic through the republican paradigm, this book draws on Chris Baldick and Robert Mighall's contention that early Gothic fiction is historical at its root; that its vital elements are cultural not psychological, rational not romantic. In 'Gothic criticism', Baldick and Mighall claim that the view of Gothic as 'anti-realist fantasy' or dream writing is a large-scale misconception that reinforces the assumption that the Gothic is to be defined 'according to the realms of psychological depth from which it is supposed to originate ... or the psychological responses it is believed to provoke'. The problem with the view of the Gothic as an irrational, non-realistic literature of nightmare is its 'prevalent de-historicising of gothic writing and its cultural referents' in favour of psychological interiority by which history is evoked only to be 'collapsed into the psychodrama enacted by "each individual", irrespective of culture, context or period'.[51] According to these critics, the cardinal error of Gothic criticism is '[t]he assimilation of Gothic fiction into romantic and pre-romantic nostalgia for the Middle Ages'. They cite the fact that very few early Gothic novels are actually situated in the Middle Ages and, more importantly, the contention that the Gothic looks backward to an idealized past displays an 'irreconcilable opposition between critical illusion and textual evidence':

> Most Gothic novels have little to do with 'the medieval world', especially not an idealised one; they represent the past not as paradisal but as 'nasty' in its 'possessive' curtailing of individual liberties; and they gratefully endorse Protestant bourgeois values as 'kinder' than those of feudal barons.

For Baldick and Mighall, this insistence on nostalgic medievalism leads to the assumption that the Gothic embodies an essentially romantic and poetic project and any affiliations with enlightened realism are dispelled in the packaging of the Gothic as a romantic or anti-enlightenment rebellion. Rather, it is 'Protestant scepticism and enlightened Whiggery' that are essential to Gothic fiction. Structured thematically around sectarian nightmares, for Baldick and Mighall, the Gothic is a staunchly anti-Catholic, 'bourgeois genre'.[52]

While Baldick and Mighall's work broadens our understanding of the importance of historical context in understanding British Gothic fiction, it is necessary to expand their thesis of 'aggressive Protestanism' and 'enlightened Whiggery' to a wider intellectual base, one that includes the faction of Whig interests in the eighteenth century. Anti-Catholicism is only one expression of a wider discursive conflict permeating the Gothic, and to restrict depictions of tyranny to monastic institutions negates the Gothic's engagement with other forms of authoritarianism. Gothic literature has always been concerned with power and the abuse of power. From the eighteenth-century British terrors of Walpole, Lewis, Godwin and Radcliffe, to the American works of Brockden Brown, the Gothic's function has been to re-enact the struggle between liberty and tyranny, sovereignty and self-government. Whether we read the Gothic as a depiction of patriarchal oppression, Catholic superstition or feudal systems of political representation, we are nonetheless describing forms of tyranny that spring from the Enlightenment debates between aristocratic defenders of constitutional order and radical dissent. The focus on

Catholicism as the mainstay of Gothic tyranny ignores the turbulent transition from subject to citizen that defined the revolutionary generation on both sides of the Atlantic. Therefore, any history of the Whigs and their role in the meaning of Gothic fiction must first acknowledge the profound schism in Whig political culture; in other words, we must distinguish the radicals from the orthodox: Milton, Paine and Hollis from Halifax, Walpole and Burke. As Marilyn Butler notes, while we think of the eighteenth-century government as stable and successful, the critique of the ruling Whig oligarchy was strong and so deeply rooted that it merged into an 'alternative ideology':

> The system's natural opponents among the politicised classes included ... elements of the old Tory country gentry, and of the urban Old Whigs, or radicals, all of whom looked back ... to the fierce doctrinaire disputes of the seventeenth century. By the second half of the eighteenth century, this opposition was generating a powerful rhetoric, heady enough to sustain the American Revolution ... salient themes include a sense of personal liberty and autonomy, a belief in civic virtue, and a hatred of corruption – all of which can be seen as symptomatic of a 'republican' tradition in Western Europe.[53]

An example of the schism operating in Whig culture appears in the correspondence between two eighteenth-century antiquarians, Horace Walpole and Thomas Hollis. As author of the first Gothic novel, *The Castle of Otranto* (1764), Walpole's attempt to 'blend two kinds of romance, the ancient and the modern', established the aesthetic material of the Gothic. Walpole's wild tale of usurpation, his animosity toward Voltaire and the 'illuminated pit of Paris' situate Walpole in opposition to contemporary radical Whigs such as Hollis.[54] For Walpole, Hollis's emphasis on 'king killing' and the legitimacy of resistance to tyrants was an anachronism. From the orthodox Whig view, republicanism ignored a century of achievement by the ruling class that strengthened the structure of the English constitution and slowly formed a balance between the people and the aristocracy, commons and cabinet.[55] Walpole's Whig politics, therefore, suggests that *The Castle of Otranto* does not represent a fear of 'the parasitic power of the past',[56] but a celebration of the material and political progress of the Enlightenment. Radical republicans, on the other hand, envisioned a gloomier world. Unlike Walpole, Hollis's concept of liberty was that of the ancient republics reflected in the minds of thinkers such as Milton, Marvell and Sidney. What these men saw in the new and growing prosperity of England was an ominous parallel to the luxury and corruption that marked the rise of tyranny in the ancient world. Civilization, they believed, was vulnerable and continually besieged by forces threatening its survival. As Gibbon had taught them,

> [n]o theory of human progress could be constructed which did not carry the negative implication that progress was at the same time decay, that culture entailed some loss of freedom and virtue, that what multiplied human capacities also fractured the unity of human personality.[57]

Progress, in other words, was inevitably a movement toward decline. This 'quarrel with modernity' reveals the complex dialectic operating at the heart of Whig culture. As Pocock notes, in the eighteenth century there existed a natural antithesis between republicanism and liberalism, classicism and progressivism: 'The Old Whigs identified freedom with virtue and located it in a past; the Modern Whigs identified it with wealth, enlightenment, and progress towards a future. Around this antithesis ... nearly all eighteenth-century philosophy of history can be organized.'[58] This Enlightenment contradiction arose out of an acute awareness of the fragility of classical republics:

> The republic was vulnerable to corruption, to political, moral, or economic changes which destroyed the equality on which it rested, and these changes might occur not accidentally, but in consequence of the republic's own virtue. Because it was virtuous it defeated its enemies; because it defeated its enemies it acquired empire; but empire brought to some citizens ... the opportunity to acquire power incompatible with equality and uncontrollable by law, and so the republic was destroyed by success and excess.[59]

The cause of liberty and equality that many radical or 'Old' Whigs promoted evoked not a superstitious medieval past returning to haunt the present, but a classical view of liberty and democracy perpetually under threat by corruption and power. Protestant scepticism, then, also encompassed a pessimistic world-view that saw the inevitable rise of tyranny and the fall of empire. Moreover, it was this 'republican tradition', so prominent in British and European Enlightenment thought, that when transmitted to the colonies, provided an explanatory structure for independence and revolution. Republicanism, therefore, was more than a form of rhetoric as Butler suggests, but a prominent discourse in Enlightenment culture, spoken everywhere in seventeenth- and eighteenth-century Europe and America. Whether Whig or Tory, the discourse of republicanism formed an essential discursive element regarding the problem of resistance within the civil order. Variously conceived of as democracy, liberty or equality, republicanism constituted an alternative world view that looked to the classical past for lessons on political theory and national identity. In the Old Whig view, there exists an overt pessimism and fear surrounding the ability of civilization to uphold the tenets of republicanism. Republicanism, therefore, is also a panic-ridden ideology animated by fears of tyranny, decay, conspiracy and corruption and it is with these ideological fears that the Gothic is deeply entangled.

The antithesis between Walpole and Hollis's world view also parallels the debates surrounding 'the myth of the Goth' that arose in the revolutionary period. Before being employed as a descriptive term for Walpole's novel, the term 'Gothic' possessed controversial political, ideological and cultural meanings. Historically, it describes the ancient Teutonic races that subverted the Roman Empire; however, in the seventeenth century, British defenders of parliamentary prerogative developed a new, politically contentious conception of the Goths, which as the various shades of Whiggery reveal, was eventually used either as a justification for resistance to tyrants or as an argument for the continuation of an organic constitutional order. For Whigs such as Robert Walpole, the ancient Gothic constitution represented a dark period of feudal slavery: 'The primitive purity of our constitution was that the people had no share in government, but were the villains, vessels, or bondsmen of the lords.'[60] Only with the advent of the Glorious Revolution was the British government free from tyranny. The orthodox Whig view of history, by contrast, advanced the theory that the Goths were morally pure, brave and humane, and, politically, the original democrats of the world. Britain's Gothic heritage signalled not only an inherent freedom lost in 1066 and regained in 1688, it reinforced a view of the British constitution's organic perfection, a return to order and continuity. For Edmund Burke, tradition, or what he saw as the natural historical and political order, was essential to freedom. It was the French revolutionaries and Enlightenment philosophers, prostrating themselves to the gods of reason and democracy, who sought to undermine freedom and re-introduce tyranny and barbarity:

> The usurpation which, in order to subvert ancient institutions, has destroyed ancient principles, will hold power by arts similar to those by which it has acquired it. When the old feudal and chivalrous spirit of *Fealty*, which, by freeing kings from fear, freed both kings and subjects from the precautions of tyranny, shall be extinct in the minds of men, plots and assassinations will be anticipated by preventive murder and preventive confiscation, and that long roll of grim and bloody maxims, which form the political code of all power, not standing on its own honour, and the honour of those who are to obey it. Kings will be tyrants from policy, when subjects are rebels from principle.[61]

Yet for radical, or 'Old' Whigs, Burke's fusion of tradition and freedom, his 'superstitious respect for kings, and the spirit of chivalry', transmogrified the Gothic past into a regressive feudal idolatry.[62] As Clery and Miles point out, 'what was at stake in these discussions was the elaboration of persuasive myths of the nation's past as a means of influencing its present and future course. In general terms, the myth of Gothic origins was fundamental to an emergent sense of British national distinctiveness'.[63] In *The Rise of the Gothic Novel*, Maggie Kilgour argues that the contrasting of Anglo-Saxon political freedom with classical tyranny, especially Roman and later French neo-classicism, is a 'peculiarly British characteristic, a sign of a national inherent love of freedom [and] liberty'.[64] Moreover, it is the political and ideological contours of this characterization that determine Gothic literature's themes of historical tyranny and usurpation, of Norman oppression and lost liberty. Yet, however fruitful the history of the Goths has been in untangling the politics of eighteenth-century British Gothic fiction, a similar influence is undeveloped in the scholarship devoted to American Gothic. Not only was this 'peculiarly British characteristic' shared by the American revolutionary generation who adopted and shaped Anglo-Saxon history for their own use, they also symbolically identified with Gothic customs and institutions. As Samuel Kliger argues, the colonists' retreat from England was the first attempt to recreate an idealized Gothic society in the New World:

> In the same sense that Americans are 'Goths', so were their Anglo-Saxon forbears who received the 'Gothic' gift of democracy as a result of the Germanic invasion of England ... Unfortunately, however, a lingering 'Roman' element in England tended at times to come to the surface of English political life. Therefore, in order to realize their 'Gothic' destiny unhampered, a band of hardy Anglo-Saxons migrated to America. The 'Gothic' pattern of life which England succeeded in establishing only in part would thus be completely realized in America.[65]

In colonial America, the term Gothic retained its Old Whig connotations of Anglo-Saxon liberty and equality, and this myth of alienation from and return to an original state of harmony and innocence would eventually provide the political mooring for American republicanism. Much of the intellectual coherence of the colonists' political arguments rested on their views of the past and the goal of revolution was in part the realization of those original Gothic ideals, unhampered by the corruption and tyranny of the present system. One of the greatest American scholars of Anglo-Saxon history was Thomas Jefferson who invoked the Saxon constitution for the American cause. Jefferson's interpretation of the Gothic past reveals much about the revolutionary generation's approach to questions of political heritage and national identity. From his readings of Rapin's *History of England* and Gordon's translation of Tacitus, Jefferson conceived of an Anglo-Saxon past in terms of a useable political heritage: 'as we have employed some of the best materials of the British constitution in the construction of our own government, a knowledge of British history becomes useful to the American politician'.⁶⁶ In *A Summary View of the Rights of British America*, he affirms the values and traditions of the Whig interpretation of history as an argument for the right to be free from the country 'which chance, not choice has placed them', and believing that Saxon rights were being abused by parliamentary exercises of tyranny, despotism and usurped power, turned the British government's own Saxon history against them as an argument for American independence. For the majority of Americans, the most characteristic view of their Gothic history was of an ideal constitution complete with an elected House of Commons in Saxon England, destroyed by the Norman Conquest, regained with modifications in the Glorious Revolution and once again challenged by the festering corruption of British politics. English history was portrayed as a continual struggle for the restoration of ancient rights and it was this struggle, according to John Adams, that had peopled America. Therefore, while the term 'Gothic' 'coexists and overlaps with the more familiar literary and aesthetic material within the semantic constellation of the British "Gothic"', it also coincides with the American conception of liberty and republican government.⁶⁷

The ambiguity and shifting about of the term is commonplace in the Gothic tradition, but the debates surrounding Gothic manners and institutions should not be viewed solely as a British phenomenon but enlarged to encompass the republican world of late eighteenth-century America. Early republicans mythologized their own national formations in much the same way as the British Whigs and, like their English counterparts, viewed their Gothic history in binary terms: one of light and liberty, the other dark and barbarous; one an ancient Elysium, the other a feudal nightmare. The recovery of the original force of this myth can also bring something of immediate value to discussions of post-war America. Confronted with the spectre of totalitarianism and the corrupting effects of conformity and mass culture, the myth of the Goth restates for a new generation the legitimacy of resistance to tyrants. The resurgence of biblical and Roman empire film epics in the 1950s and 1960s, for example, attests to the continuing relevance of this narrative. While loosely couched in spiritual themes, films such as *Quo Vadis?* (1951), *Julius Caesar* (1953), *Ben Hur* (1959), *Spartacus* (1960) and *The Fall of the Roman Empire* (1964) each depict the brutality of tyranny and the corruption of Rome while appealing to the Anglo-Saxon traits of simplicity, bravery and love of liberty. From cold war film to political and social analysis, Anglo-Saxon identity not only underlies the continuity between British and American concepts of political identity, it also supplies the imagery and iconography for contemporary America's fears of tyranny, corruption and conspiracy.

While this book is grounded in the work of historians, the choice of interpretative method accounts for the second reason for focusing on post-war Gothic fiction. It is precisely in this period that historians began to interpret American history through the paradigm of republicanism. The emphasis on ideas as the animating force of the American Revolution and early national period began in the late 1940s with the work of historians such as Caroline Robbins and Cecilia Kenyon who initiated the move toward understanding English libertarian thought and its transmission to America. Following these efforts, republicanism entered the scholarly lexicon to become 'the success story of the 1980s'.[68] It is not the burden of this book to evaluate the efficacy of the 'republican synthesis' or 'neo-Whig' framework, rather to suggest that the dominance of the liberal consensus approach on both historical interpretation and literary criticism has impeded a fuller understanding of the nation's Gothic fiction. An examination of mid twentieth-century Gothic reveals that the language of classical republicanism still had wide currency because, like their eighteenth-century forbears, post-war Americans perceived their liberty to be under threat by external treachery and internal decay. Therefore, classical republicanism's lexicon of degeneration, corruption, tyranny and conspiracy provided a familiar structure to a generation's fight against the threats of totalitarianism and mass culture. The discourse of republicanism called for a renewed civic consciousness in a period of conformity and unbridled consumer capitalism, and thereby functioned not only as an articulation or negotiation of contemporary cultural anxieties, but also as a critique of modern liberal culture. Chapter 1 provides a historical framework for discussing and analysing contemporary American Gothic. While it begins by briefly examining the shift from progressive socio-economic theories of American history to a liberal consensus approach, it is primarily concerned with tracing the development of the 'republican paradigm' that arose in the post-war period and which came to challenge the dominant approaches to American revolutionary history. Specifically, this chapter reviews the scholarship devoted to republican historiography through its most influential proponents: Caroline Robbins, Bernard Bailyn, Gordon S. Wood and J. G. A. Pocock. Opposed to the view that ideas played no part in the development of American politics and culture, these historians set out to explore the influence of classical and British libertarian thought and modes of discourse on the colonies and the importance of this transatlantic exchange on the revolution itself and on the creation of an American republic. The chapter briefly outlines some of the central assumptions of the republican tradition as advanced by these so called 'neo-Whig' historians. Subsequent chapters will each consist of three parts. The first section examines a specific assumption regarding republican ideology in late eighteenth-century America and how it functioned to refine cultural identity. The second situates the language of classical republicanism in a cold war context, arguing that while the terms may change, republican values and fears are transmitted over time and remain in tension with new liberal ideals. The final section offers a close reading of a mid twentieth-century text exploring how traditional Gothic figures continue to affirm the nation's historical fears of degeneration, corruption, deception and tyranny. Chapter 2 examines the vampire as a figure of corruption and degeneration. By reviewing the eighteenth-century cyclical theory of history and the fear of national degeneration that emerges from the idea of progress, it reveals how the concepts of corruption and degeneration were commonly expressed in metaphors of barbarity, infection and vampirism. The second part of this chapter reveals how a similar theory of history operates in cold war culture. The conception of the republic as a vulnerable organism perpetually threatened by corruption is reconstructed not as the fear of communist tyranny, but as an internal battle between tradition and progress, nature and culture. The third section offers a close reading of Richard Matheson's vampire novel *I Am Legend* (1954), arguing how the text engages with the historical theme of degeneration while articulating the central contradictions of post-war culture. Chapter 3 explores the figure of the double and the eighteenth-century concept of virtue. It argues that the fear of effeminacy, luxury and self-interest not only disclosed the gender implications of republican identity, but also represented the nation's first crisis of masculinity. The second section reveals that in the cold war era, the concept of masculine virtue manifests as an effort to shore up a liberal consensus in an age of perceived political impotence and social conformity. The third section explores the figure of the double in David Ely's novel *Seconds* (1963). It argues that the double re-emerges as a figure of failed masculinity softened not by the lures of eighteenth-century luxury and effeminacy, but by its modern corollaries: conformity and self-interest. Chapter 4 explores the concepts of conspiracy and hypocrisy in late eighteenth-century Britain and America. It argues that rather than being based in irrationality, the widespread use of conspiratorial modes of interpretation stem from the Enlightenment's engagement with the new science of causality and the rational concept of free will. In the American revolutionary context, the fear of conspiracy and hypocrisy interacts with the politics of sincerity: the need to decipher the discrepancy between words and deeds, motives and actions. Chapter 4 then explores how a similar discourse of conspiracy and dissimulation fuelled the panic of subversion and cultural decay in the post-war period. In Ira Levin's *Rosemary's Baby* (1967), the Gothic figure of the impostor or deceiver reveals the continuing interaction between motives and intentions, and hypocrisy and sincerity in the modern age. Chapter 5 examines the agrarian model of republican citizenship. It begins with a brief review of the development of a pastoral tradition in American writing and its interdependence with the discourse of republicanism. It discusses how agrarianism functioned as a way of distinguishing the Old World from the New, and the virtuous from the corrupt, and reveals that the essential threat to agrarian virtue was the rise of commerce and industrialization. The chapter then explores the republican dialectic of virtue and corruption in Truman Capote's *In Cold Blood* (1965). It argues that while Capote exploits the paraphernalia of the Gothic to explore the invasion and destruction of iconic Americans by monstrous outcasts, the characterization and structure of the narrative exposes the inherent ambiguity surrounding the values of agrarian virtue and progressive individualism in modern America.

Notes

1. Joseph Anthony Mazzeo, 'Some interpretations of the history of ideas', *Journal of the History of Ideas*, 33, 3 (1972), 379–94 (389).
2. Fred Botting, 'Preface', in Fred Botting (ed.), *The Gothic, Essays and Studies* (Cambridge: D. S. Brewer, 2001), pp. 1–6; for discussions on the Gothic's mutability see Fred Botting, *Gothic* (London: Routledge, 1996); Teresa Goddu, *Gothic America: Narrative, History, and Nation* (New York: Columbia University Press, 1997); Jerrold E. Hogle, 'Introduction', in Jerrold E. Hogle (ed.), *The Cambridge Companion to Gothic Fiction* (Cambridge: Cambridge University Press, 2002), pp. 1–20; Robert Miles, *Gothic Writing, 1750–1820: A Genealogy* (Manchester: Manchester University Press, 2002); Marie Mulvey-Roberts, 'Introduction', in Marie Mulvey-Roberts (ed.), *The Handbook to Gothic Literature* (New York: New York University Press, 1998), pp. xv–xviii; David Punter, *The Literature of Terror: Volume 1, The Gothic Tradition* (New York: Longman, 1996).
3. The term's artistic and architectural usages also intersect with its literary meanings; however, I am primarily concerned with the historical and political contours of the Gothic. For more on eighteenth-century Gothic art and architecture see Samuel Kliger, 'Whig aesthetics: a phase of eighteenth-century taste', *ELH*, 16 (1949), 135–50.
4. Goddu, *Gothic America*, p. 3.
5. Robert Miles, '"Tranced Griefs": Melville's *Pierre* and the origins of the Gothic', *ELH*, 66, 1 (1999), 157–77 (158).
6. Edward J. Ingebretsen, *At Stake: Monsters and the Rhetoric of Fear in Public Culture* (Chicago: Chicago University Press, 2001), p. 21; Leslie Fiedler, *Love and Death in the American Novel* (2nd edn; New York: Dell, 1966), p. 9.
7. Justin D. Edwards, *Gothic Passages: Racial Ambiguity and the American Gothic* (Iowa City: University of Iowa Press, 2003), p. xvii.
8. Fiedler, *Love and Death*, p. 149.
9. Ibid., pp. xi, xxiii (original emphasis).
10. Ibid., p. 6; Irving Malin, *New American Gothic* (Illinois: Southern Illinois University Press, 1962), p. 5.
11. Eric Savoy, 'The rise of American Gothic', in Jerrold E. Hogle (ed.), *The Cambridge Companion to Gothic Fiction* (Cambridge: Cambridge University Press, 2002), pp. 167–88 (p. 168).
12. Robert K. Martin and Eric Savoy (eds), *American Gothic: New Interventions in a National Narrative* (Iowa City: University of Iowa Press, 1988), p. viii.
13. Lionel Trilling, *Beyond Culture: Essays on Literature and Learning* (Middlesex: Penguin, 1963), p. 19; Chester E. Eisinger, *Fiction of the Forties* (Chicago: Chicago University Press, 1963), p. 9.
14. Russell J. Reising, *The Unusable Past: Theory and the Study of American Literature* (New York: Methuen, 1986), p. 95.
15. Ibid., p. 97; Philip Rahv, 'Fiction and the criticism of fiction', *Kenyon Review*, 18 (1956), 276–99 (280).
16. Eisinger, *Fiction of the Forties*, pp. 96, 97, 86.

Introduction

17 Philip Rahv, 'Our country and our culture', *Partisan Review*, 19 (1952), 283–326 (304).
18 Arthur M. Schlesinger, Jr., *The Vital Center: The Politics of Freedom* (Cambridge, Mass.: Riverside Press, 1949), p. 245.
19 Richard Chase, *The American Novel and its Tradition* (London: G. Bell and Sons, 1957), p. 1.
20 Ibid., pp. 2, 22.
21 Goddu, *Gothic America*, p. 7.
22 Chase, *The American Novel*, p. 37
23 Ibid., pp. 30, 36.
24 Malin, *New American Gothic*, p. 5.
25 Ihab Hassan, *Radical Innocence: Studies in the Contemporary American Novel* (Princeton: Princeton University Press, 1961), p. 31
26 David Suchoff, 'New historicism and containment: towards a post-cold war cultural theory', *Arizona Quarterly*, 48 (1992), 137–61 (142).
27 Irving Howe, 'This age of conformity', in Philip Rahv and William Phillips (eds), *The Partisan Review Anthology* (1954; London: Macmillan, 1962), pp. 145–64 (p. 151).
28 Sacvan Bercovitch, *The Rites of Assent: Transformations in the Symbolic Construction of America* (New York: Routledge, 1993), pp. 10, 11.
29 Pierre Bourdieu, *In Other Words: Essays Towards a Reflective Sociology* (Stanford: Stanford University Press, 1990), p. 190.
30 Joyce Appleby, 'Republicanism and ideology', *American Quarterly*, 37, 4 (1985), 461–73 (463).
31 Fred Botting, 'In Gothic darkly: heterotopia, history, culture', in David Punter (ed.), *A Companion to the Gothic* (Oxford: Blackwell, 2000), pp. 3–14 (p. 3).
32 Robert A. Ferguson, *Reading the Early Republic* (Cambridge, Mass.: Harvard University Press, 2004), p. 54.
33 Cathy N. Davidson, *Revolution and the Word: The Rise of the Novel in America* (Oxford: Oxford University Press, 2004), p. 312.
34 Ibid., p. 314.
35 Moses Coit Tyler, *The Literary History of the American Revolution, 1763–1783* (New York: n.p., 1897), pp. 8–9.
36 Savoy, 'The rise of American Gothic', p. 167.
37 Fiedler, *Love and Death*, p. 131.
38 Punter, *Literature of Terror*, p. 165.
39 Quoted in Robert Lawson-Peebles, *American Literature before 1880* (Harlow, England: Pearson Longman, 2003), pp. 18, 19.
40 J. G. A. Pocock, *The Machiavellian Moment: Florentine Republican Thought and the Atlantic Republican Tradition* (Princeton: Princeton University Press, 1975), p. 545.
41 J. G. A. Pocock, 'Between Gog and Magog: the republican thesis and the ideologia Americana', *Journal of the History of Ideas*, 48, 2 (1987), 325–46 (334).
42 Fiedler, *Love and Death*, p. 131.
43 Botting, *Gothic*, p. 114.
44 Charles Brockden Brown, *Edgar Huntly, Or Memoirs of a Sleep-Walker* (New York: Penguin, 1988), p. 3.

45 Clinton Rossiter, 'Nationalism and American identity in the early republic', in Sean Wilentz (ed.), *Major Problems in the Early Republic: 1787–1848* (Lexington: D. C. Heath, 1992), pp. 14–23 (pp. 14–15).
46 J. Hector St Jean de Crèvecoeur, *Letters from an American Farmer*, in Nina Baym et al. (eds), *Norton Anthology of American Literature, Vol. 1* (4th edn; New York: W. W. Norton, 1994), pp. 657–81 (pp. 659, 660).
47 William L. Hedges, 'The myth of the republic and the theory of American literature', *Prospects*, 4 (1974), 101–20 (110).
48 Michael Warner, *The Letters of the Republic: Publication and the Public Sphere in Eighteenth-Century America* (Cambridge, Mass.: Harvard University Press, 1990), p. 119.
49 Quoted in Charles Brockden Brown, *Wieland*, ed. Jay Fliegelman (New York: Penguin, 1991), p. xxvi.
50 Warner, *Letters of the Republic*, p. 120.
51 Chris Baldick and Robert Mighall, 'Gothic criticism', in David Punter (ed.), *A Companion to the Gothic* (Oxford: Blackwell, 2000), pp. 209–28 (pp. 216, 215, 218). For psychological readings of the Gothic, see Anne Williams, *Art of Darkness: A Poetics of Gothic* (Chicago: University of Chicago Press, 1995); William Patrick Day, *In the Circles of Fear and Desire: A Study of Gothic Fantasy* (Chicago: Chicago University Press, 1985); Carol Ann Howells, *Love, Mystery and Misery: Feeling in Gothic Fiction* (London: Athlone Press, 1975).
52 Baldick and Mighall, 'Gothic criticism', pp. 213, 214, 215, 226.
53 Marilyn Butler, 'Introduction', in Marilyn Butler (ed.), *Burke, Paine, Godwin, and the Revolution Controversy* (New York: Cambridge University Press, 1984), p. 3.
54 Horace Walpole, *The Castle of Otranto* (London: Oxford University Press, 1982), pp. 7, 12.
55 Caroline Robbins, 'The strenuous Whig: Thomas Hollis of Lincoln's Inn', *William and Mary Quarterly*, 7, 3 (1950), 406–53 (409).
56 Miles, '"Tranced Griefs"', 158.
57 J. G. A. Pocock, 'Gibbon's decline and fall and the world view of the late Enlightenment', *Eighteenth Century Studies*, 10, 3 (1977), 287–303 (293).
58 J. G. A. Pocock, *Virtue, Commerce, and History: Essays on Political Thought and History, Chiefly in the Eighteenth Century* (New York: Cambridge University Press, 1985), p. 231.
59 Pocock, 'Gibbon's decline and fall', 288.
60 Maggie Kilgour, *The Rise of the Gothic Novel* (London: Routledge, 1995), p. 13.
61 Edmund Burke, 'Reflections on the revolution in France and on the proceedings in certain societies in London relative to that event', in *The Works of the Right Honourable Edmund Burke*, vol. II (London: Henry G. Bohn, 1854), p. 350.
62 E. J. Clery and Robert Miles (eds), *Gothic Documents: A Sourcebook, 1700–1820* (Manchester: Manchester University Press, 2000), p. 246; Miles, '"Tranced Griefs"', 163.
63 Clery and Miles, *Gothic Documents*, p. 48.
64 Kilgour, *The Rise of the Gothic Novel*, p. 14.

65 Samuel Kliger, 'Emerson and the usable Anglo-Saxon past', *Journal of the History of Ideas*, 16, 4 (1955), 476–93 (476–7).
66 Thomas Jefferson to John Norwell (14 June 1807), Jefferson Digital Archive, University of Virginia Library, *http://etext.lib.virginia.edu* (accessed 3 March 2005).
67 Clery and Miles, *Gothic Documents*, p. 2.
68 Daniel Rogers, 'Republicanism: the career of a concept', *The Journal of American History*, 79, 1 (1992), 11–38 (11).

1

Republican Historiography

In 1985, the *American Quarterly* devoted an entire issue to the topic of republicanism and in the following year, the *William and Mary Quarterly* indexed the term for the first time in its ninety-four year history. The addition of the category 'republicanism' in these two eminent journals of history and culture reflects the intense interest and often-acrimonious debate orbiting the term since the 1960s. As one critic observed, republicanism was the one concept that could unlock the riddles of American politics and culture.[1] It represented an agreeable substitution for the increasingly pejorative term 'national' and a new found interest in language and ideology as an expression of the American political and cultural condition. Yet, for others, it was imbued with vagueness and contradiction:

> [t]o insist on the 'essence' of republicanism had the effect of driving the term *republican* into the realm of metaphor and uncertainty, making it vulnerable to a host of alternate and conflicting definitions. It would be available to signify almost anything so long as it was non-monarchical. It would become rich in overtones, useable in alternate contexts: we find ourselves speaking of republican religion, republican children, republican motherhood.[2]

By the 1980s republicanism had become a 'protean concept', a 'vocabulary' and an 'ideology', useable for a host of interpretative needs: 'The recent discovery of republicanism as the reigning social theory of eighteenth-century America has produced a reaction among historians akin to the response of chemists to a new element. Once having been identified, it can be found everywhere.'[3] The interest in republicanism represented a sea change in how historians approached revolutionary history and eighteenth-century American culture. The change took place after the Second World War and the coming of the cold war when the values and beliefs that had clarified American political and social culture were being re-evaluated and reformulated in what historians have called a 'paradigm shift of major proportions'.[4] Whether viewed as the rhetoric of classical political theory or an explanation of how ideas actually shaped events, the shift revealed that the concept of republicanism is 'bound up ... with a complex of theories about language and consciousness ... and has surreptitiously inserted into our history the conviction that reality is socially constructed'.[5]

In order to grasp the magnitude of this change, a short overview of the prevailing approaches to American history during the inter-war and post-war years is useful. Certainly, interpretations of the American Revolution and the early national period have undergone numerous transformations from the beginning when participants began to record their impressions of what was happening to subsequent views of the revolution in the setting of British imperialism. However, in the first half of the twentieth century, ideas, or the intellectual context, of early American culture receded from view and new methodologies emerged to explain the character of the nation. From the socioeconomic theories of Carl Becker and Charles Beard to the liberal consensus model advanced by Louis Hartz, Daniel J. Boorstin and Richard Hofstadter, revolutionary historiography was decidedly anti-ideological. For Progressives, who combined Marxist and Freudian thought to understand the underlying drives and interests that determine social behaviour, the revolution and the formation of the constitution was explained primarily as a conflict between different power groups where ideas were seen as merely rhetorical disguises for some hidden interest, detached from the material conditions that produced them.[6] In his introduction to *An Economic Interpretation of the Constitution*, Beard claimed that ideas were 'entities, particularities, or forces, apparently independent of all earthly considerations coming under the head of "economic"'.[7] In this evaluation, ideas were simply rationalizations modified to suit the needs of the elite and the extravagant language used to express their interests could not be taken seriously. Claims that the Tories were all 'wretched hirelings, and execrable parricides'; George III, the 'tyrant of the earth', a 'monster in human form'; that British soldiers were a 'mercenary licentious rabble of banditti' did not represent reality but merely a form of calculated deception.[8] Moreover, Americans knew very little about past republics and what they did know was 'clearly irrelevant to the discussion of the origins of republican institutions in America'. After the restoration in 1660, republican and democratic ideas 'passed into unpopularity and oblivion . . . not to be revived and re-popularized until the nineteenth century'.[9] For Progressives, the ideas of the great republican authors of the English Civil War were dead until after the American Revolution. John Locke dominated American thought and the impetus to republicanism emerged with Jefferson only after confederation:

> The colonists already had textbooks of revolution in the writings of Englishmen who defended and justified the proceedings of the seventeenth century—above all, John Locke's writings, wherein was set forth the right of citizens to overthrow government that took their money or their property without consent.[10]

However, after the Second World War, this progressive interpretation of the early national period came under assault. The shift from what has been called a Beardian paradigm to a liberal interpretation occurred just as the nation moved from political isolationism to the international arena, from the rhetoric of national exceptionalism and the concentration on social movements to the asocial politics of consensus. No longer seen as a struggle between economic interests, for liberal consensus historians American history was, and always had been, dominated by class harmony centred on self-interest. Louis Hartz's *The Liberal Tradition in America: An Interpretation of American Political Thought since the Revolution*, Daniel Boorstin's *The Genius of American Politics* (1953) and *The Americans: The Colonial Experience* (1958), and Richard Hofstadter's *The Progressive Historians: Turner, Beard, Parrington* outlined the new liberal interpretation for a post-war generation. To these post-Progressives, American thought was Lockean in its marrow: 'Locke dominates American political thought, as no thinker anywhere dominates the political thought of a nation. He is a massive national cliché.'[11] Americans took to Locke, they argued, because American society was individualistic, ambitious, proto-capitalist or, in a word, 'liberal'.[12] The ubiquity of Locke's theories of the sanctity of property and of self-regarding individuals voluntarily restraining their passions in the face of a multiplicity of interests helped to explain the reasonableness of the revolution. As Hofstadter wrote, Locke represented 'the legalistic, moderate, nonregicidal, and largely nonterroristic character of the American Revolution'.[13] The revolution was not an accumulation of seething class conflicts but a moderate and rational compromise where all demonstrations of conflict short of a Jacobin or Bolshevist revolution vanished in an all-pervasive liberal consensus.[14]

At the same time that liberal historians were working to modify the view of early American history, another form of revision was taking shape. In the late 1940s and early 1950s, a series of essays began to challenge the primacy of the consensual mode of history by exploring the influence of English libertarian thought on the American revolutionaries. For these historians, neither Beard's economics nor Hartz's Lockean individualism were the driving force behind the revolution and the early national period. Instead, they argued that colonial Americans drew their political and social attitudes from the libertarian thought of the English 'commonwealth' or 'country' polemicists of seventeenth- and eighteenth-century Britain. In 1947, Caroline Robbins looked towards Sidney's *Discourses* rather than Locke's *Essays* as a significant influence on American thought.[15] Acknowledging the contemporary ignorance of Sidney's writings and the frequent coupling of his name with Locke's, Robbins set out to uncover the nature of his influence during the revolutionary years. She revealed that like many of his contemporaries, Sidney voiced a popular theory of government against the divine right of any ruler or form of government. In his *Discourses Concerning Government*, Sidney suggested:

> As impostors seldom make lies to pass in the world, without putting false names upon things, such as our author endeavour to persuade the people they ought not to defend their liberties, by giving the name

of rebellion to the most just and honourable actions that have been performed for the preservation of them; and to aggravate the matter, fear not to tell us that rebellion is like the sin of witchcraft. But those who seek after truth, will easily find, that there can be no such thing in the world as the rebellion of a nation against its own magistrates, and that rebellion is not always evil.[16]

Unlike the 'principles of the wise and moderate Mr. Locke', Sidney justified rebellion and conspiracy in the face of tyranny and authoritarianism: 'For the radical, rebel, or revolutionary, the passionate and partisan *Discourses* provides an inspiration lacking in Locke's more temperate *Essays*.' Moreover, Robbins's essay revealed that while Sidney's inspiration faded in England after the revolution, in America his stature only increased. Conceived of as a seventeenth-century hero and martyr, his motto was adopted by various states, his story was retold in popular history books and his *Discourses* became one of the political textbooks along with the works of Milton, Harrington, Ludlow, Marvell and Locke, among others. Robbins suggests that the lack of interest in commonwealth doctrine in the contemporary 'post-Marxian world' occurred because the writings of these men did not bring about any significant constitutional change in eighteenth-century Britain, nor were they interested in issues of social and economic equality. For post-war Progressives and Liberals alike, Sidney's writings did not fulfil an interpretative need and therefore were largely ignored.[17]

Continuing her assessment of the influence of English reformers on America, Robbins followed her essay on Sidney with an examination of the republican bibliophile and philanthropist, Thomas Hollis. Another largely forgotten figure in post-war historiography, Hollis spent his life defending the seventeenth-century republican tradition and dedicated himself to the private service of English liberty. According to Robbins, Hollis 'became the most persistent and one of the most effective propagandists for radical Whig doctrines operating in the British Empire in the 1760's'.[18] While Samuel Johnson's Tory circle described him as a 'bigotted Whig or Republican', and a spreader of '"Combustibles" of sedition', Robbins uncovered his importance to eminent Americans such as Benjamin Franklin who commended Hollis's service to the cause of American liberty:

Good, not only to his own nation, and to his contemporaries, but to distant Countries, and to late Posterity; for such must be the effect of his multiplying and distributing copies of the Works of our best English writers on Subjects the most important to the Welfare of our Society.[19]

For Hollis, the American colonists represented true revolutionary principles, the faith of the real Whigs, and his benefactions of books, coins and illustrations to Harvard University reflected his support of their fight for an American Bill of Rights.[20]

Robbins's contribution to an understanding of the transmission and influence of libertarian thought to America propelled a series of essays that helped focus attention on an intellectual and ideological approach to American revolutionary thought and society.[21] While these nascent works often failed to offer an obvious relationship between English and American ideas or to define republicanism in an American context, they each helped to erode the orthodox view that ideas, particularly republican ideas, played no part in the revolution or the formation of the constitution. The turning point for republican historiography came with the publication of Robbins's 1959 groundbreaking work *The Eighteenth-Century Commonwealthmen*, the first detailed attempt to describe the English libertarian heritage that Americans drew upon. From the ideas of the Commonwealthmen, Robbins revealed the libertarian drive responsible for keeping alive the ideas of the 'Real Whigs', Harrington, Nedham, Milton, Ludlow, Sidney and Marvell who, while believing in the English constitution, also supported the separation of powers, freedom of thought and the sovereignty of the people in the face of increasing corruption and tyranny. As Robbins demonstrated, it was through the ideas of these 'Real Whigs', filtered through the writings of Robert Molesworth, John Trenchard and Thomas Gordon, that Americans developed a profound distrust of power and a fear of usurpation of liberty from the people.[22]

Following Robbins's work, the republican paradigm was fully realized with the publication of three landmark texts: Bernard Bailyn's *Pamphlets of the American Revolution: 1750–1776*, Gordon S. Wood's *The Creation of the American Republic: 1776–1787*, and J. G. A. Pocock's *The Machiavellian Moment*.[23] These volumes each contended that the breach between Britain and the colonies was to be explained primarily by understanding the circumstances as the participants perceived them. According to Pocock:

> in tracing history in terms of contemporary self-understanding – which is what the history of ideology really amounts to – one is not playing a barren game of pitting one cause against another cause, or one factor against another factor; one is exploring the contemporary perception of possibilities and impossibilities, and the limitations of that perception.[24]

Labelled the 'neo-Whig' or 'idealist' approach, these historians clarified the influence of English dissenting thought in America and the implications for American society on the intellectual life of the revolution. More significantly, they outlined the language and conceptual framework of republicanism and revealed the inherent concerns of the revolutionary generation which progressive and liberal historiography had tried to dismiss or contain. The revolution was not a smooth transition to republicanism, they argued, but an experiment punctuated by fear and despair. In this context, the classical dialects of virtue/corruption, liberty/tyranny, past/progress and authenticity/deception became the key terms to unlocking the meaning of eighteenth-century thought. For the neo-Whig historians, one solution to understanding this critical period is an awareness of the differences in political and social principle between the anti-Federalists and Federalists and, in particular, the dispute over the degree of balance between equality and the authority of the central government. Certainly, it was a generation deeply divided over its definition of social and political life. However, more important than the rivalries between opposing political parties was the fascination of the revolutionary generation with political ideology and, specifically, the ideology of republicanism. These historians viewed the whole revolutionary era as a continuing effort by the American people to decide exactly what republicanism meant to them. Arguments between Federalists and anti-Federalists were not to do with whether to have a republic, but rather what type of republic they envisioned and two modes of thought competed strenuously for the establishment of republican liberty: Protestantism and American legal thought.

The oppositional rhetoric of clergymen provided revolutionary Americans with a forceful moral dimension to the nation's fight against the British Empire, while the idea of law, reworked for an American republic from English common law and the legal treatise of the European Enlightenment, 'defined the events and capped its directions'.[25] Although individuals as diverse in political orientation as Alexander Hamilton, John Adams, Thomas Jefferson and John Taylor may have differed over the specifics of political theory, they nonetheless shared a common body of assumptions about republican political society. At its most basic level, all agreed that republicanism implied an absence of both a monarchy and an English-style aristocracy and the establishment of a government directed by the will of the people. But this usage of the term was always vague and ambiguous. It appears only once in the constitution, and in *The Federalist*, James Madison offered only a general meaning: 'we may define a republic to be, or at least may bestow that name on, a government which derives all its powers directly or indirectly from the body of the people; and is administered by persons holding their offices during pleasure, for an unlimited period, or during good behaviour'.[26] The term also encompassed a whole range of ideas regarding republican government which influenced the nation's manners and institutions. The first was that all republics were dependent on a broad distribution of virtue among its citizens. In the classical republican tradition, man was by nature a political being, and public or political liberty meant participation in government. However, liberty was only achieved when citizens were virtuous – that is, willing to sacrifice their private interests in favour of the public good. 'What is called a *republic*', wrote Thomas Paine, means the '*public good*', or the good of the whole, compared with a despotic form, which makes the good of the sovereign or of one man the only object of government. 'Every government that does not act on the principle of a *Republic*, or in other words, that does not make the *res-publica* its whole and sole object, is not a good government.'[27] The eighteenth-century classical values of public or civic virtue were not only American conceptions: virtue, and other values such as honour and sincerity that accompanied it,

> lay at the heart of all prescriptions for political leadership in the eighteenth-century English speaking world. Throughout the century

Englishmen of all political persuasions – whigs and tories alike – struggled to find the ideal virtuous leader amid the rising and swirling currents of financial and commercial interests that threatened to engulf their society.[28]

In the American context, public virtue or disinterestedness combined with the private virtues of industry, simplicity and sincerity to define the dimensions of republicanism; and it is because republics required such moral sacrifice that they are fragile polities, vulnerable to corruption and decay. The revolution had tested and refined the power of American virtue, but by the 1790s, when the crisis was over, men reverted to their naturally selfish, ambitious and extravagant ways. The greatest danger to virtue, both private and public, was commonly recognized as wealth and luxury, passion and competition, and with the return to prosperity after the economic disorder of the revolution, virtue was under threat. Profoundly aware of the historical fact that republican government never lasted for long, and challenged by the rapidly expanding commercial culture, American revolutionaries worried that the moral prerequisites of a republican order were difficult if not impossible to maintain. From their readings of both ancient and contemporary texts, they knew that all republics were vulnerable and impermanent; outside of a few European principalities, no other republican government prevailed at the time of the American Revolution. Because republican political society is characterized by individual liberty and the absence of a dominating authority, they were vulnerable to hostile attacks from without, and corruption and decay from within.

Another central idea was that the spirit and principle of a genuine republic was the promotion of equality of property among its citizens. Equality meant that no individual should be dependent on the will of another, and property made this independence possible. Americans concluded that they were naturally fit for republicanism precisely because they were 'a people of property; almost every man is a freeholder'.[29] But it was equally true that 'Power follows property', and as wealth increased, so too the tendency for power to consolidate in the hands of the few. The growing aristocracy of wealth led to the problem of faction, the internal rupture of society into competing political groups. As John Howe observes, 'Faction was virtue's opposite', and in the resulting struggles, 'passions were further aroused, internal divisions deepened and ultimately civil conflict was brought on. Such was the deadly spiral into which republican government too often fell.'[30] These fundamental assumptions reveal that rather than sunny optimism, American revolutionaries were preoccupied with fears of tyranny, corruption and national degeneration. The truth was that the once great and illustrious ancient republics were no more and Americans studied and used this knowledge to diagnose the problems of eighteenth-century England, as well as to prevent their own burgeoning nation from succumbing to a similar fate.

One of the first works to detect the pessimistic strain underlying eighteenth-century republican discourse was Bernard Bailyn's groundbreaking *Pamphlets of the American Revolution*. For Bailyn what was original about the revolution was not its social disruption but the alteration of American values, the way they looked at themselves and each other. From the agencies of newspapers, books, pamphlets, correspondence, as well as pan-Atlantic interest groups, the flow of information between Europe and the colonies was continuous, and for Bailyn the most important of these were the writings of the English dissenters:

> In every colony and in every legislature there were people who knew Locke and Beccaria, Montesquieu and Voltaire; but perhaps more important, there was in every village of every colony someone who knew such transmitters of English nonconformist thought as Watts, Neal, and Burgh; later Priestly and Price ... In the bitterly contentious pamphlet literature of mid eighteenth-century American politics, the most frequently cited authority on matters of principle and theory was not Locke or Montesquieu but *Cato's Letters*.[31]

Believing the American Revolution to be an ideological and constitutional struggle, Bailyn expected to find the influence of Enlightenment theology, common law, classical literature, as well as a certain amount of rhetoric and propaganda embedded in revolutionary writing. What he did not expect to find were those strands of thought that many historians had traditionally denounced as irrelevant, nonexistent or simply 'obtuse secularism'.[32] The first of these patterns of ideas was the pervasive influence of European Enlightenment theory and theology on the revolutionary generation. Not only were these influences relevant, he claimed, they revealed that '[c]itations, respectful borrowings from, or at least references to, the eighteenth-century European illuminati are everywhere in the pamphlets of Revolutionary America'. The ideas and writings of reformers such as Locke, Voltaire, Rousseau and Beccaria, as well as conservative thinkers such as Montesquieu, were 'quoted everywhere in the colonies, by everyone who claimed a broad awareness'.[33] The second discovery was a pattern of ideas and attitudes that flowed directly from the British tradition of radical social and political thought transmitted to the colonists by libertarians, disaffected politicians and religious dissenters whose anti-authoritarianism was bred in the upheaval of the English Civil War. Nourished by the seventeenth-century political writings of John Milton and Algernon Sidney, early eighteenth-century libertarians such as John Trenchard, Thomas Gordon, Benjamin Hoadly and Robert Molesworth, and the contemporary writings of Richard Price, Joseph Priestly and Thomas Paine, the revolutionary pamphleteers revealed an astonishing engagement with the language of radical and anti-establishment thought. This tradition, Bailyn noted, had never been applied to the origins of the American Revolution, and it was in the context of identifying and classifying these references and sources that he saw new meanings in the language of revolutionary literature. What Bailyn discovered was a lexicon of fear and suspicion, a 'vivid vocabulary' of 'slavery', 'corruption', 'conspiracy', expressed over and over in the profusion of arguments, replies, rebuttals and counter-rebuttals that made up the literature of the revolutionary period. This language was not merely the propaganda of completing interests groups, but represented a genuine fear of rising tyranny and corruption:

> These inflammatory words were used so forcefully by pamphleteers of so great a variety of social statuses, political positions, and religious persuasions; they fitted so logically into the pattern of radical and opposition thought; and they reflected so clearly the realities of life in an age in which monarchical autocracy flourished, in which the stability and freedom of England's 'mixed' constitution was a recent and remarkable achievement, and in which the fear of conspiracy against constituted authority was built into the very structure of

politics, that I began to suspect that they meant something very real to both the writers and their readers; that there were real fears, real anxieties, a sense of real danger behind these phrases, and not merely the desire to influence by rhetoric and propaganda the inert minds of an otherwise passive populace.[34]

For the colonists, the real danger to America was the violation of those principles upon which freedom rested. By 1763, Britain's 'mixed constitution', the balance of social and governmental forces was seen to be under threat by 'Jacobite remnants', 'effeminising luxury' and 'festering corruption'. In addition, there appeared to be evidence that 'nothing less than a deliberate conspiracy launched surreptitiously by plotters against liberty' was being perpetrated against America.

While conspiratorial fears were latent throughout colonial history, beginning with the Nonconformist's suspicion of the Church of England's 'formal design to root out Presbyterianism', the smouldering belief in a hidden plot directed against American liberties ignited with the institution of British policies in civil affairs: the passage of the Stamp Act, the Townsend Duties, the weakening of the judiciary and, especially, the implementation of standing armies, viewed by many as the keystone of arbitrary government, all confirmed for the colonists that the constitution was being undermined by what John Adams called the 'serpentine wiles' of the English administration. In the wake of the Boston Tea Party, Parliament 'threw off the mask' of legality and initiated a series of acts, intended to cripple the economic base of Massachusetts: the Administration of Justice Act, the Massachusetts Government Act, the Quebec Act and the Quartering Act. Once this interpretation of events took hold in the minds of the colonists, 'it could not be easily dispelled: denial only confirmed it, since what conspirators profess is not what they believe; the ostensible, for them, is not the real; and the real is deliberately malign'. It was this belief, according to Bailyn, that transformed the colonists' struggle and that in the end propelled them into revolution.[35]

Although Bailyn's work does not use the term republicanism directly, it emphasized the transatlantic influences on American institutions and employed the key terms by which republicanism would come to be identified. It was Bailyn's student Gordon Wood who would advance the view of a developing republican ideology in revolutionary America. Wood's *The Creation of the American Republic*, while less deterministic than Bailyn's *Pamphlets*, registered a similar note of surprise at the patterns of thought and conceptual language of the American patriots:

> my reading opened up an intellectual world I had scarcely known existed. Beneath the variety and idiosyncrasies of American opinion there emerged a general pattern of beliefs about the social process—a set of common assumptions about history, society, politics that connected and made significant seemingly discrete and unrelated ideas.[36]

Following Bailyn's description of revolutionary language meaning something 'very real' to both writers and readers, Wood also interprets the words of the generation not as hyperbole and propaganda but as genuine fears rooted in their culture and education. For Americans,

> the Revolution meant nothing less than a reordering of eighteenth-century society and politics ... a reordering that was summed up by the conception of republicanism ... Republicanism meant more for Americans than simply the elimination of a king and the institution of an elective system. It added a moral dimension, a utopian depth, to the political separation from England—a depth that involved the very character of their society.

According to Wood, the one source of republican inspiration acknowledged by all Whigs, English and American alike, was classical antiquity where all the great republics had flourished. The profusion of classical allusions, references, iconography and language that ran through the colonists' public and private writings revealed their investiture in creating an American neo-classical age. From their readings, Americans conceived of the ideal republic as one that avoided the downfall of the first and the sacrifice of individual interests to the greater good of the whole formed the essence of republicanism and the idealistic goal of their revolution. This ideology came to represent a final or even desperate attempt 'to realize the traditional Commonwealth ideal of a corporate society, in which the common good would be the only objective of government'.[37] Its most exact English equivalent was commonwealth, or a state belonging to the whole people rather than the crown. The people were a homogenous body, linked organically to the state and while the state was viewed as one moral whole, any clashing interests or factions were regarded as perversions and signs of sickness in the body politic.[38] Republicanism, in Wood's view, was profoundly traditional, embodying the ideal of the good society from antiquity through to the eighteenth century. Individual liberty and the public good were reconcilable because in Whig ideology liberty was public or political emphasizing not private rights against the general will but, more importantly, the public right against the interests of their rulers. This willingness to sacrifice private interests for the public good, this patriotism or nationalism was in the eighteenth century termed 'public virtue'.[39] Republics were vulnerable because in a polity that rested solely on the authority of the people, an extraordinary moral character was required. It was every man's duty to be benevolent, to subordinate their individual loves to the greater good of the whole. However, there existed an inherent conflict in this theory. Liberty means the security of property, but the security of property also begets wealth, and wealth is the source of luxury and degeneration; therefore, any attempt to regulate wealth is to restrict liberty. It is this conundrum, according to Wood, which is at the centre of republican ideology.

Wood also contends that the failure of the revolutionaries to identify a natural aristocracy resulted in the federal crisis of the 1780s and the 'end to classical politics'. The vocabulary that animated the revolutionaries in 1776, he claims, did not possess a timeless quality, and by 1787 the meaning of terms such as liberty, democracy, virtue or republicanism had undergone fundamental change: 'The Americans of the Revolutionary generation had not simply constructed a new form of government, but an entirely new conception of politics, a conception that took them out of an essentially classical and medieval world of political discussion into one that was recognizably modern'.[40] It was a shift, in other words, from republicanism to liberalism, from the classical theory of the individual as civic or active to one where the individual is primarily concerned with his own interests. According to Wood, as Federalist theory moved away from the paradigm of virtue toward self-interest, it abandoned the rhetoric of republicanism:

Once the people were thought to be composed of various interests in opposition to one another, all sense of a graduated organic chain in the social hierarchy became irrelevant, symbolized by the increasing emphasis on the image of a social contract. The people were not an order organically tied together by their unity of interest but rather an agglomeration of hostile individuals coming together for their mutual benefit to construct a society.[41]

By the end of the eighteenth century, virtue's characteristics of frugality, self-denial and simplicity were deemed too difficult to maintain in a prosperous post-revolutionary world. Classical virtue was increasingly seen as austere and anachronistic, and the burgeoning world of commerce and manners proliferated with alternatives to the ancient conceptions of virtue and liberty. Social morality became divorced from personal morality, manners replaced virtue and self-interest, a cornerstone of Federalist ideology, replaced public interest as the guiding principles of good citizenship. The effect was to 'construct a liberalism which made the state's authority guarantee the liberty of the individual's social behaviour'.[42]

In 1975, J. G. A. Pocock gave republicanism a global context and history. In *The Machiavellian Moment*, he undertook to explain how a complex of writings about republican political forms was formulated in early fifteenth-century Florence, restated in mid seventeenth-century England, and restated once more in revolutionary and Federalist America. While Bailyn and Wood claimed that the writers shaping the minds of the revolutionary generation were not Locke's heirs but the British 'commonwealth' or 'country' polemicists, Pocock traced a longer lineage through to Machiavelli and the discourse of civic humanism. And, while Bailyn and Wood viewed republicanism as an 'ideology' in the anthropological mode of Clifford Geertz, Pocock grasped a Kuhnian paradigm whose key word is language.[43] Pocock argued that the history of political ideas is also a history of political speech; that the historian of political thought is engaged in a quest for 'languages', 'idioms' and 'modes of discourse' that characterize an age:

The conduct of ideological—analysis the enterprise of showing how the historian's language is involved in the experience of his times and conveys intentions and information concerning it—ought to be an experiment in the representation of concrete actuality; we ought be able to see the historian's language shaping itself in response to actual pressures and to the end of conveying actual messages (conscious or unconscious as the case may be).[44]

The link between Florentine and American republicanism is located in the translation and migration of texts, models of rhetoric and thought patterns from one historical context to another:

> ideas—or rather the *langues* and *paroles* in which messages are conveyed—are facts: historical phenomena of varying duration, which inconveniently convey information concerning other facts that we frequently do not find it possible to accept. Some of these *langues* and *paroles* exist in forms durable enough to turn up more than once in the historical record ... the same thing can be said more than once, with effects of both continuity and discontinuity.[45]

Consequently, Pocock stresses Machiavelli instead of Locke and argues that the concept of a republic derived from Renaissance humanism was 'the true heir of the covenant and the dread of corruption the true heir of the jeremiad'. He suggests that the moment at which the 'fragility of the experiment, and the ambiguity of the republic's position in secular time, was more vividly appreciated than it could have been from a Lockean perspective'.[46] The foundation of the republic was not seen in terms of a return to nature, but as 'constituting an ambivalent and contradictory moment within a dialectic of virtue and corruption':

> There was indeed a flight from history into nature ... in terms of a flight from the Old World, from the burden of a priestly and feudal past ... but the analysis of corruption makes it clear that what was involved was a flight from modernity and a future no less than from antiquity and a past, from commercial and Whiggish Britain ... no less than from feudal and popish Europe.

It was in this 'quarrel with modernity', articulated in the humanist and neo-Harrington vocabularies, that 'American self-consciousness originated and acquired its terminology'.[47] Moreover, while Wood saw an 'end to classical ideology' after the formation of the Federalist constitution, Pocock asserts that a classical vocabulary continued to be important in shaping American thought and was kept 'alive and in tension with the consequences that followed its partial abandonment'. If America and Americans are founded on the principles of nature, then the pursuit of nature can be expressed in the dialectic of virtue and corruption: 'for this is the rhetoric of citizenship, and a cardinal assertion of Western thought has been that man is naturally a citizen'.[48] By detecting virtue in Jefferson's agrarian democracy, in frontier rhetoric and embodied in the person of Andrew Jackson, Pocock contends that 'classical history was still every man's textbook of politics'.[49] Equally, he extends his thesis of the continuation of the dialectic of virtue and corruption to the contemporary post-war generation. The conceptions and vocabularies that structured the venality in eighteenth-century public officials recurs, for example, in Eisenhower's warning of a 'military-industrial complex', in the other-directedness and one-dimensional personality of modern man and is continuous with the terms used in the classical analysis of corruption. According to Pocock, this language 'remains in many ways well suited to the purposes for which it is used; it serves to perpetuate the singular persistence of early modern values and assumptions in American culture'.[50] The quarrel with modernity, then, was not simply an eighteenth-century phenomenon, but extends over time to the present day and survives to 'furnish liberalism with one of its modes of self-criticism and self-doubt'.[51]

Criticism of the neo-Whig interpretation has been persistent and often hostile. Accused of avoiding other domains of culture, of foisting republican values on a political tradition founded on Lockean principles and of ignoring social diversity and conflict, these historians are seen to deal with ideology abstractly and without sufficient grounding in circumstances, environment and experience. The root texts of republicanism, critics argue, are in many respects as consensual as the consensus history they were designed to supplant. By insisting on the hegemony of a particular tradition, republican revisionists ignore the plurality of early America and the reality of competing ideological views in a highly literate, uncensored print culture. However, despite numerous detractors, it is now widely acknowledged that this mode of intellectual historiography has profoundly influenced our understanding of revolutionary politics and culture. It has, as Linda Kerber argues, enlarged our 'sensitivity to and respect for words as carriers of culture, and to a respect for ideology as an authentic expression of political situation and cultural condition'.[52]

While the post-war interest in republicanism provided an alternative to the world view generated by liberal capitalism, why it emerged at precisely the time it did is also worth exploring. Arguably the asocial and ahistorical approach to the study of American culture spurred many post-war intellectuals to investigate a different reality in their reading of the American past. The liberal narrative of a harmonious and moderate revolution was not an authentic depiction of events but merely reflected the contemporary vision of pluralist America basking in the glow of consensus politics. Told, with what Noam Chomsky calls 'the childlike simplicity of a fairytale', the story of liberal America in the cold war era is reassuringly familiar and uncompromising: it depicts a bipolar world projecting clear opposing categories of self and other, us and them, good and evil, American and un-American.[53] Whether political or cultural, cold war liberal narratives begin with a set of generic expectations and an implied, acquiescent audience: the spectre of international communism taking over the United States and reducing the republic to slavery, the threat of nuclear war and the urgent peril this evokes, and an appeal to the foundational narratives of freedom and democracy that supply the nation with a tradition to preserve and fight for. As Emily Rosenberg notes, these discursive strategies attempt to establish 'a single point of view from which the new post-war world is "mapped" and national security choices are understood'.[54] The consequence is a tyranny of meaning whereby the narrative becomes 'effectively monolithic and saturating, demonizing its opposite and cancelling or absorbing all mediatory and intermediate terms and kinds of activity'.[55] Arguably, in the light of this discursive tyranny, the cultural conditions were ripe for a re-evaluation of the American past and the hidden meanings of words and, therefore, republican historians set out to forge a different narrative: with their detailed focus on language and modes of discourse they uncovered not a moderate, harmonious past, but a history punctuated by fear and doubt. Equally, the lexicon of tyranny, corruption and degeneration retained their relevance in American culture well into the twentieth century because, despite the newfound comforts of the post-war era, a sense of vulnerability still consumed the American republic. As Pocock suggests, the language of classical republicanism persists into the twentieth century because the analysis of virtue and corruption 'continued to render commercial society, and the role of the self in it, problematic'.[56]

Despite the influence of this paradigm shift on American historiography, a similar republican tradition, or what Tom Paulin recently called the 'aesthetics of dissent', is muted in literary criticism.[57] In the post-war period, in particular, both progressive and idealist methods were rejected in favour of a liberal interpretation of culture. Following Pocock's thesis, this book takes the view that the language of classical republicanism did not end with the formation of the constitution and the advent of industrialization but continued to instil in the American consciousness a critique of liberal capitalism well into the twentieth century. From Theodore Roosevelt's 'Citizenship in a republic' lecture in which he extols the virtues of civic duty, 'disinterestedness' and sacrifice, to John F. Kennedy's warning against the 'corrosion of luxury' and his call for Spartan devotion to 'duty', 'honour' and the 'common cause', the conceptual language of republicanism is not only an essential part of America's cultural imaginary, but also provides the ideological scaffolding for America's deepest fears. In the mid twentieth century, Gothic fiction takes the distrust or critique of liberal principles to their logical and nightmarish extremes, re-configuring the vocabulary of corruption, tyranny and conspiracy into horrifying narratives of degeneration, infection and monstrosity. From this perspective, traditional Gothic figures such as the double, the vampire or the mass murderer function to dramatize the ongoing confrontation between the authority of traditional republican values and the liberal principles of progress and self-interest.

Notes

[1] Daniel Rogers, 'Republicanism: the career of a concept', *The Journal of American History*, 79, 1 (1992), 24, 12.
[2] Linda Kerber, 'Republican ideology of the revolutionary generation', *American Quarterly*, 37, 4 (1985), 474–95 (477).

3   Joyce Appleby, 'Republicanism and ideology', *American Quarterly*, 37, 4 (1985), 461. For a discussion of republicanism as a vocabulary, see James T. Kloppenberg, 'The virtues of liberalism: Christianity, republicanism, and ethics in early American political discourse', *The Journal of American History*, 74, 1 (1987), 9–33. On the difficulty of defining the term, see John R. Howe, Jr., 'Republican thought and the political violence of the 1790s', *American Quarterly*, 19 (1967), 147–65.
4   Lary May, 'Introduction', in Lary May (ed.), *Recasting America: Culture and Politics in the Age of Cold War* (Chicago: Chicago University Press, 1989), p. 4.
5   Appleby, 'Republicanism and ideology', 462.
6   Gordon S. Wood, 'Rhetoric and reality', *William and Mary Quarterly*, 23, 1 (1966), 3–32 (7). For Progressive interpretations of the American Revolution, see Carl L. Becker, *The Declaration of Independence: A Study in the History of Political Ideas* (New York: Random House, 1922); Philip Davidson, *Propaganda and the American Revolution, 1763–1783* (Chapel Hill: University of North Carolina Press, 1941); Arthur M. Schlesinger, *Prelude to Independence: The Newspaper War on Britain, 1764–1776* (New York: A. A. Knopf, 1958).
7   Charles A. Beard, *An Economic Interpretation of the Constitution of the United States* (1913; New York: Macmillan, rev. edn 1935), p. x.
8   Quoted in Wood, 'Rhetoric and reality', 9.
9   George M. Dutcher, 'The rise of republican government in the United States', *Political Science Quarterly*, LV, 2 (1940), 199–216 (200, 203). This overview is indebted to Robert E. Shalhope's essay, 'Toward a republican synthesis: the emergence of an understanding of republicanism in American historiography', *William and Mary Quarterly*, 29, 1 (1972), 49–80.
10 Charles A. Beard and Mary R. Beard, *The Rise of American Civilization*, vol. 1 and 2 (New York: Macmillan, n.d.), p. 187.
11 Louis Hartz, *The Liberal Tradition in America* (New York: Harcourt Brace, 1955), p. 140.
12 Rogers, 'Career of a concept', 14.
13 Richard Hofstadter, *The Progressive Historians: Turner, Beard, Parrington* (New York: A. A. Knopf, 1968), p. 162.
14 Rogers, 'Career of a concept', 13–14. See also Daniel J. Boorstin, *The Genius of American Politics* (Chicago: Chicago University Press, 1953).
15 Caroline Robbins, 'Algernon Sidney's *Discourses Concerning Government*: textbook for revolution', *William and Mary Quarterly*, 4, 3 (1947), 267–96.
16 Algernon Sidney, *Discourses Concerning Government* (1698), www.constitution.org/as/dcg_000.htm, section 36 (accessed 5 August 2005).
17 Robbins, 'Algernon Sidney', 292, 294. The novelty of Robbins's essay is evident in the journal's editorial: 'Miss Robbins' article on Sidney's *Discourses* is the first of a series of essays that the *Quarterly* plans to publish on the relation between English political "classics" and the eighteenth-century English radicals and the revolutionary principles of the American patriots of 1776. Scheduled for later publication are studies of Hume and the Federal Constitution, Thomas Hollis, "republican bibliophile," Bolingbroke in America, and Whig translators of the Greek and Roman classics' (295–6).

[18] Caroline Robbins, 'The strenuous Whig: Thomas Hollis of Lincoln's Inn', *William and Mary Quarterly*, 7, 3 (1950), 412. The editor's note, for example, reads: 'When in 1947 Miss Robbins and the editors of the *Quarterly* originally planned this article on Thomas Hollis we thought of it primarily as an amusing sketch of an eighteenth-century eccentric whose main claim to fame consisted in being obsessed by a great subject—LIBERTY ... In the process of research, however, Miss Robbins discovered the detailed Diary begun by Hollis in 1759, which reports *all* of his manifold activities in "the cause" of public liberty during the 1760's. With the Diary as a guide it was then possible to show for the first time ... that though he is a minor figure in the politics of his day, he is of major significance for understanding the strength—and weaknesses—of English radicalism and of pro-American sentiment in England on the eve of the Revolution' (406).

[19] Quoted in Robbins, 'Strenuous Whig', 408.

[20] For Hollis's contribution to America's republican iconography, see Caroline Winterer, 'From royal to republican: the classical image in early America', *The Journal of American History*, 91 (2005), 1264–90.

[21] See, for example, Douglass Adair, 'The tenth Federalist revisited', *William and Mary Quarterly*, 8 (1951), 48–67; Douglass Adair, '"That Politics May be Reduced to a Science": David Hume, James Madison, and the tenth *Federalist*', *Huntington Library Quarterly*, 20 (1957), 343–60; Neal Riemer, 'The republicanism of James Madison', *Political Science Quarterly*, 69 (1954), 45–64; Neal Riemer, 'James Madison's theory of the self-destructive features of republican government', *Ethics*, 65 (1954), 34–43; Cecelia Kenyon, 'Men of little faith: the anti-Federalists on the nature of representative government', *William and Mary Quarterly*, 12 (1955), 3–43; H. Trevor Colbourn, 'Thomas Jefferson's use of the past', *William and Mary Quarterly*, 15, 1 (1958), 56–70.

[22] Shalhope, 'Toward a republican synthesis', 58.

[23] Bernard Bailyn, *Pamphlets of the American Revolution: 1750–1776*, vol. 1 (Cambridge, Mass.: Harvard University Press, 1965); Gordon S. Wood, *The Creation of the American Republic, 1776–1787* (Williamsburg: University of North Carolina Press, 1969); J. G. A. Pocock, *The Machiavellian Moment: Florentine Republican Thought and the Atlantic Republican Tradition* (Princeton: Princeton University Press, 1975).

[24] J. G. A. Pocock, *Virtue, Commerce, and History: Essays on Political Thought and History, Chiefly in the Eighteenth Century* (New York: Cambridge University Press, 1985), p. 75.

[25] Robert A. Ferguson, *Reading the Early Republic* (Cambridge, Mass.: Harvard University Press, 2004), p. 53.

[26] James Madison, *The Federalist*, George W. Carey and James McClellan (eds) (Indianapolis: Liberty Fund, 2001), p. 194.

[27] Thomas Paine, *The Rights of Man*, ed. Gregory Claeys (Indianapolis: Hackett Publishing, 1992), p. 140 (original emphasis).

[28] Gordon S. Wood, *The Radicalism of the American Revolution* (New York: A. A. Knopf, 1992), p. 105.

[29] Quoted in Wood, *Radicalism of the American Revolution*, p. 234.

30. Howe, 'Republican thought', 158, 159.
31. Bailyn, *Pamphlets*, p. 344.
32. Ibid., p. ix.
33. Ibid., pp. 24, 23.
34. Ibid., p. ix.
35. Ibid., pp. 56, 61, 42, 60.
36. Wood, *Creation of the American Republic*, p. viii.
37. Ibid., pp. 47, 48, 54.
38. Ibid., pp. 58–9.
39. Ibid., pp. 61, 68.
40. Ibid., p. viii.
41. Ibid., p. 607.
42. Pocock, *Virtue, Commerce, and History*, p. 50.
43. Geertz contends that ideologies emerge and take hold at precisely the time when a society begins 'to free itself from the immediate governance of the received tradition'. Clifford Geertz, 'Ideology as cultural system', *The Interpretation of Cultures* (New York: Basic Books, 1973), p. 219.
44. J. G. A. Pocock, 'Between Gog and Magog: the republican thesis and the ideologia Americana', *Journal of the History of Ideas*, 48, 2 (1987), 326.
45. Ibid., 329.
46. *Idem, Machiavellian Moment*, p. 545.
47. Ibid., pp. 545–6.
48. Ibid., p. 527.
49. Ibid., p. 537.
50. Ibid., p. 548.
51. *Idem*, 'Between Gog and Magog', 341.
52. Kerber, 'Republican ideology', 474.
53. Noam Chomsky, *Deterring Democracy* (London: Vintage, 1992), p. 10.
54. Quoted in Ernest May (ed.), *American Cold War Strategy: Interpreting NSC68* (Boston: Bedford Books, 1993), p. 161.
55. Virginia Carmichael, *Framing History: The Rosenberg Story and the Cold War* (Minneapolis: University of Minnesota Press, 1993), p. 6.
56. Pocock, 'Between Gog and Magog', 344.
57. Tom Paulin, *Crusoe's Secret: The Aesthetics of Dissent* (London: Faber, 2005).

2

Vampires and the Cyclical Theory of History

> It is an unpleasing part of history, when corruption begins to prevail, when degeneracy marks the manners of the people, and weakens the sinews of the state. If this should ever become the deplorable situation of the United States, let some unborn historian, in a far distant day, detail the lapse, and hold up the contrast between a simple, virtuous, and free people, and a degenerate, servile race of beings, corrupted by wealth, effeminated by luxury, impoverished by licentiousness, and become the *automatons* of intoxicated ambition.
>
> Mercy Otis Warren (1805)[1]

In Stephen King's vampire novel *Salem's Lot* (1975), Ben Mears contemplates the history of his hometown; reviewing the names on the local war memorial he decides 'This town has the wrong name. It ought to be Time' (p. 170).[2] Before the vampire infestation, time in Jerusalem's Lot was seen to operate on a different schedule: a predictable timetable in which everything stayed the same and nothing nasty ever happened. While the names of the dead stretched from the revolutionary war to Vietnam, the Lot's knowledge of the country's history and torment remained 'academic' (p. 42). But as Ben discovers to his cost, the Lot's veneer of virtue and historical stasis masks an inner corruption; beneath the bucolic surface of the old-fashioned republic lurks a community in the throes of decay.

Commercial progress in the form of conglomerates had slowly 'eaten up the last of the independents' (p. 64) consuming the town's industry while behind closed doors, infidelity, domestic violence, infanticide and religious doubt festered and burst. Initially, the signs of rot are only palpable in the air, in the smell of 'something bad, like spoiled meat' (p. 50); in the odour of 'old corruption' (p. 137) and in the ghost of Hubert Martsen. But with the arrival of Kurt Barlow and Richard Straker, the town's final trajectory toward degeneration is complete. Weakened by corruption from within, it is invaded by an Old World terror: the urbane and courtly vampire.

King's narrative of the downfall of small-town America is organized around a theory of history which views civilization as perpetually threatened by corruption and the corrosive effects of time. As the prologue suggests, history is not static or progressive but cyclical:

> It is not the first town in American history to just dry up and blow away, and will probably not be the last, but it is one of the strangest. Ghost towns are common in the American Southwest, where communities grew up almost overnight around rich gold and silver lodes and then disappeared almost as rapidly when the veins of ore played out, leaving empty stores and hotels and saloons to rot emptily in desert silence. (p. 6)

Because Jerusalem's Lot remained inattentive to the outside world and therefore to the insidious infiltration of power and corruption, it begins and ends as a ghost town, a movement affirmed in the progression from virtue to corruption which the vampire cynically exploits. Ben's task is to return to the past, to search history for the cause of national degeneration and the return of the vampire. As the narrative reveals, whether moral corruption or the unbridled quest for power unleashed the vampire, the cause of the infestation invariably lies within.

The view of history as a perpetual cycle of birth, growth and inevitable decline has been a part of the narrative of America since the revolution and a central theme of the nation's Gothic literature. The concept of republicanism begins with the radical perception that history was a struggle between two parallel sets of opposing principles: in political terms, between liberty and power; in ethical or moral terms, between virtue and corruption. Intertwined with these oppositions is the belief that world events are conceptualized through a theory of history whereby the rise and fall of nations follows a pattern in which virtue leads to liberty, which in turn engenders progress and power, followed inevitably by corruption, tyranny and degeneration. While early republicans believed America was only beginning the first stage of its development, just how it would avoid the downfall of the first was the central concern of the age and explains the continuing fear of tyranny or unchecked power in the American consciousness. During the cold war period, in particular, narratives of invasion or infestation register the widespread fear of totalitarianism and nuclear erasure. Popular narratives, in particular, often portray America in the grip of an emergency or what Susan Sontag calls the 'imagination of disaster',[3] dramatizing the need for group consensus or the lone maverick sacrificing himself to save humanity. Post-war tales of vampire infestation, on the other hand, often begin in the fatalistic aftermath of disaster where no hero or group cohesion can emerge. The vampire, by its very nature presents a pessimistic view of history as inevitable and repetitive. Charles Beaumont's 'Place of meeting', imagines a world in which 'gas bombs', 'disease' and 'flying pestilences' cover the earth in 'three days and three nights'.[4] In this tale, national degeneration is the result of man's scientific hubris and quest for power; the only survivors in this destroyed civilization are a collection of vampires who, after scouring the earth for signs of life, return to their graves until humanity rebuilds: 'It ain't the first time. It ain't the last … it'll start all over again and folks'll build their cities— new folks with new blood—and then we'll wake up (pp. 374–5). Like King's *Salem's Lot*, Beaumont's tale begins where it ends: the narrative, like history is cyclical; only after total destruction can the process of regeneration or rebirth ensue. Richard Matheson's 1954 vampire novella *I Am Legend* reveals a similar theme. Employing the popular metaphor of infection in its depiction of a world overrun by vampires, Matheson's text engages with the contemporary fears of communist takeover, while enacting for a new generation, the theory of civilization perpetually under threat by corruption and the movement of time. In a post-war context, the conceptual language of this fear is re-configured in the liberal categories of nature versus culture.

Vampires and the Cyclical Theory of History

Degeneration and the eighteenth-century cyclical theory of history

> The best instituted governments, like the best constituted animal bodies, carry in them the seeds of their destruction: and though they grow and improve for a time, they will soon tend visibly to their dissolution. Every hour they live is an hour the less that they have to live. All that can be done therefore to prolong the duration of a good government, is to draw it back, on every favourable occasion, to the first good principles on which it was founded. When these occasions happen often, and are well improved, such governments are prosperous and durable. When they happen seldom, or are ill improved, these political bodies live in pain or in languor, and die soon.
>
> Bolingbroke, *The Patriot King* (1738)[5]

Historians identify three distinct theories of history operating in American culture during the eighteenth century: the millennial revival, the cyclical theory and the idea of progress. The first conception comes from the revivalists of the Great Awakening. This 'supernaturalist interpretation' viewed history as the unfolding revelation of divine purpose. Human history was a work of redemption which would only be completed with the second coming of Christ and the establishment of his millennial kingdom on earth.[6] Revivalists such as Jonathan Edwards believed that the new world had been 'reserved for recent discovery and the conversion of the heathen aborigines' in order to fulfil God's promise of the establishment of Christ's kingdom. The central controversy arising from the Great Awakening concerned the method of God's governance. For the revivalists, God intervened through special providences and direct inspiration to guide men through the historical process. Anti-revivalists, on the other hand, believed God achieved his ends through laws learned in scripture and through the observation of nature. The work of the divine spirit operates upon the reason, bringing about a change in the temper of mind, disciplining the unruly passions in accordance with the new and clearer insight into the nature of divine truth. It is only through the use of reason and Scripture men would discover and do God's will. 'The plain truth is, an *enlightened Mind*, and not *raised Affections*, ought always to be the Guide to those who call themselves Men.' As Persons observes, 'Enlightened thinkers commenced by glorifying reason as a disciplinary agency, and only gradually did the course of events suggest its use as a revolutionary solvent.' While neither the revivalists nor their opponents rejected the millennial hope, or the testimony of Scripture that Christ would return to judge mankind, there nonetheless emerged two radically different concepts of the second coming and it was out of the anti-revivalist line of thought that the second concept of history emerged. The new view of history saw historical movement in the operation of a universal moral law, the effect of which was an endless cyclical movement analogous to the life cycle of an organism: 'Societies and nations rise and fall in endless sequence according as they observe or disregard those universal moral laws ordained by God and graven upon men's consciences for their governance and happiness.'[7] To the enlightened clergy the cyclical theory possessed a didactic function: history was teaching by example and the decline and fall of empires represented a divine judgement on the corruption of men and the body politic. The main feature of this revised millennial hope was the belief that mankind would advance toward the millennium and toward a state of civil harmony and religious and political liberty.

These ideas and attitudes were not peculiar to the clergy. For the secular thinkers of the period, the cyclical schematic of world history also provided a projection into the future which placed Americans at the beginning of a libertarian and economic uprising. 'We have it in our power to begin the world over again', wrote Paine. 'A situation, similar to the present, hath not happened since the days of Noah until now. The birthday of the new world is at hand, and a race of men perhaps as numerous as all Europe contains, are to receive their portion of freedom from the event of a few months.'[8] From this secular point of view, rational thought, with its emphasis on the material world, often melded comfortably with religious faith. In *The Church's Flight Into the Wilderness*, the Reverend Samuel Sherwood contemplates 'free trade' in his sermon, and how, through the Continental Congress, 'the spirit of liberty might spread and circulate with commerce'.[9] The cyclical view of history, therefore, performed a mediatory function readily accommodating both the revivalist and secular theories of history. Many Americans agreed with Charles Rollin that 'history may properly be called the common school of mankind, equally open and useful to great and small, to princes and subjects, [because] history when it is well taught becomes a school of morality'. It was Rollin's ability to fuse theological and secular elements that was especially attractive to Americans:

> Whilst all things are in motion and fluctuate upon earth; whilst states and empires pass away with incredible rapidity, and the human race, vainly employed with these outward appearances, are also drawn in by the same torrent, almost without perceiving it; there passes in secret an order and disposition of things unknown and invisible, which, however, determines our fate to all eternity.[10]

Religious and secular thought came together partly because the republic emerged from a revivalist Bible culture, but also because both reason and faith were necessary to explain the wide-scale changes occurring in post-revolutionary culture.[11]

The third conception of history was embodied in the idea of progress which issued from the moralism of the cyclical theory and the millennial hope of the revivalists. As leading evangelicals realized that the second coming was not imminent or that their hopes were premature, they worked to keep it alive by encompassing historical possibilities. For the more enlightened members of the clergy, the survival of the millennial vision was made possible by measuring progress in moral terms. The idea of progress posited history as a linear, irreversible continuum ushering in the progressive notion of liberty within a virtuous republic. Human nature was perfectible through reason and education, and history was a steady movement from savagery towards peace and prosperity. America, Jefferson wrote, was 'a rising nation ... advancing rapidly to destinies beyond the reach of mortal eye'. While it was unclear what direction the country would take, for like-minded optimists, tolerance, equality and the pursuit of 'industry and improvement' would work to 'close the circle of our felicities'.[12] Republican principles, it was argued, whether religious or secular, would ensure virtue thereby avoiding the cyclical pattern of rise and fall, and inculcating a linear movement towards progress and freedom.

Yet, for many Americans cyclical theory was less about millennial utopianism or secular progress than about national degeneration. In much eighteenth-century writing, images of the rising glory of America competed strenuously with a discourse of loss and dissolution. In addition to an awareness of liberty's vulnerability to corruption, faction and power was the understanding of the historical forces at work to undermine a republican government. History consisted of the rise and fall of empires and this cycle of birth, maturity and decline was directly related to the character and behaviour of the people. The cyclical theory of history assumed that once republics reached a certain level of accomplishment, the manners of the people would change. Progress and prosperity would not secure virtue but introduce vice and hasten corruption.[13] As Pocock observes, there is a dimension of 'historical pessimism' in America's utopian thought; the Jeffersonian vision of the 'chosen people' is not guaranteed by nature; for civic virtue to last, it requires an apocalyptic framework for its own affirmation. 'When manners are corrupt, not even the Constitution can be counted upon. Even in America, the republic faces the problem of its own ultimate finitude, and that of its virtue, in space and time.' As Machiavelli had taught them, virtue was finite and when used up, catastrophe followed.[14] While many clung to the image of America as a pastoral Eden, even the proponents of republicanism understood that the country was under constant threat by the movement of history and the inevitable corruption of man. Over the course of time, increased commerce would lead to the love of riches that in turn would lead to the want of luxury and power, the ultimate precursors to corruption and tyranny. In the republican tradition, inherited agrarian values exemplified a 'civic and patriot ideal in which the personality was founded in property, perfected in citizenship but perpetually threatened by corruption'. Virtue, in other words, could 'develop only in time, but is always threatened with corruption by time'.[15] Borrowing Bolingbroke's metaphor of the infected animal body, Reverend David Tappan places this fear in an American context:

> Experience proves that political bodies, like the animal economy, have their periods of infancy, youth, maturity, decay, and dissolution. In the early stages of their existence their members are usually industrious and frugal, simple in their manners, just and kind in their intercourse, active and hardy, united and brave. Their feeble, exposed, and necessitous condition in some sort forces upon them this conduct and these habits.

> The practice of these virtues gradually nourishes them to a state of manly vigor. They became mature and flourishing in wealth and population, in arts and arms, in almost every kind of national prosperity. But when they have reached a certain point in greatness, their taste and manners begin to be infected. Their prosperity inflates and debauches their minds. It betrays them into pride and avarice, luxury and dissipation, idleness and sensuality, and too often into practical and scornful impiety. These and other kindred vices, hasten their downfall and ruin.[16]

For religious leaders such as Tappan, the loss of virtue renders man incapable not only of preserving liberty, but also of 'bearing the blessings' of equality. The survival of the republic is subject not only to God's judgement but equally to the behaviour of individuals. In this conception, morality and liberty are interdependent, and when civilization reaches its zenith, it inevitably becomes 'infected' and dies.

For many of the revolutionary generation, the cyclical view was an attempt to understand the moral and social basis of politics. Since Machiavelli, the classical world had been the inspiration for politicians and particularly those of the radical Whigs, which informed much of America's understanding of antiquity. As a result, America's view of the classical past was glossed by the didactic popularizations and translations of eighteenth-century authors. Rollin's *Ancient History* (1730–8) and *Roman History* (1738–41), Gibbon's *Decline and Fall of the Roman Empire* (1776–88) and Volney's *Ruins* (1791) all worked to undercut the idea of progress; each impressed upon a generation, no matter how optimistic, the fragility of the republic and its vulnerability to the corrosive effects of time. As Wood observes, since the aim of these works was to discover 'the principal causes of that degeneracy of manners, which reduc'd those once brave and free people into the most abject slavery', their view of antiquity was 'highly selective, focusing on decline and decadence'. It was the pessimistic literature of Romans such as Cicero, Sallust, Tacitus and Plutarch, filtered through the pens of Enlightenment thinkers that spoke directly to the revolutionary generation and which validated their diagnosis of the illness permeating Great Britain and which would soon infect the republic. Antiquity became 'a kind of laboratory in which autopsies of the dead republics would lead to a science of social sickness and health matching the science of the natural world'.[17] It was 'undeniably evident', wrote one observer, 'that some malignant disorder has seized upon our body politic, and threatens at least an interruption of our advances to manhood, if not a political dissolution'. 'LUXURY, LUXURY, the great source of dissolution and distress, has here taken up her dismal abode; infectious as she is, she is alike caressed by rich and poor', destroying 'that simplicity of manners, native manliness of soul, and equality of station, which is the spring and peculiar excellence of a free government'.[18] Cyclical theory held that corruption acted like a cancer, metastasizing through the state, eating at its vitals until the state died. What made the ancient republics great and what ultimately destroyed them was not the force of arms but the character and spirit of the people. It was power, wealth and a desire for a life of ease, distinction and elegance that softened the nation and foreshadowed degeneracy. Frugality, industry, temperance and simplicity, these were the characteristics of a virtuous society. Republics, in other words, 'died not from invasion from without but from decay from within'.[19] Thomas Jefferson sought a legal remedy for the degenerative effects of time: 'It can never be too often repeated, that the time for fixing every essential right on a legal basis is while our rulers are honest, and ourselves united. From the conclusion of this war we shall be going downhill.'[20] Although Jefferson remained hopeful that America's decline could be curtailed by the diffusion of knowledge and a balanced constitution which would 'unite common efforts for the common good', others envisioned a more precarious future. Mercy Warren Otis, for example, disagreed with Jefferson's appraisal and argued for moral and ethical solutions to the problem of corruption. In *History of the American Revolution* (1805), she claimed that 'fixing every essential right on a legal basis' would be useless unless the people themselves were virtuous. Precisely as Greece, Rome, Venice and Geneva had fallen, so too had England's 'republican opinions'. With the freedom of the nation under wane, England had become 'an ungrateful, dissipated nation', fallen into 'barbarism'.[21] Warren's *History* questions the competing theory of uni-linear progress: there was no evidence that history contained an inherent principle that would naturally lead to man's perfectibility or that history moved in one desirable direction indefinitely. On the contrary, all past republics had been consumed from within and to ignore this fact and to trust in the authority of the constitution was to be lulled into a false sense of security, and to abdicate responsibility for one's own actions. Therefore, while the sentiments of the Jeffersonians suggested a cautious belief in progress when founded on law, others were not so sure. As Stow Persons observed, the revolutionary generation had 'a keen sense of the precariousness of the felicity which they enjoyed, of the moral and social conditions which would make its continuation possible, and of the ultimate likelihood of its dissipation'.[22]

The view of corruption as a horrid, rapidly consuming contagion gave rise to a theory of history that was designed to unite secular republican thought and morality in a single interpretative framework, a theory that pitted American virtue against the corruption of the Old World. The fusion of republican ideology, cyclical theory and religious doctrine harmonized for a diverse American population the moral teachings of history. As Cohen suggests, 'what Jefferson might have called weakness, [others] called sin. Where Adams might have seen a cause and effect relationship between debauchery and tyranny, [others] discerned punishment from Heaven.'[23] Yet, whether religious or secular, the eighteenth-century fear of corruption, tyranny and degeneration revealed a conception of history as repetitive and inevitable; and because corruption was commonly expressed in metaphors of infection, barbarity and automation, in the eighteenth-century mind it also became allied with the consumptive and oppressive habits of the vampire.

The use of the term 'vampire' in the English language is believed to have originated in 1732 with the sensational case of the Serbian farmer Arnold Paul who apparently had fallen victim to a vampire and lived to tell the tale. It was Paul's story that informed two of the eighteenth century's most influential works on vampirism: Dom Augustin Calmet's *Dissertations sur le apparitions des anges, des démons et des esprits, et sur les revenants et vampire de Hongrie, de Bohême, de Moravie, et de Silésie* (1746), and Guiseppe Davanzati's *Dissertazione sopra I Vampiri* (1744). Identified as *revenant, upir, nosferatu* or *vrykolakas*, in Calmet's construction, vampires were materialistic peasants, usually apostates, excommunicated Christians or victims of murder or plague who preyed on their family or neighbours. But in the eighteenth century, the concept of a bloodsucking parasite already had other rhetorical uses. For a generation preoccupied with the abuse of power, the vampire came to signify a specific kind of political corruption. Shortly after the Arnold Paul story broke in 1732, an article in the *The Craftsman* proposed that the stories circulating about the Hungarian vampire also functioned as 'satirical Invective' against oppression:

> The Account, you'll observe, comes from the Eastern Part of the World, always remarkable for the *Allegorical Style*. The States of *Hungary* are in Subjection to the *Turks* and *Germans*, and govern'd by a pretty hard Hand; which obliges them to couch all their Complaints under *Figures* . . . These *Vampyres* are said to torment and kill the *Living* by *sucking out all their blood*; and a *ravenous Minister*, in this part of the World, is compared to a *Leech* or *Bloodsucker*, and carries his Oppressions beyond the Grave, by anticipating the *publick Revenues*, and entailing a perpetuity of *Taxes*, which must gradually drain the Body Politick of its Blood and Spirits. In like manner, Persons who groan under the burthens of such a *Minister*, by selling or mortgaging their estates, torment their *unhappy Posterity*, and become *Vampyres* when dead. *Paul Arnold*, who is call'd a *Heyduke*, was only a *ministerial Tool*, because it is said he had kill'd but 4 Persons, whereas, if he had been a *Vampyre* of any Rank, we shou'd probably have heard of his *Ten Thousands*.[24]

In the eighteenth-century popular imagination, the figure of the vampire represents the degenerative effects of luxury and self-interest; not simply an anthropological oddity or a figure of Christian superstition, the bloodsucking parasite was also a handy term of abuse levelled against corrupt community leaders. The metaphorical use of the term 'vampire' in *The Craftsman* suggests the word was already in common usage before the Arnold Paul story. Charles Forman, for example, employed the term in 1688 to describe the corruption of the merchant class. In *Some Queries and Observations Upon the Revolution of 1688*, written in the same year, but not published until 1741, Forman writes:

> Our Merchants indeed, bring money into their country, but it is said, there is another Set of Men amongst us who have as great an Address in sending out again to foreign Countries without any returns for it,

which defeats the Industry of the Merchant. These are the Vampires of the Publick, and Riflers of the Kingdom.[25]

Here, vampires are linked to private interest, profiteering and plunder, a theme repeated by Voltaire in his *Philosophical Dictionary* (1764):

> We never heard a word of vampires in London, not even Paris. I confess that in both these cities there are stock-jobbers, brokers, and men of business who sucked the blood of the people in broad daylight; but they were not dead, though corrupted. These true suckers lived not in cemeteries but in very agreeable palaces.[26]

Voltaire's comment forges a relationship between vampires and money speculators: the corrupt business class sucks the life blood in pursuit of its own aristocratic pretensions. In 1770, William Pitt, Earl of Chatham, referred to the Treasury as that '*moneyed interest*', 'that bloodsucker' and 'muckworm, that calls itself the friend of government'.[27] The widespread use of the signifier vampire to denote the corrupting and degenerative effects of commerce and power was particularly relevant in America as the New England preacher Edward Payson exclaimed in his 1804 anniversary address: 'Luxury is the first, second and third cause of the ruin of republics. It is the vampire which soothes us into fatal slumber while it sucks the lifeblood of our veins.'[28] Regardless of political or religious affiliation, in the conceptual language of corruption, the vampire is inextricably associated with luxury, power and degeneration, a theme that would continue to resonate into the twentieth century.

Degeneration, disease and cold war vampires

On 20 January 1953, General Dwight D. Eisenhower swore the presidential oath of office on not one, but two Bibles. The first belonged to George Washington and was used for his presidential inauguration in 1789; the second was a gift from Eisenhower's mother upon his graduation from the Military Academy at West Point. While not the first president to swear his oath on two Bibles (Harry Truman also used two), together they function as a symbolic rendering of what, by 1953, was a dominant discursive strategy in cold war discourse: the melding of the moral and political categories of virtuous citizenship. By laying claim to a universal moral authority, Eisenhower forges a link between swearing an oath before God and his role as the nation's leader, between the institutions that embody power and the Christian precept of faith. Reminiscent of the eighteenth-century's revised millennial hope, Eisenhower's oath reaffirms the long-held belief that faith in God and the hopes for America are inseparable.

The two Bibles also establish linkages between the national narrative and cold war foreign and domestic policy. Washington's Bible appeals to the authority of the founding fathers and the discourse of republicanism. It is a turn towards history constructing a continuity of purpose and tradition while at the same time precluding contradiction and dissent. Eisenhower's West Point Bible reinforces the sacred alliance between the military and motherhood, between the role of God in the security of the nation and the economic and foreign policies that support this alliance. The two Bibles create, with double emphasis, a vision of a national consensus, a representation of a symbolic 'us', thereby positioning his audience on the side of family, of government, of history and of God. However, there is a fundamental paradox at the heart of this postwar narrative of America. After establishing the frame that will inform his speech, Eisenhower begins to lay out a plot of impending disaster:

> The world and we have passed the midway point of a century of continuing challenge. We sense with all our faculties that forces of good and evil are massed and armed and opposed as rarely before in history. This fact defines the meaning of this day.[29]

The mid twentieth century is, according to Eisenhower, a 'time of tempest', a time that has seen thrones 'toppled', 'vast empires' destroyed and the birth of 'new nations'. It is a time infused by shadow and the fear of inevitable repetition: 'How far have we come in man's long pilgrimage from darkness toward light? Are we nearing the light – a day of freedom and peace for all mankind? Or are the shadows of another night closing in upon us?'[30] While a great believer in the beneficence of progress, Eisenhower, like many of his American forefathers, expressed a concern for the 'disastrous rise of misplaced power', a power locked in the movement of time:

> This trial comes at a moment when man's power to achieve good or to inflict evil surpasses the brightest hopes and the sharpest fears of all ages. We can turn rivers in their courses, level mountains to the plains. Oceans and land and sky are avenues for our colossal commerce. Disease diminishes and life lengthens. Yet the promise of this life is imperiled by the very genius that has made it possible. Nations amass wealth. Labor sweats to create—and turns out devices to level not only mountains but also cities. Science seems ready to confer upon us, as its final gift, the power to erase human life from this planet.[31]

Eisenhower's speech reverberates with the discourse of cyclical decline, with David Tappan's warning against amassed 'arts and arms' and the inevitability of corruption. It also represents one of the essential contradictions in post-war liberal culture. On the one hand, Eisenhower's optimistic hope for the future is founded on tradition and the moral category of virtue. Like many of his enlightened forefathers, he believes in the idea of progress and the ability of man to control his historical destiny. Just as Jefferson thought that industry and improvement would 'close the circle of our felicities', Eisenhower views liberty and material progress as inextricably linked:

> Moral stamina means more energy and more productivity, on the farm and in the factory. Love of liberty means the guarding of every resource that makes freedom possible—from the sanctity of our families and the wealth of our soil to the genius of our scientists.

Yet this vision of a progressive republic liberated by material wealth and moral virtue is tempered by an opposing narrative: the growth of wealth, Eisenhower knows, breeds power, which in turn begets corruption.

> For our own country, it has been a time of recurring trial. We have grown in power and in responsibility. We have passed through the anxieties of depression and of war to a summit unmatched in man's

history ... In the swift rush of great events, we find ourselves groping to know the full sense and meaning of these times in which we live.³²

Implicit in the warning is a deep suspicion of the perfectibility of man and of the progressive movement of history in time.

By the end of his presidency, Eisenhower's fear of the future took on an urgent tone, and in his farewell address he cautioned the nation against what he saw as the dangerous growth of complacency and power:

> As we peer into society's future, we—you and I, and our government—must avoid the impulse to live only for today, plundering, for our own ease and convenience, the precious resources of tomorrow. We cannot mortgage the material assets of our grandchildren without risking the loss also of their political and spiritual heritage. We want democracy to survive for all generations to come, not to become the insolvent phantom of tomorrow.

For Eisenhower, corruption and national dissolution is predicated not only in the want of ease, but also in the 'technical revolution' and in 'the acquisition of unwarranted influence ... by the military-industrial complex', that monolithic unification of industrial and military machinery of defence.³³ Democracy in this vision is at risk of becoming a mere 'phantom', destroyed by luxury and scientific hubris. Ironically, for all its protestations against nostalgia for the past, the liberal narrative reproduces the conceptual language of the early republic. Its ultimate admonition is against the encroachment of corruption from the effects of power; rather than being free from the chains of history, liberalism, as Reinhold Niebuhr paradoxically acknowledged, 'simply [recovers] ancient truths which [it] never should have forgotten'.³⁴

If corruption and degeneration was still the language of post-war America, vampirism, too, still functioned as one of its primary metaphors. The vampire's return challenges the idea of time as progressive and ordered, and of man moving ever forward to a state of perfection. In a political culture determined to contain ambiguity of meaning as well as social and political deviance, the vampire is the ultimate enemy: an equivocal and barbaric other, an invading pathogen whose virulence is matched only by its duplicity and insatiable hunger for power.

For cold warriors such as Eisenhower, J. Edgar Hoover and George Kennan among others, the logic of counter-subversion is most potently expressed in the Gothic metaphors of disease, degeneration and predatory, primitive energy. Communism, like vampirism, functions metonymically for everything that is perceived as corrupt, degenerate or 'Other' in culture. For J. Edgar Hoover, communism in America signalled the invasion of a paradoxically 'modern primitive' who uses 'blood purge' to achieve domination: 'Something utterly new has taken root in America . . . a communist mentality representing a systemic, purposive, and conscious attempt to destroy Western civilisation and roll history back to the age of barbaric cruelty and despotism.'[35] The Gothic resonance in Hoover's language is located in the fear of degeneration and tyranny, and in the threat to progress that the communist (and the vampire) embodies. Similarly for Eisenhower, communists represent the dangerous, single-minded tyrant who knows 'no God but force, no devotion but its use', and if left unchecked, will proliferate and 'feed upon the hunger of others'.[36] Eisenhower's language marks the violence, profanity and diabolical powers of the primitive enemy. Unchristian, regressive and negative, the communist, like the vampire, is the dark double of the ideal citizen. Employing the metaphor of the body, George Kennan links communist tyranny with physical disease: 'Much depends on the health and vigor of our own society. World communism is like a malignant parasite which feeds only on diseased tissue. This is the point at which domestic and foreign policies meet.'[37] Kennan's rhetoric signals the ultimate threat of communist (vampiric) activity: the consumption and eventual degeneration of the body politic. Kennan's villain is the germ within, or what Hoover called the 'barbarian in modern dress', 'virtually invisible to the non-communist eye, [and] unhampered by time, distance, and legality'.[38]

Underlying the metaphors of communist infection, the figure of the vampire also allows for an interrogation of the quarrels that existed within the political centre itself. One of the central assumptions of 1950s culture was that political ideology was organized around the themes of consensus and containment as articulated in pluralist discourse. Centrists adopted an 'us' or 'them' framework to denote dissidence, whereby anything that threatened consensus was discredited as 'Other'. And while the 'Other' was certainly communism, it was also whatever the centre was not. As cultural historians Peter Biskind and Victor Navasky have pointed out, during the cold war, ideological positions were informed by a host of cultural oppositions that emerged after the Second World War: science versus the military, government versus the individual, private versus public, culture versus nature. 'The Red Menace theory', argues Biskind, 'stands in the way of thinking through the idea of the Other ... The Soviet threat was as much a function of the squabbles between Democrats and Republicans as it was a reality ... Indeed, the red nightmare was so handy that had it not existed, American politicians would have to invent it.'[39] Therefore, while government figures such as Hoover, Eisenhower and Kennan may have conceived of the subversive within as a genuine threat to American security, subversion was always ambiguously defined and, as a result, readily functioned as a polemical device for dehumanizing political opponents. As Carey McWilliams observed, 'Without a witch hunt, there would be no witches, and witches are never hunted without a reason. Witch hunts are a means by which, in time of storm, the belief in witches is exploited in order to control men's thoughts and to police their loyalties.' For McWilliams, there was no real enemy, no evil Other, only what he called 'imaginary monsters of error'.[40] The cold war, in other words, was more than a battle between rival political ideologies, it was a war between Eisenhower and MacArthur, Teller and Oppenheimer and, one might add, between McWilliams and Schlesinger:

> the cold war was really three simultaneous conflicts: a global confrontation between rival imperialism and ideologies, between capitalism and Communism ... a domestic clash in the United States between hunter and hunted, investigator and investigated ... and, finally, a civil war amongst the hunted, a fight within the liberal community itself, a running battle between the anti-Communist liberals and those who called themselves Progressives, the so-called anti-anti-Communists.[41]

In the language of pluralism, if the centre was modern, the Other was ancient. If the centre was civilized, the Other was primitive. If the centre was scientific and technological, the Other was natural.

If the centre was 'normal', the Other was abnormal, radical, extreme; if the centre was culture, the Other was nature.[42]

Like other popular texts of the era, Richard Matheson's *I Am Legend* dramatizes the dialectics operating at the heart of post-war political culture. On one level, its imagery of predatory, mindless hordes of vampires thematically fulfils the role of anti-communist horror and the political darkness, uniformity and automata of the communist psyche. In this reading, the text allegorizes the central fears of the generation: the invasion of America by a monstrous and monolithic global power, and the subversion of societal values from within. However, implicit in the narrative structure of 'us' versus 'them', the text also mirrors the clashing ideologies between nature and culture which existed within the political establishment itself, ideologies which resonate with the classical language of virtue and corruption and the fear of progress. In the 1950s, the political centre rejected the notion that America was founded on the principles of nature. In pluralist ideology, nature is primitive, dangerous and ultimately dystopian; it implies a naive, nostalgic and sentimental turn to the past and a belief in the perfectibility of man. If nature could be viewed as an escape from corruption, it also represents a flight from modernity and the future. Nature then, becomes analogous to the eighteenth-century concept of republican virtue, which post-war liberals dismissed as obsolete and immature. Culture, on the other hand, is civilized, rational, technological and progressive. Pluralists identified the centre with the highest achievements of humanity, with scientific production and with the future. The past, in their view, was redundant; virtue anachronistic. The Other in culture were extremists, those who still believed in utopian promises, who distrusted culture and who either repudiated consensus or battled for authority over it. 'We must grow up now', wrote Schlesinger, 'and forsake the millennial dream.'[43]

I Am Legend

There are vampires and vampires and not all of them suck blood.
Fritz Leiber, 'The girl with the hungry eyes'[44] (1949)

I Am Legend tells the story of Robert Neville, presumably the last survivor of a devastating pandemic unleashed in the aftermath of war. Instead of killing its victims outright, the plague turns the population into marauding vampires that congregate nightly on Neville's lawn. Neville's daily struggle is the fortification of his defences, and the surveillance and destruction of those who had once been his friends and neighbours. Using *Dracula* (1897) as his material guide, he initially employs folkloric remedies to ward off and kill the creatures. He cultivates garlic, hangs mirrors and carves wooden stakes. When superstition and legend no longer prove effective, Neville turns to science to dismantle the legend of the vampire. Focusing on the disciplines of immunology and virology, Neville discovers that vampirism is caused by an anaerobic bacterium. Dubbed *vampirus*, it is the germ within the vampire that caused the plague and the downfall of civilization. When Neville sees a woman wandering in the daylight, he believes he has finally found another survivor to ameliorate his horrific isolation. However, he soon realizes that she is in fact a spy for a new, mutated breed of vampire who, after discovering a way to survive in the daylight, plan to eliminate Neville and the other vampires.

In Matheson's dystopian narrative, the vision of progress as sequential time and a dominated future is undercut from the onset by the return of the vampire and the trope of 'the last man'. Just why the vampire has returned to the modern world of track housing and supermarkets is unfathomable. The solution, Neville decides, is to revisit his own history: 'Maybe if he went back. Maybe the answer lay in the past, in some obscure crevice of memory. Go back then, he told his mind, go back' (p. 51).[45] As the narrative switches from the present to the past, Neville considers the events leading up to the epidemic. Clues lie in his time as a soldier in Panama, in the bombings that followed and in the war that 'nobody won' (p. 56) but which unleashed dust storms, plagues of insects and disease. The vampire's return, he surmises, coincides with the execution of military power that, over the course of time, destroyed the world leaving only Neville, inexplicably immune to infection.

The theme of time as cyclical and corrosive is the organizing mode of the text. As a figure of degeneration and tyranny, the vampire refutes the idea of progress, signalling instead the rise of power and corruption, and the inevitable movement towards decay. And, as in other post-war narratives of invasion and infection, in *I Am Legend*, the enemy is internal and Neville's fight for survival is conceptualized through the language of nature versus culture.

Nature and culture are pitted against one another in this book through the depiction of Neville's survivalist struggles and through an internal clash within Neville himself. From the beginning of the narrative, the vampires are clearly associated with otherness and, therefore, with nature. Borrowing the popular Manichaean pattern of thought, Neville employs a simplistic 'us' versus 'them' binary to distinguish himself from the creatures:

> Outside, on the lawn, the dark figures stood like silent soldiers on duty. As he watched, some of them started moving away, and he heard them muttering discontentedly among themselves...There was no union among them. Their need was their only motivation. (p. 23)

Unnamed and homogenous, in the oppositional rhetoric of nature versus culture, the vampires are corrupt automatons driven purely by instinct and appetite: 'He could still see them out there, the white-faced men prowling around his house, looking ceaselessly for a way to get in at him' (p. 22). Spying through his peephole, the vampires, Neville observes, 'circle each other like wolves, never looking at each other once, having hungry eyes only for the house and their prey inside' (p. 65). The vampires are not only undead, but are linked to the untamed and primitive force of nature. This is in direct contrast to the depiction of Neville who exemplifies the rational Anglo-Saxon hero bravely defending his home against intruders. Reminiscent of the cold war communist hunter, Neville's daily activities consist of shoring up his defences and surveying, ferreting out and killing vampires. As the only survivor of the plague, Neville is characterized as the embattled individual waging a survival-of-the-fittest Darwinian struggle against a dehumanized enemy. He is, in the social science parlance of the era, 'inner-directed', a self-sufficient, warrior-like individual reliant on his own strength and inner values: 'Morality... had fallen with society'; in this destroyed world, Neville is 'his own ethic' (p. 62).

This binary is disrupted, however, by Neville's own drives and unrestrained violence. His preference for force as a solution to the vampire problem reveals his own extremist tendencies. Not only are the vampires infected, but they are also repeatedly victims of Neville's chaotic and indiscriminate violence:

> He kept firing the pistols until they were both empty. Then he stood on the porch clubbing them with insane blows . . . And when they tore the guns out of his hands he used his fist and elbows and butted with his head and kicked them with his big shoes. (p. 47)

Even after discovering the cause of the vampire infection, Neville nonetheless continues to kill arbitrarily because an 'experimental fervor had seized him and he could think of nothing else' (p. 39). Acknowledging that he had never been 'analytical', Neville, too, is governed by instinct. In the shifting boundaries between barbarism and civility, Neville displays both insatiable fear and desire for the vampires: 'Every night . . . he'd think about the women. Deep in his body, the knotting heat began again' (p. 19). Like the bloodless vampires outside his door, Neville too, paces the room, drained of colour. The repetition of the imagery points to the uneasy parallels between Neville and the vampires. In the fallen world of the text, the distinction between culture and nature is a fragile one.

The eruption of dangerous and natural drives is not merely threatening to the individual, but has a destabilizing impact on the community's social structure. When the virus took hold, the first hallowed shibboleth to perish was the family which is infiltrated and destroyed. Neville's daughter is burned in a communal fire established by the government to dispose of plague victims. Unwilling to see his wife's body destroyed in the same way, Neville breaks the law by burying her in the ground resulting in her return as a vampire. While children are purified by fire, wives and mothers return as fatal seductresses who unleash a dangerous sexuality: 'The women were out there, their dresses open or taken off, their flesh waiting for his touch, their lips waiting for my blood, my *blood!* (p. 33). Predatory and sexual, the female vampires signal the return of dominant, natural principles which Neville must resist: 'It was the women who made it so difficult, he thought, the women posing like lewd puppets in the night' (p. 19). To ward off the impulse, Neville engages in symbolic acts of penetration: 'Robert Neville's hands fumbled on the stake and mallet. It was always hard when they were alive; especially with women. He could feel that senseless demand returning again, tightening his muscles' (p. 26). The irrationality of the vampire and of his own violent desire leads Neville to abandon folkloric explanations and turn to reason to dismantle the myth. Initially, Neville is contemptuous of science; prone instead to nostalgia and superstition, he 'fought the acquisition of . . . logic and mechanical facility every inch of the way' (p. 27). It is only when folkloric methods prove ineffective does he decide, 'things should be done the right way, the scientific way' (p. 27). If there is to be a rational answer to the problem 'he could only find it by careful research' (p. 77).

The shift from folklore to science marks Neville move from nature to culture; from a preference for force to the use of science; rather than reacting with primitive violence, he now seeks a logical explanation for the presence of the vampire and, potentially, even a cure. His eventual discovery that the population is infected with a germ also leads Neville to reappraise the status of the vampires: 'It was the germ that was the villain. The germ that hid behind obscuring veils of legend and superstition' (p. 88). As his scientific experiments begin to unravel the legend, Neville discovers that there are in fact varieties of vampires which he categorizes into various types: the 'true vampires' or 'the living dead' (p. 38) who can be terminated by folkloric methods including exposure to sunlight; the 'long dead', those vampires 'who had originally started the plague', and who were still 'cheating death' (p. 68); the still living but infected who are not yet vampires and cannot be eliminated by traditional means; and the merely insane who, while 'thinking themselves true vampires', are actually only 'demented sufferers' (p. 116). Through the process of differentiation, Neville begins to see them as victims, more sinned against than sinning, and by embracing the therapeutic, substitutes supernatural horror for pathology. And while man-made technology was initially responsible for unleashing the dangerous germ from the past, science, he decides, is now the only hope for defeating it. Neville's rejection of superstition also functions as a social curative. Reason and experimentation quells both his random violence and his sexual desire; as he begins to focus on virological explanations for the cause of the epidemic, hypodermic syringes replace wooden stakes as preferred methods of penetration. It is science that will eventually hold the key to the vampire: rationality not superstition, culture not nature. In the pluralist ideology of nature versus culture, Neville has tempered his extremist habits; his renewed interest in a scientific and therapeutic approach to the vampire problem registers his status as a man of the liberal centre and, therefore, of culture.

The dilemma for Neville is the cyclical nature of vampire existence. Progressive science cannot explain the vampire's timelessness and Neville invariably finds himself once again turning to history for answers. The germ is not a product of modern times; rather the source of the infection stems from the ancient world: 'He thought of the fall of Athens . . . Before anything could be done, the city had fallen. Historians wrote of bubonic plague. Robert Neville was inclined to believe that the vampire had caused it' (p. 78). The classical allusion links the current vampire infection to the fall of empire and the discourse of degeneration. The germ infecting his neighbours is not a new phenomenon; rather vampirism is merely a symptom, a manifestation of a long dormant organism that has returned because it has found current culture amenable to its survival: 'Certain kinds of bacilli, when conditions became unfavorable for life, were capable of creating, from themselves, bodies called spores . . . Later, when conditions were more favorable for survival, the spore germinated again, bringing into existence all the qualities of the original bacillus' (p. 88). Couched in scientific terms, Neville's research restates the theory of corruption as inevitable and repetitive. In the cyclical framework, the disease has always been present and waiting for a moment of vulnerability to re-infect humanity. In Neville's world, the right conditions are linked to war and to scientific over-development. And while science in the form of bombs has unleashed the germ, it was nature that dispersed the spores. The germ is not a result of technology gone wrong, but the timeless product of power and corruption.

The discovery of another human being marks a shift in the novel from the last man's struggle for physical survival to the realization that humanity is not lost and that through his own ignorance and fear, Neville has indiscriminately killed the living along with the dead. The appearance of Ruth also reveals that science has not offered the cure that Neville had hoped for. The belief that culture would neutralize the distinctions between us and them, the living and the dead is rendered problematic with the arrival of the mutated new breed. Nature defeats Neville's scientific efforts because the natural world has supplied a way for the germ to adapt to change; because, as Neville realizes, germs mutate. In spite of science, 'in the end the germ will win': 'If I didn't kill them, sooner or later they'd die and come after me. I have no choice; no choice at all' (p. 146). Nature cannot be defeated by culture. Science is a 'trap'; killing is justified on the grounds that a society peopled by vampires cannot be cured, that they represent the ultimate threat to the individual and civilization. Nature adapts, corruption is innate and history will inevitably repeat itself.

With the appearance of Ruth the narrative of degeneration comes full circle. The extremist values that characterized Neville in the beginning are now ironically reversed or replicated by the mutated vampires. While Neville initially positioned himself as the lone individualist waging an 'us' versus 'them' battle against the vampires, the language of the new breed is the conciliatory 'we':

> I know now that you were just as much forced into your situation as we were forced into ours. We *are* infected ... What you don't understand yet is that we're going to stay alive. We've found a way to do that and we're going to set up society again slowly but surely. (p. 154)

Unlike the isolated individual, they band together and work as a group to destroy Neville, who is now the 'other', the real vampire and ultimate figure of tyranny. Although Ruth offers him an opportunity to escape, Neville decides to surrender and 'throw himself on their new justice system' (p. 160), but, as he soon discovers, they have no intention of allowing him to live. Replicating Neville's random killing, the new breed make no distinctions between the living and the dead: 'The dark-suited men ... surrounded the [vampires], held their flailing arms, and drove razor-tipped pikes deep into their bodies. Blood spouted out on the dark pavement and the vampires perished one by one' (p. 158). The imagery of the breed's clumping boots, dark suits, dark cars and spotlights hint at the authoritarian overtones of the new society. Reminiscent of Hoover's G-men, their sole purpose is to hunt and exterminate the other vampires. When Neville complains that they appear to relish killing, Ruth responds:

'Maybe you did see joy on their faces ... It's not surprising. They're young. And they *are* killers—assigned killers, legal killers. They're respected for their killing, admired for it' (p. 167). That man can learn to enjoy killing is, she reminds Neville, an old story, and for the first time, Neville is forced to come to terms with his own complicity in murder; that in the minds of the new society, he is the abnormal one, the other:

> Abruptly that realization joined with what he saw on their faces—awe, fear, shrinking horror—and he knew that they *were* afraid of him ... He was an invisible specter who had left for evidence of his existence the bloodless bodies of their loved ones. (p. 169)

While appearing to match Neville's brutal violence to the vampires, Ruth justifies their actions on the grounds that, 'New societies are always primitive ... In a way we're like a revolutionary group repossessing society by violence. It's inevitable. Violence is no stranger to you. You've killed. Many times' (p. 166). Unlike Neville, who tried to control his future, Ruth understands that history is deterministic, a series of cycles periodically purged by the flames of war, followed by birth and growth. For the new society to survive, all forms of corruption must be eliminated. Neville, Ruth explains, is 'the last of the old race' (p. 167). With Neville's death, the cycle of history will be renewed and a new civilization born. As the 'new people of the earth' (p. 170), the new breed believe they have mastered both culture and nature. While still infected by the germ, a new drug prevents them from perishing and returning as vampires: 'The blood feeds the germs, the drug prevents its multiplication. It was the discovery of this pill that saved us from dying, that is helping us to set up society again slowly' (p. 155). Science once again has provided the means for survival, but although they dream of founding a new Eden free of tyranny and corruption, the new society is by no means a utopian ideal. Humanity in this form is still a highly vulnerable perversion marked by violence and extremist overtones.

In the Gothic imagination, culture or progress is often a movement towards decline and an open invitation to corruption and tyranny. Like other products of cold war culture, *I Am Legend* imagines a future where the pursuit of military power and scientific progress leads to devastation. However, Matheson's text does not ennoble nature over culture; instead, the novel's bleak ending suggests a repudiation of both conservative and liberal values. Man-made technology and nature's germs are equally destructive and equally responsible for national degeneration. In *I Am Legend*, the boundaries between us and them, self and other, hunter and hunted disappear with the death of Neville and the creation of the new society. But the mutated breed, with their visions of a virtuous republic, is in fact a totalitarian regime representing the endgame of Eisenhower's military-industrial complex, the dissolution of the republic and the return to tyranny. The warnings of history unheeded, the technical revolution unleashes a long dormant corruption. As Neville realizes in the last moments of his life, history does indeed repeat itself: 'Full circle, he thought while the final lethargy crept into his limbs. Full circle. A new terror born in death, a new superstition entering the unassailable fortress of forever. I am Legend' (p. 170).

Notes

1. Quoted in Lester H. Cohen, 'Explaining the revolution: ideology and ethics in Mercy Otis Warren's historical theory', *William and Mary Quarterly*, 37, 2 (1980), 200–18, 215.
2. Stephen King, *Salem's Lot* (1975; New York: Simon & Schuster, 1999). Further references will appear in parentheses in the text.
3. Susan Sontag, *Against Interpretation* (New York: Dell Publishing, 1967), p. 222.
4. Charles Beaumont, 'Place of meeting', in Alan Ryan (ed.) *The Penguin Book of Vampire Stories* (London: Penguin, 1987), pp. 371–5 (p. 374).
5. Quoted in Stow Persons, 'The cyclical theory of history in eighteenth-century America', *American Quarterly*, 6, 2 (1954), 147–63 (147). The following section is indebted to Persons's article.
6. Ibid., 148–9.
7. Ibid., pp. 151, 152.
8. Thomas Paine, *Common Sense* (London: Penguin, rev. edn 2004), p. 69.
9. Samuel Sherwood, 'The Church's flight into the wilderness: an address on the times', *Political Sermons of the American Founding Era, 1730–1895* (1 April 1776), ed. Ellis Sandoz, part II: 1774–81, *http://oll.libertyfund.org/Texts/LFBooks* (accessed 3 June 2006).
10. Quoted in Cohen, 'Explaining the revolution', 217.
11. Robert A. Ferguson, *Reading the Early Republic* (Cambridge, Mass.: Harvard University Press, 2004), p. 14.

12. Thomas Jefferson, 'First inaugural address', in Robert Birley (ed.), *Speeches and Documents in American History: Vol. 1: 1776–1815* (London: Oxford University Press, n.d.), pp. 251–6, p. 251.
13. John R. Howe, Jr., 'Republican thought and the political violence of the 1790s', *American Quarterly*, 19, 1 (1967), 162.
14. J. G. A. Pocock, *The Machiavellian Moment: Florentine Republican Thought and the Atlantic Republican Tradition* (Princeton: Princeton University Press, 1975), pp. 540, 541. See, for example, Machiavelli's *Discourses on Livy*, trans. Judith Conway Bondanella and Peter Bondanella (Oxford: Oxford University Press, 2003).
15. Pocock, *Machiavellian Moment*, pp. 507, 527.
16. Quoted in Persons, 'Cyclical theory of history', 152–3.
17. Gordon S. Wood, *The Creation of the American Republic, 1776–1787* (Williamsburg: University of North Carolina Press, 1969), pp. 51, 52.
18. Quoted in ibid., pp. 415, 418.
19. Ibid., p. 53.
20. Thomas Jefferson, *Notes of the State of Virginia*, The Avalon Project, Yale Law School, http://www.yale.edu/lawweb/Avalon/jefifram.htm (accessed 14 January 2004).
21. Quoted in Cohen, 'Explaining the revolution', 207.
22. Persons, 'Cyclical theory of history', 156.
23. Quoted in ibid., 217.
24. Quoted in Richard Davenport-Hines, *Gothic: 400 Years of Excess, Horror, Evil and Ruin* (London: Fourth Estate, 1998).
25. Quoted in Katharina M. Wilson, 'The history of the word "vampire"', *Journal of the History of Ideas*, 46, 4 (1985), 580–1.
26. Quoted in J. Gordon Melton (ed.), *The Vampire Book: The Encyclopedia of the Undead* (Farmington Hills, MI: Visible Ink Press, 1999), pp. 538–9.
27. William Pitt, Earl of Chatham, 'Speech to the House of Lords', *The Speeches of Lord Chatham* (2 November 1770), http://classicpersuasion.org/cbo/chatham/chat11.htm (accessed 12 August 2006).
28. Edward Payson, *Memoir and Selected Thoughts*, vol. 1, http://pbministries.org/articles/payson/the_works_vol_1/payson_vol_1.htm (accessed 14 June 2006).
29. Dwight D. Eisenhower, 'First inaugural address' (20 January 1953), The Dwight D. Eisenhower Library, http://www.eisenhower.archives.gov/1stinaug.htm (accessed 19 July 2004).
30. Ibid.
31. Ibid.
32. Ibid.
33. Eisenhower, 'Farewell address' (17 January 1961), The Dwight D. Eisenhower Library, http://www.eisenhower.archives.gov/farewell.htm (accessed 19 June 2004).
34. Quoted in Arthur M. Schlesinger, Jr., *The Vital Center: The Politics of Freedom* (Cambridge, Mass.: Riverside Press, 1949), p. ix
35. J. Edgar Hoover, *Masters of Deceit: The Story of Communism in America* (London: Dent and Sons, 1958), p. 319.
36. Eisenhower, 'First inaugural address'.
37. George Kennan, *Memoirs: 1925–1950* (London: Hutchinson, 1967), p. 559.

38 Hoover, *Masters of Deceit*, pp. 81, 99.
39 Peter Biskind, *Seeing is Believing: Or How Hollywood Taught Us to Stop Worrying and Love the 50s* (1983; London: Bloomsbury, 2001), p. 111.
40 Carey McWilliams, *Witch Hunt: The Revival of Heresy* (Westport, CT: Greenwood Press, 1950), pp. 3, 121.
41 Victor S. Navasky, *Naming Names* (New York: Viking Press, 1980), p. 3.
42 Biskind, *Seeing is Believing*, p. 111.
43 Schlesinger, *The Vital Center*, p. 254.
44 Fritz Leiber, 'The girl with the hungry eyes', in Alan Ryan (ed.), *The Penguin Book of Vampire Stories* (New York: Penguin, 1987), p. 335.
45 Richard Matheson, *I Am Legend* (New York: Orb, 1995). Further references will appear in parentheses in the text.

3

The Double and Republican Masculinity

☙

> In the end, more than they wanted freedom, they wanted security. They wanted a comfortable life, and they lost it all – security, comfort and freedom. When . . . the freedom they wished for was freedom from responsibility, then Athens ceased to be free.
> Edward Gibbon, *The Decline and Fall of the Roman Empire*

In 1796, the popular German author Jean Paul coined the term doppelgänger in his romantic narrative of self-creation and self-destruction. To gain freedom from his unhappy marriage, the eponymous hero Siebenkäs fakes his own death and assumes the identity of Leibgeber, a cosmopolitan libertine whose indulgences lead nearly to destruction. In Paul's subsequent novel, *Titan* (1803), an uncanny reversal occurs: Leibgeber encounters Siebenkäs and thinking he has seen himself, finally goes insane.[1] Since these first encounters with the doppelgänger or 'double goer', tales of duality and fractured identity have been a recurring motif in Gothic fiction. As Kelly Hurley has shown, in the Gothic the human body loses its claim to 'a discrete and integral identity', occupying a liminal existence between 'human/beast, male/female, civilized/primitive, by which cultures are able meaningfully to organize experience'. Whether a figure of Faustian excess, diabolical agency or unconscious drives, the double assumes these oppositions in response to the hazardous encroachment of modernity.[2] Moreover, while Gothic narratives of duality are predominantly about men, they actively engage issues of masculine destabilization, re-working plots of hidden depravity and fears of feminization. According to Hurley, narratives that chart the re-making or construction of the male subject arise from a general anxiety about the nature of human identity permeating late Victorian and Edwardian culture, an anxiety generated by scientific theories of degeneration and the abhuman.[3]

While recent Gothic criticism has revealed the instability of an essentialist construct of human sexuality, situating narratives of male fragmentation and destabilization within British *fin de siècle* scientific discourses cannot account for the rise of the double in late eighteenth- and early nineteenth-century American fiction, or explain its persistence in the mid twentieth century. The American plot of the double life needs to be historicized through a different lens because the fear of what C. Wright Mills calls 'the feminization of male subjectivity' predates scientific discourses of degeneration. Accordingly, the self's 'condition of rupture, disjunction, [and] fragmentation' will be discussed in terms of the republican theory of virtue and the ideology of masculinity that sustains it.[4] This approach necessarily evokes a different set of oppositions than those normally associated with the rise of the double. As Brian Baker argues, the 'split' in Gothic masculinity goes back to the Gothic's beginnings and arises from 'a fundamental paradox at the heart of post-Enlightenment constructions of the subject'.[5] While Baker employs the dyad of reason/ passion to analyse the figure of the double, theorized through a republican paradigm, the discursive fields associated with Gothic representations of male duality exhibit classical oppositions: freedom/ tyranny, public good/self-interest and virtue/ corruption. These polarities not only inform eighteenth-century masculine identity, but continue to resonate in twentieth-century narratives of fractured male subjectivity. The post-war years provide a particularly salient example of the modern American crisis of national and gender identity among men. In the Kennedy years, for example, the double re-emerges as a figure of failed masculinity, softened not by the lures of eighteenth-century luxury and effeminacy but by its twentieth-century corollaries: conformity and self-interest. In eighteenth-century republican discourse, the fantasy of freedom from social and political responsibility registers the decline of civic virtue and the threat of national degeneration. Similarly, in a cold war context, the complexities and contradictions evinced by the liberal centre produce ideologically and socially decentred male subjectivities. In David Ely's dystopian novel *Seconds*, the fragmented subject tests the sustainability of masculine identity in a period dominated by the tensions between 'feminized' conformity and 'manly' freedom. The task of remaking oneself, the novel reveals, is not freedom from the collective, but a horrifying descent into the nightmare of emasculation and tyranny.

The decline of virtue: 1776–1795

> Mr. Printer, I saw a man [bring] a lamb to market.—Lambs command cash and cash pays taxes—but the good countryman went to a store and bought a feather—5 shillings for a feather, Mr. Printer. Sugar, coffee, gauzes, silks, feathers, and the whole life of baubles and trinkets ... what an enormous expence! ... My countrymen are all grown very tasty.
>
> Benjamin Franklin[6]

The period of peace following independence should have been a time of celebration and expectation; instead, victory heralded a new panic. Throughout political life – in the public press, sermons, speeches and private correspondence – there ran an overwhelming sense of crisis and despondency. The whole country, observed John Quincy Adams, was 'groaning under the intolerable burden of ... accumulated evils'. 'Never', claimed Moses Mather, 'was there greater danger of evils, in this land, since the first settlement of it than now.'[7] While community leaders accepted that extravagancies will accompany the 'blessings of freedom', few people anticipated the widespread social change that characterized the years of transition between the end of the revolution and the formation of a national government. The generation expected that in a time of great upheaval, the morals of the people would be affected, but as Mercy Otis Warren observed, 'such a total change of manners in so short a period ... was never known in the history of man'.[8] The war had not produced the effect 'expected from it upon the manners of the people'; nor had it 'rendered them more worthy, by making them more virtuous, of the blessings of free government'. The revolution, it seemed, had not led to liberty and equality after all, but resulted in what John Adams called 'democratic despotism'. Just as the British had perverted their power, now Americans were perverting their liberty. 'Have we fought for this?', 'Was it with these expectations that we launched into a sea of trouble, and have bravely struggled through the most threatening dangers?' These were the often-repeated questions of the age.[9]

The source of such apprehension and disillusionment was the detection of an alarming growth in public idleness, licentiousness and rapacity. As early as 1779, Samuel Adams was decrying the 'inundation of levity, vanity, luxury, dissipation'. Americans were 'No longer governed by that pure, disinterested patriotism, which distinguished the Infancy of the Contest'.[10] Instead, unfettered liberty had left the population prey to the destructive influences of 'stockjobbing, speculation, dissipation, luxury and venality':

> The people grow less steady, spirited, and virtuous, the seekers more numerous and more corrupt, and every day increases the circles of their dependents and expectants, until virtue, integrity, public spirit, simplicity, and frugality, become the objects of ridicule and scorn, and vanity, luxury, foppery, selfishness, meanness, and downright venality swallow up the whole society.[11]

What was at stake was the character of American society. As the new republic in a world of monarchies, Americans sought to represent themselves as new freedom-loving republicans and legitimate heirs of Europe's Enlightenment culture.[12] The world, they knew, was watching: 'We, my countrymen,' declared Candidus, 'have a character to establish.' Yet, just what form this character would take was unclear. Americans, it seemed, had had a sudden failure of nerve: 'A foreigner could hardly believe we were that brave people who so nobly struggled for our Independence.' 'Are not our manners becoming soft and luxurious, and have not our vices begun to shoot?'[13] The key term commonly employed in these jeremiads is luxury, the Western concept most often drawn upon to denote corruption and tyranny. As John Sekora notes, through much eighteenth-century writing is a typology of values and characters that all lead to the ancient concept of luxury:

> The main Western philosophical systems posited perfect (i.e. absolute) forms of degradation as well as models of perfect virtue and freedom. To describe the decline into depravity of an individual or group, they created various theories of entropy, the concept of luxury being among the most prominent.[14]

Virtue is associated with freedom and equality, with civic participation and patriotism. Luxury represents the degeneracy of these values: it denotes self-interest, corruption and tyranny. As Charles Rollin observed,

> Carthage is destroyed, because its avarice, perfidiousness, and cruelty, have attained their utmost height. The like fate will attend Rome, when its luxury, ambition, pride, and unjust usurpations, concealed beneath a specious and delusive show of justice and virtue, shall have compelled the sovereign Lord, the disposer of empires, to give the universe an important lesson in its fall.[15]

Republicanism was supposed to free men's selfish ambition; instead, dangerous self-interest threatened to destroy the communion and benevolent duty the revolutionaries fought for. Unless the lust for wealth and power was curtailed, degeneration would surely follow.

Evidence of the republic's impending descent into luxury and corruption was the establishment of various social clubs such as the Tea Assembly or Sans Souci Club as it was popularly known. Ostensibly an innocuous social club formed to amuse the nouveau riche of Boston, it soon came to symbolize everything that was wrong in the new republic. Modelled on British and French manners, dancing and card playing, the values of the club were in sharp contrast to the Spartan asceticism of traditional community leaders. While members and supporters charged its critics with envy and malice, others saw a more threatening development and launched a vituperative attack on the club:

The Double and Republican Masculinity

> Did ever effeminacy with her languid train, receive a greater welcome in society than at this day. New amusements are invented, new dissipations are introduced, to lull and enervate these minds already too much softened, poisoned and contaminated by idle pleasures, and foolish gratifications. We are exchanging prudence, virtue and economy, for those glaring spectres luxury, prodigality and profligacy. We are prostituting all our glory as a people, for new modes of pleasure, ruinous in their expences, injurious to virtue, and totally detrimental to the well being of society . . . Why do you thus suffer all the intemperances of Great-Britain to be fostered in our bosom, in all their vile luxuriance?[16]

Here luxury and the corruption of the British monarchy coalesce to form the central threat to republican liberty. As Seamus Deane observes, the 'definition of the English and of the French national character became an integral part of the contemporary analysis of both the American and French Revolutions, and the Enlightenment'.[17] Just as France provided a useful contrast in underscoring what was distinctive about England's constitutional and cultural forms, England and France provided a contrast for America's burgeoning national and political character. For those still clinging to the vision of a Christian Sparta, the values of the Sans Souci Club were not the follies of a youthful republic but suggested the pernicious influence of the *ancien régime*. Federalists and anti-Federalists alike were quick to find patterns of British or French tyranny behind the crisis. In a letter to Mercy Otis Warren, John Adams wrote we should 'deplore that spirit of dissipation, vanity and knavery, which infects so many Americans and threatens to ruin our manners and liberties, in imitation of the old world'. In a similar vein, Samuel Adams complained that citizens 'are imitating the Britons in every idle amusement and expensive foppery which it is in their power to invent for the destruction of a young country'. John Eliot, on the other hand, blamed the French:

> French etiquette, French manners and customs, cannot be altogether fashionable, if we abide by our constitutions or laws. Nor ought we to imitate any nation in Europe. We are a people *per se*. We ought to be original, therefore, in our manners, and independent of other nations, of their follies and vices, as of anything else.[18]

The important belief was that all republican governments were dependent upon a broad distribution of virtue among the people: 'Liberty was realized when the citizens were virtuous—that is, willing to sacrifice their private interests for the sake of the community.' Private virtues were important, but public virtue, the sacrifice of private desires for the public interest, was crucial: 'To be completely virtuous citizens, men . . . had to be free from dependence and from the petty interests of the marketplace. Any loss of independence and virtue was corruption.' '"No virtue, no Commonwealth." It was that simple.'[19] It was precisely because republics required private and civic virtue that they were extremely fragile and vulnerable to internal decay. While optimists such as Benjamin Rush believed that education could 'convert men into republican machines', gloomy prognosticators such as Theophilous Parsons wondered if American virtue could possibly last:

> The most virtuous states have become vicious . . . The morals of all people, in all ages, have been shockingly corrupted . . . Shall we alone boast an exemption from the general fate of mankind? Are our private and political virtues to be transmitted untainted from generation to generation, through a course of ages?

Many were doubtful. Once an erosion of virtue was evident, it was an open door to 'deceivers, betrayers and destroyers'.[20]

While these jeremiads seem to have nothing, overtly, to say about gender, the eighteenth-century concept of republican virtue was premised on an ideology of masculinity. As historian Carroll Smith-Rosenburg points out, in addition to striving for a new constitution, Americans were also constructing 'a new *homo nationalis*, a new *homo Americanus*', which, despite the republic's claim to social diversity, was 'male, white, and increasingly middle-class'.[21] Eighteenth-century virtue, therefore, came to refer 'not only to female private morality but more importantly to male public spirit, that is, to the willingness of citizens to engage actively in civic life and to sacrifice individual interests for the common good'.[22] Whether loyalist or republican, Federalist or anti-Federalist, virtue was an inherently masculine trait inherited from the revitalized Renaissance republicanism of Machiavelli who equated virtu with acts of bravery,

The Double and Republican Masculinity

military heroism and civic activism. In the American republic, virtue was also often termed manliness, a quality repeatedly characterized as resistance from British tyranny. In the Declaration of Independence, Jefferson wrote, '[The King] has dissolved Representative Houses repeatedly, for opposing with manly firmness his invasions on the rights of the people.'[23] Benjamin Goodhue, similarly equated manliness with resistance: 'We shall be compelled shortly to either manfully oppose the injuries We endure . . . or submissively submit to the degrading terms those haughty Despots choose to impose.'[24] If the virtues of courage, resistance and public duty were inherently male, the opposites – cowardice, submission and luxury – were castigated as feminine, weak and unpatriotic. The charges of effeminacy directed against the members of the Sans Souci Club, for example, underpin the centrality of masculine virtue in the formation of the new republic. In the gendered language of republican ideology, soft manners, foppery and the want of luxury lead to damaging countertypes of failed or unhealthy masculinity, the precursors to cultural degeneration and political oppression.

The perceived crisis of moral and national reputation represented more than a momentary reaction to the exhilaration of independence: it marked the transformation from the early colonial ethos of communal manhood where terms such as individuality and self-reliance had little place, to the late eighteenth-century's celebration of the self-made man in the new Federal constitution.[25] Not only did the inundation of luxury represent a threat to virtue's Spartan asceticism and disinterestedness, it also demonstrated a transgression against the dominant image of republican masculinity which needed censuring. Accusations of luxury or luxurious living, therefore, functioned as a central method of exclusion. According to Sekora, 'Luxury readily accommodated, even encouraged, belief in historical division of mankind into a virtuous "we" standing against a luxurious "they".' Luxury stood for 'persons, thoughts, and behaviour that have been branded as unacceptable. Individually and collectively, all represent "the Other"—that which is beyond the pale.'[26] While the gender implications of this exclusion may be muted in the writings of eighteenth-century commentators, the fear of feminization is evident everywhere in the lexicon of virtue and corruption, freedom and tyranny, common good and self-interest. Escalating consumerism rendered men passive and weak, mere prostitutes in the marketplace; it was this condition, Americans were repeatedly warned, that led to the fall of empires:

> Did we consult the history of Athens and Rome, we should find that so long as they continued their frugality and simplicity of manners, they shone with superlative glory; but no sooner were effeminate refinements introduced amongst them, than they visibly fell ... and became timid, dependent, slavish and false.[27]

The post-revolutionary crisis of virtue is important in the discussion of American Gothic because it exposes the political logic behind narratives of fractured or alienated male subjectivity. The threat to republican virtue marks the early delineation of American masculine identity, an identity repeatedly portrayed as polarized and crisis-ridden. The crisis occurred during the political transformation from public to private interests, from republican or civic humanist ideology to a liberal paradigm predicated on self-interest and rising commercial exchange. This shift inaugurated a tension between individualism and collectivism that would resonate for the next two centuries. Just as the Jeffersonian desire for the simple values of an agrarian society based on the common good collided with the values of a commercial society governed by individual self-interest, in the mid twentieth century, the battle within the corporate liberal centre pitted individualism against the collectivism of the group, the inner-directed personality against the outer-directed, the active against the passive. Moreover, in both eras it was the force of consumerism that presented the greatest threat to masculine identity: in the eighteenth century, rising commerce was seen to create dependence and instilled in men effeminate values in place of authentic male virtue. Similarly, in the post-war era, men were seen to have sacrificed their volition to the power of consumerism and corporate structures, rendering them weak and feminized and, therefore, susceptible to the tyranny of conformity and totalitarianism.

The Double and Republican Masculinity

The threat of luxury in the age of cold war

> We are, I am afraid, in danger of losing something solid at the core. We are losing that Pilgrim and pioneer spirit of initiative and independence — that old-fashioned Spartan devotion to 'duty, honor, and country'. We don't need that spirit now, we think. Now we have cars to drive and buttons to push and TV to watch — and pre-cooked meals and prefab houses. We stick to the orthodox, to the easy way and the organization man. We take for granted our security, our liberty, and our future — when we cannot take any one of them for granted at all.
>
> John F. Kennedy (1960)[28]

The founding fathers' bequest to the twentieth century was a panic-ridden ideology of effeminizing luxury and perpetual decline. In the tense climate of cold war politics, Americans once again were facing a crisis of character and the spectre of intolerable evil. 'Twentieth century man', wrote Arthur Schlesinger, Jr., is 'tense, uncertain, adrift. It is a time of troubles, an age of anxiety. The grounds of our civilization, of our certitude, are breaking up under our feet, and familiar ideas and institutions vanish as we reach for them, like shadows in the falling dusk.'[29] If the disillusionment had a traditional ring, the cause of the modern malaise was equally familiar: 'We are heading for the classical condition of private opulence and public squalor. Let no one forget that through history this condition had led to the fall of empires.'[30] 'The United States', declared John F. Kennedy, had 'gone soft — physically, mentally, spiritually soft.' Virtue, that bulwark of republicanism, was once again threatened by the 'slow corrosion of luxury' and the 'erosion of courage'.[31]

The seminal work expressing the contemporary crisis was Schlesinger's *The Vital Center*. Employing the sexual and bodily metaphors that structured pluralist discourse, Schlesinger set out to diagnose the failure of freedom in contemporary post-war life in an effort to restore the liberal tradition of tough-mindedness. The essence of the crisis, according to Schlesinger, is internal: it is a conflict between the 'doers' and the 'wailers', between Progressives and anti-communist liberals, between sentimentality and activism, the flight of responsibility and civic duty. It is an old fight, he adds, resulting in America's 'permanent crisis':

> There is no more exciting time in which to live – no time more crucial or more tragic. We must recognize that this is the nature of our age: that the womb has irrevocably closed behind us, that security is a foolish dream of old men, that crisis will always be with us.[32]

Schlesinger's call is for a 'new radicalism', a new language of consensus, a synthesis of cold war liberals and corporate capitalists into a coalition of moderates that make up the bipartisan alliance of the centre.

Often cited as a turning point for American liberalism, the rhetoric and imagery of *The Vital Center* propelled the surge of discourses on emasculated conformity that permeated the 1950s and 1960s. David Riesman's *The Lonely Crowd*, William H. Whyte's *The Organization Man*, Robert Lindner's *Must You Conform?* (1956), Philip Wylie's *A Generation of Vipers* (1942, 1955), Schlesinger's 'Crisis of American masculinity' (1958), C. Wright Mill's *White Collar* (1951), and *Look* magazine's series on 'The decline of the American male' (1958) all placed conformity and masculinity under renewed scrutiny.[33] While they varied in terms of emphasis, each plotted a narrative of duality and emasculation. Whether 'other-directed' conformist made selfless by an affluent mass society, victims of overbearing mothers or parasitic women or sexually distorted by puritanical norms, each traced a shift in the male character from the rugged inner-directed men of yester-year to the weak, soft, emasculated man of the mid twentieth century. William Whyte's *The Organization Man*, in particular, affixed the memorable term for the individual duped into a sense of 'belongingness' as he toils in the white-collar factory. The 'organization ethic', according to Whyte, 'rationalizes the organization's demands for fealty and gives those who offer it wholeheartedly a sense of dedication in doing so . . . it converts what would seem in other times a bill of no rights into a restatement of individualism'. The central principles of this new ethic are 'a belief in the group as the source of creativity; a belief in "belongingness" as the ultimate need of the individual; and a belief in the application of science to achieve the belongingness . . . Man exists as a unit of society. Of himself, he is isolated, meaningless.' Man's duty is to the group, his 'obligation to the here and now'.[34]

While pluralism claimed a non-ideological diversity, the political and sociological discourses of the era reveal that liberalism's overt aim was to corral extremists, those errant individuals who existed outside the centre. Regardless of the quarrels for authority that existed within the centre itself, the new consensus encoded a rigid gender identity: just as eighteenth-century luxury and idleness were scorned as emasculating and threatening to a virtuous republican character, the post-war rise of consumerism and conformity were linked to the loss of male potency. In the cold war complex of gendered dualisms, those residing outside the centre assumed a submissive, feminine role; they were soft, limp, possibly homosexual and, ultimately, a threat to national security.

Kennedy and the cult of masculinity

One hundred and eighty years after John Adams identified a critical juncture in American political life, another presidential hopeful told Americans that they were once again perched on the cusp between greatness and decline. In his acceptance speech for the Democratic Party nomination, John F. Kennedy claimed America stood 'on the edge of a New Frontier—the frontier of the 1960's—a frontier of unknown opportunities and perils—a frontier of unfulfilled hopes and threats'. Answering Schlesinger's call for a revival in courageous leadership, Senator Kennedy told his audience that 'courage—not complacency—is our need today—leadership—not salesmanship. And the only valid test of leadership is the ability to lead, and lead vigorously.'[35] For cold war liberals, Kennedy was a new breed of man who 'saw America as the founding fathers had seen it', a man who would re-instil those ancient qualities of republican virtue seen to be increasingly necessary in global power politics, and a man who, 'by affirming the obligation to act in the face of complexity and chaos . . . lifted his own generation out of its superficial disillusion, its transient love affair with impotence and self, and imbued it with new convictions of purpose and hope'.[36] Kennedy was not only the incarnation of the virile 'vital center' Arthur Schlesinger had imagined years earlier, but also represented the much-needed antidote to the liberal crisis in masculinity.[37] By combining the discourse of civic virtue with the rhetoric of the new frontier, Kennedy's career was premised on what Robert Dean calls an 'ideology of masculinity' which he used to justify his claim to presidential power.[38] Invoking resonant images from America's stoic republican heritage and frontier expansiveness, Kennedy campaigned on a platform of courage and toughness: 'In the decade that lies ahead . . . the American Presidency will demand more than ringing manifestos issued from the rear of the battle. It will demand that the President place himself in the very thick of the fight.'[39] The founding fathers, claimed Kennedy:

> were not the captives of their own doubts, the prisoners of their own price tags. Their motto was not 'every man for himself'–but 'all for the common cause.' They were determined to make that new world strong and free, to overcome its hazards and its hardships, to conquer the enemies that threatened from without and within . . . Today some would say that those struggles are all over–that all the horizons have been explored–that all the battles have been won–that there is no longer an American frontier.

Kennedy was anxious to remind voters that the battle was not over, that, in his view, the 'increasing evidence of a lost national purpose and a soft national will' was placing the republic at risk. Echoing Schlesinger's 1949 question, 'Can we win the fight?', Kennedy's question of the new frontier was 'Are we up to the task – are we equal to the challenge?'

> That is the choice our nation must make–a choice that lies not merely between two men or two parties, but between the public interest and private comfort–between national greatness and national decline–between the fresh air of progress and the stale, dank atmosphere of 'normalcy'–between determined dedication and creeping mediocrity.[40]

As Dean notes, the ideology of masculinity 'organizes the "performance" of an individual's role in society and draws boundaries around the social category of manhood'. In its prescriptive form, this ideology 'imagines and constructs a narrative identity that lends coherence to the self'. Yet, in its proscriptive form, 'it rules out certain ways of imagining and acting in the world'.[41] The soft versus hard, effeminate versus masculine, public versus private dichotomies that structure Kennedy's speeches readily function to reduce political positions to dualistic and feminized images. Yet, the strange amalgam of frontier individualism and civic virtue also represents concepts traditionally antagonistic in political thought. In the rhetorical choice he offers the nation, his preferences seem clear: it is public interest not private comfort that lead to national greatness. The effect of combining two ideological traditions is the creation of a muscular national identity premised on individual courage and collective participation. As a new liberal, Kennedy wants it both ways: the ability to celebrate individual endeavour but only in the interests of the public good. His use of terms such as 'soft', 'comfort', 'mediocrity' and 'decline' also reveal a shared suspicion that the values of civic virtue he extols are endangered by the effeminizing effects of modern luxury and individual self-interest. And it is this ideological contradiction that, in the mid twentieth century, leads to the self's condition of rupture and fragmentation.

Republican masculinity in David Ely's Seconds

> Man is not truly one, but truly two . . . It was the curse of mankind that these incongruous faggots were thus bound together – that in the agonized womb of consciousness these polar twins should be continuously struggling.
> Robert Louis Stevenson, *Dr Jekyll and Mr Hyde*[42]

David Ely's novel of post-war male duality and emasculation consciously engages with contemporaneous social and political discourses concerned with diagnosing the condition of the American male in the mid twentieth century. The narrative abounds with Kennedy's rhetoric of the new frontier, with Schlesinger's womb imagery and with the 'hidden persuaders' of corporate 'groupthink' culture. From this perspective, *Seconds* is the product of a specific and unique moment in time. Yet, underpinning its mid-century topicality, it is also possible to situate Ely's Gothic tale within a larger historical context. Like Kennedy's fusion of republican and liberal discourses, the central themes of the novel rework the conflict between civic virtue and self-interest in the post-war era. In *Seconds*, the desire for freedom from responsibility not only results in the decline of manly virtue and thereby liberty, but also in the terrifying rupture of the self.

Seconds tells the story of a 'liberal republican' bank executive who receives a telephone call from his friend Charley who had apparently committed suicide several months before.[43] Charley refers the banker to a company offering a service vaguely described as 'rebirth'. For a fee, the company will fake his death, provide cosmetic surgery and reinvent him as a moderately successful freelance artist. Once confirmed as a client, the flabby, middle-aged banker is transformed into the young, virile Antiochus Wilson, free to enjoy his bachelor existence unencumbered by family ties and professional responsibilities, 'In short, you are alone in the world, Mr. Wilson, absolved of all responsibility except to your own interests and desires. Isn't it marvellous, sir?' (p. 57) Unable to reconcile his internal self with the freedom from responsibility that his new body affords, Wilson becomes a threat to the integrity of the organization and after several warnings, is deemed a security risk and ultimately eliminated.

Before his transformation, Wilson's 'grey tailored suit, his spotless shoes, and his homburg' (p. 8) register his status as the quintessential symbol of complacent masculinity in an era of unbridled consumer capitalism. Unnamed and ubiquitous, he is emblematic of the two-dimensional stereotype indicated in the popular slogans of the period: the 'man in the grey flannel suit' and the 'organization man'. At his initial interview with the company, Wilson sums up his career: 'I went to business school ... and then I went into banking ... I'm earning a substantial salary, I've built a home and have a summer place, I own a boat and two cars' (p. 21). Wilson's résumé is important, the company tells him, because it is a useful reminder 'of the context of [his] problems' (p. 22), which in Wilson's case is his organization man status and the ethic of belongingness that underlines it. As William Whyte describes it, 'belongingness' is a belief in 'the sacredness of property, the enervating effect of security, the virtues of thrift, of hard work and independence' . Yet, it is also an ethic fraught with anxiety:

> He honestly wants to believe he follows the tenets he extols, and if he extols them so frequently it is, perhaps, to shut out a nagging suspicion that he, too, the last defender of the faith, is no longer pure. Only by using the language of individualism to describe the collective can he stave off the thought that he himself is in a collective as pervading as any

ever dreamed of by the reformers, the intellectuals, and the utopian visionaries he so regularly warns against.[44]

The organization man's nagging suspicion that his beliefs are corrupted is what generates referrals to the company. Despite his material success, Wilson exhibits symptoms of alienation and dissatisfaction: 'As for reminding me of my problems . . . you may have a point there.' He admits to a 'sensation of remoteness', of 'erosion' and tremors of 'anxiety' (p. 22). He is, in effect, the ideal client because the company relies on men like Wilson who are receptive to the idea of starting over and the notion of freedom from responsibility.

The whole concept of rebirth on which the story turns exposes the post-war crisis of male identity. Reminiscent of the sexually charged dualisms that organize the sociological and political discourses of the era, rebirth, and its Frankenstein suggestiveness, uses medical science to negate the role of women in the regeneration of men. Solely a male concern, the organization's goal is not to create life, but to restructure and monitor representations of masculinity. Wilson is referred to the company because he is a 'white-collar' man, a condition C. Wright Mills identified as fundamentally disjointed: 'Internally, they are split, fragmented; externally, they are dependent on larger forces.'[45] When asked to describe his initial reaction to hearing the fantastic proposal of rebirth, Wilson acknowledges this condition: 'I was being drawn in some peculiar way, but my habitual self acted as a kind of brake . . . And that's about the way I feel right now—divided' (p. 26). For Wilson, the appeal of rebirth lies not only in the unleashing of primitive drives, but in a return to innocence and childlike irresponsibility: 'I wondered if I would be a man and an infant at the same time, something innocent but also knowing' (p. 24). Rebirth is both a release from, and a retreat to, the womb: an escape from the mediocrity of his organization man existence through acquiescence and passive surrender.

The womb metaphor looms large in Ely's text: it is the place to which the anxious man flees in his flight from anxiety. From the moment Wilson makes contact with the company, he is literally and figuratively treated as a child in utero. In adherence to the company's clandestine requirements, Wilson wears a cap and overalls, and covers his face with dust. The effect is the erasure of all surface features that signalled his prior identity; like a newborn child, Wilson is cleansed of all social and ideological colourings. Despite the indignity, Wilson submits to the prescribed role: 'I must say I, um, feel like a character in a play, or something' (p. 12). Blindfolded and locked in the back of a windowless truck, he notes, 'it was not an unpleasant ride', and for 'the first time in years' he experiences 'the sensation of irresponsibility' (p. 14). Upon arrival at the company's offices, Wilson is directed to an enclosed circular reception area before being moved to the 'delivery room'; ensconced in the womb-like refuge of the company, Wilson prepares to be reborn.

In the initial stages of Wilson's transformation, the company behaves like a corporate liberal establishment, preferring therapy over coercion. As Wilson himself observes, the company resembles one of those 'over modernized ... advertising agencies' (p. 18), peopled by what Vance Packard called the 'hidden persuaders', those public relations and advertising executives who use depth psychology to sell products and services. Characteristic of post-war suspicion of brainwashing techniques, Packard explores what he regards as an endemic system of manipulation beyond the level of individual consciousness: 'Large scale efforts are being made to channel our unthinking habits, our purchasing decisions, and our thought processes by the use of insights gleaned from psychiatry and the social sciences ... so the appeals which move us are often, in a sense, "hidden".'[46] Once assessed for his suitability and commitment, Wilson is placed in the hands of nurses, doctors and guidance advisers who speak the language of the 'depth manipulator'. In deciding his new career, his guidance counsellor states: 'I think the creative wish-pattern there is pretty self-evident ... your obsessive motivations strongly indicate artistic pursuits as being basically responsive to your particular development as an integrated human being' (p. 55). In the process of rebirth, everything is justified on the grounds of making the client happy. The company, Wilson is told, is 'very up to date. The whole idea is to treat the client as a complete person and make him feel at home ... the difference is that we *care* ... Really' (p. 48, original emphasis). When Wilson continues to exhibit symptoms of anxiety, the company uses sex as a means to sell him freedom: 'I frequently find this necessary with our more sensitive clients', a nurse tells him. 'Not that I mind, really ... it's part of the job' (p. 46). When Wilson ejaculates prematurely, the woman immediately assumes a maternal role: '"You just cuddle up and forget about everything," she went on, drawing his head down so that his face nestled into the warmth of her bosom. "That's the boy. That's the good boy"' (p. 49). In *Seconds*, the ambiguous boundary between female sexuality and motherhood registers Wilson's intransitive state as he moves from resistance towards passive dependency and rebirth. And because her manipulation strategies are packaged as helpful services rather than as a form of masculine destruction, Wilson harbours no guilt for his transgression. Indeed, the company's tactics do not strike him as fantastic because the 'whole framework of the operation was businesslike and efficient . . . and superficially, quite familiar' (p. 48). With the process of emasculation complete, Wilson willingly sells his mediocre existence for a chance at personal freedom. However, the Faustian exchange is superficial, enacted only on the surface of Wilson's body, and the act of rejuvenation ultimately divides him against himself. Masculinity, Wilson discovers, is not a stable construct, but a role which has to be constantly performed and reasserted.

Initially, Wilson is pleased with his new identity. Examining his reflection, he is confronted not by a 'craven creature' but by a 'handsome and self-possessed man of the world' (p. 75). He sees a 'stamp of real character in that rugged, masculine face, which, the longer he studied it, seemed to suggest that here was a man who might have performed feats of courage and daring' (p. 65). With the evidence of his prior weakness and timidity erased, he feels confident enough to 'rush out of the house and commit the Lord knew what act of libertinism' (p. 75) and claims 'he owes it to himself to act like a man' (p. 75). Yet, a deep disparity exists between his authentic emotions and his new features. His attempts to act out his new role cannot resolve the fact that he is, at heart, 'impotent' and 'soft', 'a sheep in wolf's clothing' (p. 77). Wilson faces the stark realization that his manufactured self has no centre, that the change in his physical body has not transformed his inner being. Rather than lending coherence to the self, Wilson's metamorphosis has merely created a disjointed and fragmented identity. Sensing a 'divergence between his exterior and interior selves' (p. 77), Wilson feels betrayed: 'what right did the company have to manufacture a façade for him that was so completely at odds with his inner nature?' (p. 79). Beneath the virile surface, Wilson remains an 'outer-directed man' who, with no core self or identity, is merely a 'succession of roles and encounters'.[47]

Out of this admixture of anxiety and confidence emerge the reborns and their Kennedyesque promise of a new frontier. Whenever Wilson shows signs of maladjustment, he receives a call from Charley who reminds him of the unique opportunity the company has offered him: 'You've got what almost every middle-aged man in America would like to have. Freedom. Real freedom' (p. 82). Wilson, Charley claims, is a pioneer in a new frontier, 'the frontier of personal freedom' (p. 82). As the company's apparent success stories, the reborns position themselves as the wave of the future, the radical 'doers' that have achieved personal freedom from conformity and responsibility. Yet, despite these reassurances, Wilson's masculine identity remains unfixed: 'I've been thrown suddenly from one kind of world into another, quite different, and I'm having to discover myself as a person, as a man, all over again' (p. 73). Wilson's attempts to imagine himself as an autonomous individual are frustrated by his authentic self which repeatedly manifests itself in a composite of assertions, actions and references which disrupt the intended bond with the company's reborns. When individuals from his past reappear in his life, he feels 'exposed' and is almost 'betrayed ... into making a terrible gaffe' (p. 89). These uncanny confrontations are deliberate tests of Wilson's loyalty, tests he fails miserably and which ultimately expose him as a threat to the company's objectives. It is not merely Wilson's social presentation that is being policed by the brotherhood: in the high stakes of gender politics, it is his masculine performance that is exposed and any slippage of the mask would make visible his unhealthy or excluded masculinity. While the company sets the coordinates of manhood, Wilson finds himself pulled in two directions: on the one hand, Charley reminds him of his previous level of dissatisfaction and desire for freedom; on the other, in granting freedom, the company requires acquiescence and adjustment. The choice Wilson faces is a bleak one: it is the choice between what Norman Mailer called a 'quick death by the state' or 'slow death by conformity'.[48] After his near exposure, it becomes increasingly apparent to Wilson that in choosing freedom, he has merely sublimated himself to another group. Wilson's emasculation and lack of vigilance has left him ripe, in Schlesinger's terms, for 'permeation and conquest'.[49]

From the moment Wilson is reborn, the process of existential degeneration begins. The deference with which he was initially treated vanishes and Wilson confronts the reality of the company's operation. Life and death are mere commodities produced with assembly line efficiency. 'You think you're the only one today? Not on your life' (p. 52). The company's 'flesh mechanics', Wilson is told, produce 3,000 men a year. The sinister cadaver procurement section relies on a steady influx of dead bodies to meet the requirements of the living who want be reborn. It is a cynical never-ending cycle of death and rebirth: 'They handed you all that crap about love and rebirth, and now you find out it's just a butcher shop, like everything else' (p. 53). His transformation, then, signals not a rebirth but a stillbirth: Wilson, in effect, is reborn dead. When the dreadful nature of the company's operation is confirmed, the reflection of the self-possessed man is replaced by 'a wolfish stranger who had gobbled up that plump banker and stolen his eyes' (p. 60). Out of these eyes, Wilson sees nothing but vast expanses of emptiness and corruption (p. 60). The resident doctor is dressed 'not in a surgeon's smock but in a black suit, like a clergyman's [and] his face bore the scars of some terrible accident, which gave him an impressive expression of spiritual agony' (p. 51). The personal assistant, assigned to help Wilson through his initial period of adjustment resembles a 'mortician's assistant maintaining a discreet composure for the sake of the bereaved, while at the same time covertly sniffing for the taint of physical corruption' (p. 64). Everyone and everything around him signals incompleteness, remoteness and death. From the 'empty frames' and 'blank canvases' in his fake studio, to the lifeless landscape beyond the window, Wilson is 'exposed to nothingness' (p. 73) until, eventually, even his physical integrity begins to disintegrate: 'The figure in the glass had the appearance of reality, of being a living man, and yet was without substance . . . a fleshless apparition . . . a two-dimensional representation of a man' (p. 110). For Wilson, the promise of freedom has failed and in his fragmented state, he perceives only corruption and decay.

Underlying the inherent sociological discourses surrounding male duality are the sinister echoes of cold war weaponry that forged a nexus between cultural and political life. In addition to its use of helpful therapists, the company also drugs, blackmails and psychologically manipulates Wilson in a bid to sell him freedom. The company president, who is called in when there is 'a soul worth saving' (p. 40), restates the case for Wilson: 'It isn't blackmail . . . it's just a kind of insurance, that's all. It's easier to go forward . . . when you know that you can't go back' (p. 38). Although initially the company subscribes to the centre's preference for therapy over force, once Wilson demonstrates autonomy within the corporate structure, he is no longer working within the bounds of consensus. Wilson's quest for autonomy represents the radical extremist whose goal is to undermine rather than reinforce pluralist values for which he is punished, and the company, as a stand in for the state, ultimately reverts to sinister methods to rein him in. The company draws on the methods and language of secret societies: the reborns are a 'brotherhood' and a 'fraternity' of men whose continued freedom is dependent on secrecy and deception. When Wilson violates this code, he is reprimanded: 'you're one of us, after all. You just have to set yourself to act in good faith, to trust . . . and to accept (p. 97). Yet, concomitant with this fraternity is an elaborate system of surveillance born out of a complete lack of trust and fear of betrayal. Away from the auspices of the organization, company employees and their manufactured reborns no longer function as helpful experts and friends, but as spies and inquisitors. While seemingly benevolent, the company is in fact a totalitarian regime, a representative of what Whyte called the 'new enemy': 'In the 1984 of Big Brother one would at least know who the enemy was . . . but in the other kind of 1984 one would be disarmed for not knowing who the enemy was, and when the day of reckoning came . . . they would be a mild-looking group of therapists who, like the Grand Inquisitor, would be doing what they did to help you.'[50]

The reality of the company's tyranny becomes clear when, believing the 'masterful and beneficent' organization still 'has his best interest at heart' (p. 132), Wilson returns to seek a new identity. This time, however, the woman who had so effectively mothered him into submission no longer recognizes him, and instead of the nurturing womb-like waiting area, Wilson is directed to a room full of uniformed and tranquillized middle-aged men. Stripped of their individuality, this 'collection of misfits and failures' (p. 138) live out a passive existence of 'quiet, domestic activity' (p. 31) until their bodies are required for another fake death. Despite his insistence that their change in identity represents the final barrier to freedom, Charley, in fact, has been imprisoned by the company for over a year. As a previous failure, he was destined for the dreaded cadaver procurement section but because he referred Wilson, he was allowed to remain alive as his sponsor. Charley, in effect, had named names, and his constant rallying calls were not the exhilaration of freedom, but the cries of a desperate man trying to avoid his own destruction. As Wilson soon realizes, the Faustian exchange offered to the company's clients is a cynical double cross: rebirth does not lead to freedom; for the timid and frightened like Wilson, the burden of freedom offers only a 'nightmare filled with nameless horrors'.[51] The fraternal *esprit de corps* that initially defined the reborns experience is gone and their denouement signals the final stage of failed masculinity at the hands of totalitarian control. The utopian dream of freedom from responsibility has left them unmanned and dependent. Even the company president is disillusioned about creating a community of free men. His dream, he tells Wilson, was built on a fallacy: 'My clients were men who were ready to abandon their original identities . . . I can't imagine what possessed me to think that these gentlemen would be likely to do much better just because I gave them a new face and a new name' (p. 156). Like Frankenstein, he no longer controls the creatures he has created: the men rebel while the company itself morphs into a 'modern concern', an unwieldy corporate machine endlessly churning out failures.

With his status as a failure confirmed, Wilson is denied contact with those whose initial job it was to sell him freedom. Instead, he is introduced to Dr Redfield, a PhD in history, whose job is to guide him through the process of death. Dr Redfield's specialization is, appropriately, the fall of Rome, providing an historical allusion to the degenerative effects of corruption and desire for freedom from responsibility. Dr Redfield understands that the company is in reality an agent of decline, peddling utopian dreams to alienated and dissatisfied men. His function is not to give Wilson a new body but to extract names of potential clients. Wilson can save his life but only if he can come up with a name, any name, of another man who might be receptive to the company's unique services: 'It is a word of mouth operation', Wilson is told, 'You don't want the company to suffer any further on your account, do you now? Be a good fellow, Wilson, and give us a hand' (p. 147). Wilson's refusal to cooperate seals his fate and with the realization that he will not be given a second chance at rebirth, Wilson's sense of corporeal materiality fragments even further, 'he seemed to be more divorced from his body than before, as if it were gradually . . . acquiring an independent existence. If it got up and walked away, he wondered, would he remain in the little room . . . and if he did, what would he consist of?' (p. 157). With the fragmentation of the self almost complete, only Wilson's material body retains some value for the company. Instead of another identity, he will go to the over-burdened cadaver procurement section; in a macabre reversal, Wilson is given a second chance at death.

The insistence on individual choice and action, combined with the liberal ethic of consensus reveals an inherent contradiction between when the company behaves like a corporate liberal consensus-builder and when it reveals its radical or extremist tendencies. Wilson is at once placed in the irreconcilable position of being offered freedom from conformity by complying with another form of conformity, forcefully if necessary. Ely's text does not offer any closure on the issue but merely confirms man's essential alienation in an increasingly polarized political world. With the notion of consensus repudiated, the question of who holds authority over the centre is no longer relevant. The individual and the group are irrevocably at odds. As the company president attempts to convince him that his death will at least give an opportunity to another man, the novel's closing line expresses the dark fatalism of Wilson's choice: 'It doesn't really matter' (p. 159). Wilson's passive acceptance of his fate depicts the futility of resistance from encroaching power of the corporate state. In *Seconds*, the only form of manly resistance is death.

As a product of post-war culture, the political ambiguity of the text reflects the underlying tensions of the period. On the one hand, *Seconds* can be read as a liberal cautionary tale warning against the lure of totalitarianism. Wilson is targeted for rebirth because he is weak and vulnerable to utopian promises. His desire for social and political irresponsibility places him outside the political centre and undermines the cult of masculine toughness deemed necessary to defeat the cold war enemy. In effect, Wilson's new body becomes a subversive replica, an expression of the failed, unadjusted polity of pluralism. On the other hand, the novel's dystopian vision unveils the political centre's strategies of repression and the subjugation of difference required for the maintenance of conformity and normative masculinity. Consensus, the narrative suggests, is bankrupt, individual freedom is an illusion marked not by man's susceptibility to utopian promises, but by betrayal and corruption. Wilson is offered the opportunity to play the role of self-interested individual, free from the social constraints of marriage and family but only within the bounds of the group, a condition that paradoxically requires him to surrender his individual freedom which leaves him fragmented and emasculated.

However, the cold war narrative of fragmented masculinity also restates in modern terms the historical values that set the parameters of male identity since the early national period. In the conceptual language of virtue and corruption, manliness is predicated on public interest and resistance to tyranny. Wilson's abdication of responsibility for his own self-interest and his passive surrender to authority signals in historical terms his lack of virtue; in choosing private comfort and mediocrity, Wilson is characterized as effeminate, unpatriotic and an agent of national decline. While the goal of rebirth is ostensibly to reconcile self-interest with the concept of freedom, the contradiction cannot be sustained. Without the moral restraints of virtue, unfettered liberty ultimately leads to corruption and the undoing of the self; the difficulty for twentieth-century man, the double reveals, is that these concepts are not unified narratives but a compendium of fictions generated by a culture of suspicion and rigid gender proscriptions.

Notes

[1] Gerhart Hoffmeister, 'From Goethe's *Wilhelm Meister* to anti-*Meister* novels: the Romantic novel between Tieck's *William Lovell* and Hoffman's *Kater Murr*', in Dennis F. Mahoney (ed.), *The Literature of German Romanticism*, vol. 8 (New York: Camden House, 2004), pp. 79–100 (p. 84).
[2] Kelly Hurley, 'British Gothic fiction, 1835–1930', in Jerrod E. Hogle (ed.), *The Cambridge Companion to Gothic Fiction* (Cambridge: Cambridge University Press, 2002), pp. 189–208 (p. 190).
[3] Idem, *The Gothic Body: Sexuality, Materialism, and Degeneration at the Fin de Siècle* (Cambridge: Cambridge University Press, 1996), p. 5.
[4] Robert Miles, *Gothic Writing, 1750–1820: A Genealogy* (Manchester: Manchester University Press, 2002), p. 3
[5] Brian Baker, 'Gothic masculinities', in Catherine Spooner and Emma McEvoy (eds), *The Routledge Companion to Gothic* (London: Routledge, 2007), p. 165.

6 Quoted in Carroll Smith-Rosenburg, 'Dis-covering the subject of the "Great Constitutional Discussion"', 1786–1789', *The Journal of American History*, 79, 3 (1992), 841–73 (854–5).
7 Quoted in Gordon S. Wood, *The Creation of the American Republic, 1776–1787* (Williamsburg: University of North Carolina Press, 1969), pp. 393, 403.
8 Quoted in Charles Warren, 'Samuel Adams and the Sans Souci Club in 1785', *Massachusetts Historical Society Proceedings*, 60 (1927), 318–44 (319).
9 Quoted in Wood, *Creation of the American Republic*, pp. 424, 404, 395–6.
10 Quoted in ibid., p. 415.
11 Quoted in Warren, 'Samuel Adams', 319; quoted in John R. Howe, Jr., 'Republican thought and the political violence of the 1790s', *American Quarterly*, 19, 1 (1967), 157.
12 Carroll Smith-Rosenberg, 'The republican gentleman: the race to rhetorical stability in the new United States', in Stefan Dudink, Karen Hagemann and John Tosh (eds), *Masculinities in Politics and War: Gendering Modern History* (Manchester: Manchester University Press, 2004), pp. 61–76 (p. 61).
13 Quoted in Wood, *Creation of the American Republic*, pp. 423, 393, 424.
14 John Sekora, *Luxury: The Concept in Western Thought, Eden to Smollett* (Baltimore: John Hopkins University Press, 1977), p. xii.
15 Quoted in William Gribbin, 'Rollin's histories and American republicanism', *William and Mary Quarterly*, 29, 4 (1972), 611–22 (614).
16 Quoted in Warren, 'Samuel Adams', 322.
17 Seamus Deane, *The French Revolution and Enlightenment in England, 1789–1832* (Cambridge, Mass.: Harvard University Press, 1988), p. 2.
18 Quoted in Warren, 'Samuel Adams', pp. 320, 344.
19 Gordon S. Wood, *The Radicalism of the American Revolution* (New York: A. A. Knopf, 1992), p. 104; *Creation of the American Republic*, p. 418.
20 Quoted in Wood, *Creation of the American Republic*, pp. 426, 427; quoted in Howe, 'Republican thought', 157.
21 Carroll Smith-Rosenberg, 'Dis-covering the subject', 844.
22 Ruth H. Bloch, 'The gendered meanings of virtue in republican America', *Signs: Journal of Women in Culture and Society*, 13, 1 (1987), 37–58 (38).
23 Thomas Jefferson, 'Declaration of independence', Robert Birley (ed.), *Speeches and Documents in American History: Vol. 1: 1776–1815* (London: Oxford University Press, n.d.), pp. 1–5 (p. 1).
24 Quoted in Anthony E. Rotundo, *American Manhood: Transformations in Masculinity from the Revolution to the Modern Era* (New York: Basic Books, 1993), p. 16.
25 Ibid., p. 15.
26 Sekora, *Luxury*, p. 50.
27 Warren, 'Samuel Adams', 322.
28 John F. Kennedy, 'Are we up to the task?', *The Strategy of Peace* (New York: Harper Collins, 1960), p. 200.
29 Arthur M. Schlesinger, Jr., *The Vital Center: The Politics of Freedom* (Cambridge, Mass.: Riverside Press, 1949), p. 1.
30 Idem, *The Politics of Hope* (London: Eyre and Spottiswoode, 1964), p. 89.

31 John F. Kennedy, *Freedom of Communications: Final Report of the Committee on Commerce, United States Senate: Part I, The Speeches, Remarks, Press Conferences, and Statements of Senator John F. Kennedy, August 1 through November 7, 1960* (Washington, 1961), pp. 51, 54, 55.
32 Schlesinger, *Vital Center*, pp. 3, 5, 10.
33 The theme of crisis is widespread across all disciplines dealing with masculinity. See, for example, Roger Horrocks, *Masculinity in Crisis: Myths, Fantasies and Realities* (Basingstoke: Palgrave Macmillan, 1994); Cyndy Hendershot, *The Animal Within: Masculinity and the Gothic* (Ann Arbor: University of Michigan Press, 1998); Clare W. Anthony, *On Men: Masculinity in Crisis* (London: Chatto and Windus, 2000); Sally Robinson, *Marked Men: White Masculinity in Crisis* (New York: Columbia University Press, 2000); Anthony W. Clare, *On Men: Masculinity in Crisis* (London: Chatto and Windus, 2000); Stephen J. Ducat, *The Wimp Factor: Gender Gaps, Holy Wars, and the Politics of Anxious Masculinity* (Boston: Beacon Press, 2004).
34 William H. Whyte, Jr., *The Organization Man* (New York: Anchor, 1956), pp. 6, 7.
35 'Address of Senator John F. Kennedy accepting the Democratic Party nomination for the presidency of the United States' (15 July 1960), John F. Kennedy Library and Museum, http://www.jfklibrary.org/Asset+Tree/Asset+Viewers/Audio+Video+Asset+Viewer.htm?guid=%7BB9D9721F-64AB-4624-800D-C38EFE69241B%7D&type=Audio. On the Kennedy administration's cultivation of the cult of masculinity, see Garry Wills, *The Kennedy Imprisonment: A Meditation on Power* (New York: Pocket Books, 1983); Bruce Miroff, *Pragmatic Illusions: The Presidential Politics of John F. Kennedy* (New York: MacKay, 1976); Arthur M. Schlesinger, Jr., *A Thousand Days: John F. Kennedy in the White House* (Boston: Houghton Mifflin, 1965); David Halberstam, *Best and the Brightest* (New York: Ballantine, 1969); Richard J. Barnet, *The Roots of War: The Men and the Institutions behind U.S. Foreign Policy* (New York: Penguin, 1973); Robert D. Dean, 'Masculinity as ideology: John F. Kennedy and the domestic politics of foreign policy', *Diplomatic History*, 22, 1 (1998), 29–62.
36 Schlesinger, *Politics of Hope*, p. xv.
37 K. A. Cuordileone, '"Politics in an Age of Anxiety": cold war political culture and the crisis in American masculinity, 1949–1960', *The Journal of American History*, 87, 2 (2000), 1–25 (2).
38 Dean, 'Masculinity as ideology', 29.
39 'The presidency in 1960', address by Senator John F. Kennedy, National Press Club, Washington DC, 14 January 1960), John F. Kennedy Library and Museum, http://www.jfklibrary.org/Historical+Resources/Archives/Reference+Desk/Speeches/JFK/JFK+Pre-Pres/1960/The+Presidency+in+1960.htm.
40 'The presidency in 1960'.
41 Dean, 'Masculinity as ideology', 30.
42 Robert Louis Stevenson, *Dr Jekyll and Mr Hyde* (1886; London: Penguin, 1994), p. 71.
43 David Ely, *Seconds* (London: Four Square, 1963), p. 10. Further references to the novel will appear in parentheses in the text.

44 Whyte, *Organization Man*, pp. 5–6.
45 C. Wright Mills, *White Collar: The American Middle Classes* (New York: Oxford University Press, 1951), p. ix.
46 Vance Packard, *The Hidden Persuaders* (1957; London: Penguin, 1981), p. 11.
47 David Riesman, Nathan Glazer and Revel Denney, *The Lonely Crowd: A Study of the Changing American Character* (1950; New Haven: Yale University Press, 1969), p. 139.
48 Quoted in Wilfred A. McLay, 'The hipster and the organization man', *First Things*, 43 (1994), 23–30 (25).
49 Schlesinger, *The Vital Center*, p. 37.
50 Whyte, *Organization Man*, p. 31.
51 Schlesinger, *The Politics of Hope*, p. 242.

4

Conspiracy and Hypocrisy *in* Rosemary's Baby

> When danger is all around, every thing is of course suspected: and when the ordinary connection between causes and effects cannot be traced, men have no means of distinguishing between the probable and the improbable; so that their opinions are dictated by their prejudices, their impressions, and their fears.
>
> John Playfair (1814)[1]

In his essay on communism, motherhood and cold war movies, Michael Rogin identifies three major moments in the history of demonology in American politics. The first moment is racial: America's economic and political development, along with its cultural identity, is rooted in the violent expropriation of Indian land and the exploitation of black labour. According to Rogin, 'a distinctive American political tradition, fearful of primitivism, disorder, and conspiracy developed in response to peoples of color'. This tradition, he claims, draws its power from the 'alien threat to the American way of life, and sanctions violent and exclusionary responses' to perceived otherness.[2] The second demonological moment surrounds the class and ethnic conflicts that permeated American political culture from the 1870s to the New Deal. No longer threatened by 'Indians' or 'blacks', subversives were embodied in the 'working class "savages" and alien "reds" of urban, industrializing America'. Seen as fostering disloyalty and radical agitation, immigrants became the new threat to the

American way of life. The third moment occurred during the cold war as the Soviet Union replaced the immigrant working class as the main source of anxiety. Rather than a conflict between workers and capitalists, immigrants and natives, the red scare pitted Moscow's agents against a national security apparatus. In all three stages, Rogin argues, the subversive other has 'threatened the family, property, and personal and national identity'. The essential difference between the modern forms of demonology and earlier expressions is that as racial and cultural differences disappeared, subversives melted into their surroundings and danger 'shifted from the body to the mind'. Perceived threats, in other words, became internalized, irrational and paranoid. Consequently, cold war cinema's representations of conspiracy and demonology were conscious anti-communist propaganda and 'unintentional registers of anxiety' which 'reflected, shaped, and expressed the buried dynamics of a repressive political consciousness'. Equally, American demonology's insistence on opposition and difference derives from 'forbidden desires for identity with the excluded object'. In Rogin's analysis, cold war cultural and political productions 'register the collapse of demonological polarization in a return of the politically and psychologically repressed'.[3]

The view that America's conspiratorial fears are rooted in paranoia and repression has a long history in American political thought. Richard Hofstadter's influential 'The paranoid style in American politics' traces this 'paranoid style' from the Illuminati scare of the 1790s through to the anti-Masonic, anti-Catholic, nativist and populist fears of the nineteenth century, to the recent Fascist and Communist conspiracies of the twentieth. For Hofstadter, the term 'paranoid' is appropriate because 'no other word adequately evokes the qualities of heated exaggeration, suspiciousness, and conspiratorial fantasy' he had in mind. While not going so far as to suggest that politicians are 'certifiable lunatics', he claims that they suffer from a 'political pathology' and therefore are fit subjects for the application of 'depth psychology'.[4] Moreover, Hofstadter borrows the clinical term to suggest that politicians past and present utilized this particular style for nationalistic and political purposes:

> In the paranoid style, as I conceive it, the feeling of persecution is central, and it is indeed systematized in grandiose theories of conspiracy.

But there is a vital difference between the paranoid spokesman in politics and the clinical paranoiac: although they both tend to be overheated, oversuspicious, overaggressive, grandiose, and apocalyptic in expression, the clinical paranoid sees the hostile and conspiratorial world in which he feels himself to be living as directed specifically against him; whereas the spokesman of the paranoid style find it directed against a nation, a culture, a way of life whose fate affects not himself alone but millions of others.[5]

Underlying the paranoid style is a 'fundamentally Manichean psychology': the enemy is both totally evil and totally unappeasable. As a 'perfect model of malice, a kind of amoral superman: sinister, ubiquitous, powerful, cruel, sensual, luxury-loving ... he is a free, active demonic agent'. At the same time, the enemy is also 'a projection' of the 'ideal and the unacceptable aspects of the self'; the paranoid, he claims, imitates the enemy while calling for his destruction. According to Hofstadter, although the villains change over time, this mentality is primarily linked to an ultra-conservative argument: the paranoid style is a radical mode used to meet the interests of the political right who, because their demands are unrealistic and unrealizable, 'cannot make themselves felt in the political process'.[6] Like other liberal historians of the post-war period, Hofstadter's interpretative interests are clear: his purpose is to banish radical or extreme modes of thought from the pluralist centre; acknowledging his argument is 'a bit one-sided', his aim is to understand the 'symbolic aspects' of politics.[7]

Conspiracy and deception are also common themes of Gothic fiction and, like the historical and sociological approaches to the topic, tend to be read through the rubric of psychology. William Godwin's *The Adventures of Caleb Williams* (1794), Charles Robert Maturin's *Melmoth the Wanderer* (1820), and James Hogg's *The Private Memoirs and Confessions of a Justified Sinner* (1824), are each characterized as pathological because they enact 'a classical psychology of paranoia whereby the self is threatened by and pursued by its own unaccommodated residues'.[8] Similarly, in the American Gothic, the subject is always in the process of abjecting its irrational 'other' which continually returns in the form of the uncanny. Eric Savoy, for example, argues that Brockden Brown's achievement was to reposition 'history' in a 'pathologized return of the repressed whereby the present witnesses the unfolding and fulfilment of terrible destinies incipient in the American past'.[9] In contrast, this chapter argues that the Gothic's concern with conspiracy has a history that transcends the common idioms of 'repression' and 'paranoia'. In particular, it reveals that when approached from an ideological perspective, the discourse of conspiracy is rooted not in irrationality, but in the eighteenth-century debates surrounding the nature of free will and the scientific observations of cause and effect. In the early American republic, the new science of causality provided an explanatory structure for the developing relationship between government and citizens, and the widespread concern surrounding authenticity and hypocrisy. As republican citizens, individuals were expected to know with whom they were dealing and what their true intentions were. Specific individuals, in other words, did and said things and therefore were personally accountable for what happened.[10] It was the disparity between an individual's words and deeds, motives and actions that in the eighteenth century often led to charges of dissimulation. In the Gothic, villainy often points to conspiracy and deception. From duplicitous monks, persecutory doubles and confidence tricksters, the Gothic re-enacts the drama of ferreting out forms of duplicity. That the impostor often takes centre stage reveals the Gothic's urge to unmask or unveil the corrupting effects of dissimulation. Similarly, in twentieth-century fiction, the figure of the conspirator functions not as a return of the psychologically repressed, but as a means of examining the nature of deception in a culture atrophied by the effects of consumerism and mass media.

Conspiracy and hypocrisy in the eighteenth century

As Bailyn and other historians have noted, the tendency to view events through the aperture of deception and hidden design was particularly acute in the writings of American revolutionaries: whether loyalist sympathizers, suspicious Whigs or radical democrats, Americans often adopted conspiratorial and duplicitous modes of interpretation to explain the threat to republican liberty. Thomas Jefferson commonly resorted to conspiratorial explanations when describing the motives of King George III: 'Single acts of tyranny may be ascribed to the accidental opinion of a day; but a series of oppressions, begun at a distinguished period, and pursued unalterably thro' every change of ministers, too plainly prove a deliberate, systematical plan of reducing us to slavery.'[11] During the constitutional struggle of the 1780s, the Federalist James Madison argued:

> men of factious tempers, of local prejudices, or of sinister designs may, by intrigue, by corruption or by other means, first obtain the suffrages, and then betray the interests of the people ... it is to be remarked that however small the republic may be, the representatives must be raised to a certain number in order to guard against the cabals of a few.[12]

The widespread belief in the prevalence of plots and schemes was not a uniquely American reaction but a dominating theme of eighteenth-century culture, Whig and Tory alike. While Jefferson was accusing the British king of 'systematical plans', George III was equally attributing colonial resistance to 'turbulent and seditious persons, who, under false pretenses, have but too successfully deluded numbers of my subjects in America'. In a rhetorical counterpart to Jefferson's claim that there was a 'design to reduce [the colonies] under absolute despotism',[13] George III claimed:

> The authors and promoters of this desperate conspiracy have in the conduct of it derived great advantage from the difference of our intentions and theirs. They meant only to amuse, by vague expressions of attachment to the parent state and the strongest protestations of loyalty to me, whilst they were preparing for a general revolt ... The rebellious war now levied is ... manifestly carried on for the purpose of establishing an independent empire.[14]

In his 'Thoughts on the cause of the present discontents', Edmund Burke describes the nature of deceit in the early years of George III's reign. The discontents of the British nation were, according to Burke, all out of proportion to the perceived causes. The widespread alarm was not due to any 'external calamity', 'pestilence or famine', 'no unsuccessful war' or system of oppressive taxation. Therefore, it could only be explained by hidden causes, by the existence of a *'double cabinet'*, a 'shadow of ministers' operating 'behind the curtain'. It was a 'cabal of the closet', a 'backstairs influence and clandestine government' that was at work against the will of the people.

> [W]hilst they are terrifying the great and opulent with the horrors of mob government, they are by other managers attempting . . . to alarm the people with a phantom of tyranny in the nobles. All this is done upon their favourite principle of disunion, of sowing jealousies amongst the different orders of the state, and of disjointing the natural strength of the kingdom; that it may be rendered incapable of resisting the sinister designs of wicked men, who have engrossed the royal power.[15]

So, if not delusion and paranoia, what lay behind the eighteenth century's preoccupation with deception? According to Gordon S. Wood, to understand how so many reasonable and sophisticated people could believe in conspiracy and hidden design, 'we should begin by taking their view of events at face value and examine what it rationally implied'.[16] Wood eschews the tendency of contemporary historians to explain the revolution and the conspiratorial beliefs of its leaders in psychological terms. The 'search for identity', the rejection of the 'mother' country or 'fatherly' king is, according to Wood, 'being wrung dry of every bit of psychological significance it may contain'.[17] His task is to enlarge the view of malevolent conspiracies and fear of subversion to encompass the culture of the eighteenth century. The widespread resort to conspiratorial interpretations cannot be explained by modern psychohistory but through an examination of the Enlightenment's attempt to explain human behaviour in an increasingly scientific, rational and complicated world. According to Wood, in the late eighteenth century, conspiracy and deception were the only morally coherent and intellectually satisfying explanations for the obvious discrepancy between men's words and deeds, and denotes a significant change from the Machiavellian conception of conspiracy as a common feature of political theory to a period of bewilderment and unprecedented suspicion. Historians chart this change to the expansion and increasing complexity of the political world including economic and demographic growth, shifting class structures, greater mobility and independence, and the development of more complicated and impersonal human relationships. Moreover, the public's increasing access to the secrets of politics also meant that the actions of various groups, interests and classes were often suspected but not easily deciphered. However, as the behaviour of individuals became more difficult to explain, the enlightened of the age were attempting to do just that. It was out of this contradiction that the widespread resort to conspiratorial interpretations of events grew:

> Conspiratorial interpretations—attributing events to the concerted design of wilful individuals—became a major means by which educated men ordered and gave meaning to their political world. Far from being symptomatic of irrationality, this conspiratorial mode of explanation represented an enlightened stage in Western man's long struggle to comprehend his social reality. It flowed from the scientific promise of the Enlightenment and represented an effort . . . to hold men personally and morally responsible for their actions.[18]

What the belief in conspiracy rationally implied was a causal explanation. With the publication of Isaac Newton's *Philosophiae naturalis principia mathematica* (1687) came the widely held belief that social, economic and political phenomena could be explained, not by the workings of providence, but by the laws of cause and effect. The new science of mechanistic causality became the new paradigm in which to uncover the mysteries of natural phenomena and, more significantly, the moral world of human affairs. All causes produced effects and every effect had a related cause. This science shaped new laws, predictions and regularities of behaviour; while many people held fast to the Christian belief in God's control over nature, others came to see God as a mere clockmaker in a world that ran itself.[19] The new science of natural philosophy also advanced the belief that moral laws, or chains of cause and effect in human behaviour, could work the same as in the physical world. To avoid the mechanical necessitarianism implied in this approach, philosophers evoked the notion of free will. While Newton proposed the idea of God-like 'active principles' as causal agents of motion and gravity, moral philosophers looked towards the minds and hearts of men for the moral equivalents of physical energy: '[m]en's motives or will thus became the starting point in the sequential chain of causes and effects in human affairs. All human actions and events could now be seen scientifically as the products of men's intentions'.[20] It was the specific intentions or designs, and the particular passions and interests of individuals that explained all social phenomena. If events happened, it was because individuals willed them to happen. Good intentions and beliefs would lead to good actions, while evil motives would result in evil actions. However, as Bernard Mandeville perceived, the moral connection between cause and effect was not always straightforward: there existed the fundamental paradox of 'Private vices, Publick benefits', that could not be explained through causal necessity.[21] Evil intentions often produced good effects and vice versa. One explanation for this paradox was the Protestant concept of providence: the 'incomprehensible chain of causes' was the work of the mysterious hand of God. Yet, for the rationally minded this was a step backwards: the only logical explanation for linked human action was some form of dissimulation; the actor, in other words, had to be concealing his real motives.

The suspicion that individuals were hiding their true intentions for political gain is expressed in the numerous charges of hypocrisy that characterized much of the political writing of the early national period. In a letter concerning the Federalist John Marshall, Jefferson wrote:

> Though [John] Marshall will be able to embarrass the republican party in the Assembly a good deal, yet upon the whole, his having gone into it will be of service. He has been hitherto able to do more mischief acting under the mask of republicanism than he will be able to do throwing it plainly off. His lax lounging manners have made him popular with the bulk of the people of Richmond, and a profound hypocrisy with many thinking men of our country. But having come forth in the full plenitude of his English principles, the latter will see that it is high time to make him known.[22]

Donning the mask of republicanism is inherently threatening to the well-being of the nation: it revealed a support of English principles and, therefore, an interest in domination. True republicans, Jefferson suggests, do not wear masks, and do not act a part to gain popularity or political favour. This was the height of hypocrisy, and hypocrisy was the handmaiden of the aristocracy and, therefore, of inequality, oppression and tyranny.

Conspiracy and Hypocrisy in Rosemary's Baby

The ubiquity of terms such as misrepresentation, pretence, counterfeit and impostor in eighteenth-century writing reveals the generation's preoccupation with the discourse of duplicity and, significantly, its interdependence with the concept of republican liberty. It was not simply a Whiggish distrust of centralized government or the Christian tradition of a deceitful Satan that was fundamental to the age's susceptibility to conspiratorial interpretations: individuals who were neither radical Whigs nor devout Protestants nonetheless believed in conspiracies. As Wood argues, 'what was fundamental is that American secular thought – in fact, all enlightenment thought of the eighteenth century – was structured in such a way that conspiratorial explanations of complex events became normal, necessary, and rational'. Deciphering the concealed or partially exposed wills of human beings was what being enlightened was all about:

> It was precisely this task of tracing, predicting, disclosing, and connecting motives and events that American Whig leaders had set for themselves in the debate with Great Britain . . . and became another example of their application of science to human affairs . . . a humanization of Providence, an impassioned attempt to explain the ways of man to man.[23]

But with the onset of the French Revolution, such personalistic and rationalistic modes of explanation could no longer account for the widespread upheaval. As John Playfair observed, with the French Revolution 'a body was put in motion sufficient to crush whole nations under its weight'. No one 'had the power or the skill to direct its course'. As a consequence, 'a year was magnified into an age; and . . . in a few months one might behold more old institutions destroyed, and more new ones projected or begun'.[24] What was required to explain the complexity and scale of the revolution was an elaborate organization involving thousands of individuals linked by a sinister design. Only the machinations of secret societies and associations could be behind such chaos and turmoil.

The assumption that insurrectionary associations, influenced by the likes of Jefferson, Paine and Voltaire, were working to bring down government and religion had wide currency in 1790s counter-revolutionary and anti-Jacobin discourse on both sides of the Atlantic.

In the minds of Federalist leaders, democratic societies were secretly working 'to unhinge the whole order of government, and introduce confusion, so that union, the constitution, the laws, public order and private right would be all the sport of violence or chance'.[25] As Vernon Stauffer noted,

> from the day the first of these sinister Societies was established ... the public mind found itself wrought upon by a new species of excitement, by suggestions of tricks and plots, by appeals to passion and unreasoning fear, all conspiring to inject into the national spirit an element of haunting suspicion from which it was not soon to be cleared.[26]

The fear of subversive organizations was entrenched by President George Washington who, in 1794, suggested a causal link between the Whiskey rebellion and democratic societies. In his address to Congress on 19 November, he claimed:

> In the four western counties of Pennsylvania a prejudice, fostered and embittered by the artifice of men who labored for an ascendancy over the will of others by the guidance of their passions, produced symptoms of riot and violence ... From a belief that by a more formal concert their operation might be defeated, certain self-created societies assumed the tone of condemnation.[27]

Washington's denunciation of these 'associations of men' or 'self-created societies' was seized upon by Federalist leaders, editors and orators who were at pains to inform the public about the pernicious nature of these organizations. The phrase 'self-created societies' in particular was seen to be applicable to the Jacobin clubs of France. Although the attacks issued from the press and the pulpit effectively destroyed the credibility of the democratic societies, their demise did not efface the fear that artifice and malevolent design were working to undermine the new republic. The humiliation of the XYZ affair and the threat of war with France evinced a form of Francophobia that climaxed with the introduction of the Naturalization and Alien and Sedition Laws which were intended, as Robert Goodloe Harper declared, to stave off 'a domestic – what ... shall I call it? – a conspiracy, a faction leagued with a foreign power to effect a revolution or a subjugation of this country'.[28] The Federalist campaign to root out foreign and domestic subversives found unwavering support in the clergy, who blamed the rise of deism on Jacobin plotting. Disturbed by the liberalizing tendency of the age, the clergy attempted to 'renew cohesion within Church and state by pointing to a threat even more alarming than Jacobinical violence and heresy'.[29] That threat was the seditious order of the Bavarian Illuminati.

If Americans had not already been primed to believe in the possibility of a grand conspiracy on the part of Jacobin forces to destroy the republic, it was vividly brought to their attention on 9 May 1798 when Jedidiah Morse rose to the pulpit to deliver his Thanksgiving Day sermon. Morse told his congregation of a secret European organization known as the Illuminati whose malevolent influence had sparked the French Revolution:

> Kings, princes, and rulers in all governments, ... priests and ministers of religion of all denominations ... are reviled and abused ... [and] fraud, violence, cruelty, debauchery, and the uncontrolled gratification of every corrupt and debasing lust and inclination of the human heart exists in the place of religion.[30]

It was this order, according to Morse, that was the fruit of the French Revolution and the Jacobins were merely the open manifestation of the hidden system of the Illuminati. More terrifying was the fact that 'the Order has its branches established and its emissaries at work in America. The affiliated Jacobin Societies in America have doubtless had as the object of their establishment the propagation of the principles of the illuminated mother club in France.'[31] So significant were the 'awful events' that Morse felt compelled to warn his parishioners:

> I hold it a duty, my brethren, which I owe to God, to the cause of religion, to my country and to you, at this time, to declare to you, thus honestly and faithfully, these truths. My only aim is to awaken you and myself a due attention, at this alarming period, to our dearest interests. As a faithful watchman I would give you warning of your present danger.[32]

The response to Morse's sermon was electric: pulpits throughout New England reverberated with anti-Illuminati agitation. On 19 June 1798, David Tappan, professor of divinity at Harvard, cautioned his students against a recent system 'which . . . has for its ostensible object THE REGENERATION OF AN OPPRESSED WORLD TO THE BLISSFUL ENJOYMENT OF EQUAL LIBERTY'.[33] Samuel McCorkle of North Carolina warned of Illuminati plotting in *Work of God for the French Revolution*, and Timothy Dwight, president of Yale, himself no stranger to finding irreligion and anarchy afoot in the republic, delivered a similar warning in his Fourth of July sermon:

> The sins of these enemies of Christ, and Christians, are of number and degrees which mock account and description. All that the malice and atheism of the Dragon, the cruelty and rapacity of the Beast, and the fraud and deceit of the false prophet, can generate or accomplish, swell the list. No personal or national interest of man has been un-invaded; no impious sentiment, or action, against God has been spared; no malignant hostility against Christ, and his religion, has been unattempted . . . Shall we, my brethren, become partakers of these sins? Shall we introduce them into our government, our schools, our families? Shall our sons become the disciples of Voltaire . . . or our daughters the concubines of the Illuminati?[34]

The source for these and many other explosive sermons, orations and newspaper articles was the publication of two texts on the subject of illuminism and Freemasonary: John Robison's *Proofs of a Conspiracy against All Religions and Governments of Europe* and Abbé Augustin Barruél's four volume *Mémoires pour servir à l'histoire du Jacobinisme*. Considered the founding documents of the conservative interpretation of the French Revolution, their influence was widespread in both Europe and America. Barruél claimed that the revolution was caused by Voltaire, Rousseau and other *philosophes*, who plotted with the Freemasons and the Illuminati to destroy the monarchy in France. The American clergy played down the Freemason conspiracy in deference to well-known members, such as Benjamin Franklin and George Washington, and instead focused their ire on the Illuminati, a defunct order founded in 1776 by Adam Weishaupt, professor of canon law at the University of Ingolstadt. Stimulated by the works of Rousseau, the ideals of republicanism and natural rights, Weishaupt and his followers sought to bring reason, enlightenment and liberty to the world through the reform of man and society. Although originally allied with notions of equality and humanitarian rationalism, the term 'illuminati' was appropriated by counter-revolutionaries as an epithet of abuse levied towards political and religious opponents. Evidence of this ideological divide is manifest in the profusion of letters on the subject of illuminism. In 1797, Edmund Burke, for example, wrote to Abbé Barruél after receiving a copy of the first volume of the *Mémoires*:

> I cannot easily express to you how much I am instructed and delighted by the first Volume of your History of Jacobinism. The whole of the wonderful narrative is supported by documents and proofs with the most juridical regularity and exactness. Your reflexions and reasonings are interspersed with infinite judgement, and in their most proper places, for leading the sentiments of the reader, and preventing the force of plausible objections. The tendency of the whole is admirable in every point of view, political, religious, and, let me make use of the abused word, philosophical . . . I forgot to say, that I have known myself, personally, five of your principal conspirators; and I can undertake to say from my own certain knowledge, that so far back as the year 1773, they were busy in the plot you have so well described, and in the manner, and on the principle you have so truly represented.— To this I can speak as a witness.[35]

Burke and Morse link the Illuminati with the terror of the French Revolution, with subversive democratic clubs and with the circulators of publications such as Paine's *Age of Reason*. Democrats, on the other hand, found no subversion in Weishaupt's philosophy. In a letter to James Madison, Thomas Jefferson wrote:

> I have lately by accident got sight of a single volume (the 3rd) of the Abbé Barruél's 'Antisocial Conspiracy', which gives me the first idea I have ever had of what is meant by the Illuminatism against which 'Illuminate Morse', as he is now called, and his ecclesiastical and monarchical associates have been making such a hue and cry . . . Wishaupt seems to be an enthusiastic philanthropist. He is among those (as you know the excellent Price and Priestly also are) who

believe in the infinite perfectibility of man. He thinks he may in time be rendered so perfect that he will be able to govern himself in every circumstance, so as to injure none, to do all the good he can, to leave government no occasion to exercise their powers over him, and, of course, to render political government useless. This, you know, is Godwin's doctrine, and this is what Robison, Barruél, and Morse have called a conspiracy against all government.[36]

Jefferson's invocation of Priestly, Price and Godwin forges a link between illuminism, anti-Federalism and British oppositional politics. To Federalists, as well as many Tories in England, the prime mover of the French Revolution was Voltaire. Viewed as the great infidel, he deliberately plotted to undermine Christianity and encouraged the anti-monarchical feeling out of which the revolution grew. Moreover, Thomas Jefferson was frequently charged with being Voltaire's emissary in America. His role as ambassador to France, his support of the French Revolution, his interest in French philosophy and his deism all led to charges of infidelity. Before Robison and Barruél's texts appeared in America, pamphleteers and newspaper writers were arguing the case against Jefferson and other democrats. During the presidential election campaign of 1800, Jefferson's opponents accused him of being in league with the Illluminati and part of a worldwide conspiracy to destroy government and Christianity. In both England and America, it was the publication of Burruél's *Mémoires* that crystallized Voltaire's and, for many, Jefferson's guilt.[37]

While many twentieth-century historians dismissed the story of the Bavarian Illuminati as a momentary divergence, republican historiography reveals that the vocabulary of conspiracy, deception and dissimulation was at the centre of European and American counter-revolutions. So real were these fears that in the aftermath of revolution both England and America instituted forms of legislation aimed at suppressing opposition. In Britain, the fear of Jacobinism led to the suspension of habeas corpus, the famous treason trials and the introduction of draconian measures to repress dissent. The passage of the Alien and Sedition Acts, the prosecution of *The Rights of Man* and the 'Twin Acts' against 'treasonable practices' and 'seditious meetings' revealed what the belief in conspiracy and dissimulation had unleashed on the opposite side of the Atlantic. As Tise observes, the Illuminati experience of 1798 introduced 'a new terminology into the American parlance . . . revolutionary, brigand, Jacobin, infidel, illuminate, enthusiast, anarchist, liberal, conservative'.[38] The fear of conspiracy also introduced a new phantom enemy into America culture: a Gothic figure that, next to the ubiquitous tyrant, fuelled the apocalyptic fears of political and moral degeneration that would linger for the next two centuries. Perhaps the most famous example of an early American Gothic phantom is Benedict Arnold, the universally abhorred and enigmatic figure of the revolutionary era. Arnold's treason represented, in stark terms, the discrepancy between man's words and deeds. What was particularly troubling for Americans was not only Arnold's act of conspiracy for which he was never prosecuted, but the failure of those close to him, such as Washington, to spot his duplicity. As a general in the revolutionary army and war hero several times over, Arnold symbolized the qualities of republican virtue, honour and sincerity of character, a crucial trait to a country engaged in rebellion. For some, Arnold represented the vulnerability of the republic; his act of treason for personal gain was viewed as an example of the nation's slide towards corruption and loss of virtue, a sign that the New World was slowly turning into a replica of the Old. For others, Arnold was simply a lonely traitor, an aberration or a Gothic villain. In a direct address to Arnold, the *Pennsylvania Packet* frames his actions in the language of deformity, monstrosity and distortion:

> I took up my pen with an intent to shew a reflective glass, wherein you might at one view behold your actions, but soon found such a horrid ugly deformity in the outlines of your picture, that I was frightened at the sight, so the mirrour dropped and broke to pieces! each of this discovered you to be a gigantick overgrown monster, of such a variety of shapes, all over ulcerated, that it is in vain to attempt to describe them.[39]

Whether secular or spiritual explanations, or a conflation of the two, gave meaning to his actions, Arnold came to represent the ultimate hypocrite, the 'ungraspable phantom of an ideological nightmare'.[40]

If conspiracy, hypocrisy and hidden design formed the grammar and vocabulary for much of the thought of the 1780s and 1790s, they were also the central themes of British and American Gothic fiction.

It is out of this political and ideological milieu that Mathew Lewis's *The Monk*, Anne Radcliffe's *The Italian*, William Godwin's *Caleb Williams*, Karl Grosse's *Horrid Mysteries* and Brockden Brown's *Wieland* and *Ormond* emerge. Gripped by an atmosphere of conspiratorial claims and counterclaims, the Gothic on both sides of the Atlantic was characterized as a world of 'forged plots, spies, informers, and false witnesses'.[41] It is axiomatic that in the Gothic nothing is quite as it appears: perceptions are distorted and unreliable, senses are betrayed and accepted definitions of reality blur or disappear. Attempts at decoding individual intention, of gauging sincerity and puzzling over the discrepancy between words and deeds are often the primary tasks of Gothic protagonists. Charles Brockden Brown's novel *Wieland; Or the Transformation* (1798), in particular, explores the concepts of causality and deception in a culture undergoing transformation from one that assumed stable relations between appearance and reality to one confronted with deceptive appearances, mixed motives and the growing discrepancy between thoughts and actions, words and deeds.[42] For Brown, moral obligations such as sincerity and benevolence often contradict one another or lead to evil consequences. In both *Arthur Mervyn* (1800) and *Edgar Huntly*, for example, good intentions backfire, while in *Wieland* Carwin admits to setting in motion 'a machine over whose progress [he] had no control'.[43] Believing that motives and intentions are unreliable determinants in judging moral responsibility, Brown's characters repeatedly grapple with the unintended consequences of behaviour. In *Wieland*, all the characters are deceived, all mistake appearances and question motives. Believing in a traditional moral order whereby outward actions reveal inward intention, Clara finds herself questioning the determinism of cause and effect:

> From the death of my parents, till the commencement of this year, my life had been serene and blissful ... but now, my bosom was corroded by anxiety. I was visited by dread of unknown dangers, and the future was a scene over which clouds rolled, and thunder muttered. I compared the cause with the effect, and they seemed disproportioned to each other. All unaware, and in a manner which I had no power to explain, I was pushed from my immoveable and lofty station, and cast upon a sea of troubles (p. 69).

Clara is 'powerfully affected by [Carwin's] first appearance' and is 'bewitched by his countenance and his tones' (p. 123) and, although his sentiments were 'accompanied with that degree of earnestness which indicates sincerity', Clara remains 'wholly uncertain' whether Carwin is someone to be 'dreaded or adored, and whether his powers have been exerted to evil or to good' (p. 71). Decoding Carwin's concealed intentions is what propels the plot forward and by the end, both Clara and Wieland realize the futility of judging moral responsibility through individual action: 'Let that man who shall purpose to assign motives to the actions of another, blush at his folly and forbear. Not more presumptuous would it be to attempt the classification of all nature, and the scanning of supreme intelligence' (p. 146.) Through their experiences, Brown's characters begin to question both Enlightenment rationalism and religious enthusiasm. No one, Brown suggests, ever acts purely out of reason or moral principles; to do so leads to false assumptions and mistaken beliefs. Both Wieland's religious enthusiasm and Playel's devotion to reason equally lead to delusion. Only Clara acknowledges that the mix of these systems of thought is an uneasy one: 'The will is the tool of the understanding, which must fashion its conclusion on the notices of sense. If the senses be depraved, it is impossible to calculate the evils that may flow from the consequent deduction of the understanding' (p. 39).

In addition to investigating the moral complexity of life, Brown's fiction draws on the contemporary theme of an Illuminati conspiracy. Published at the height of the panic, many of his novel's central characters are allied with mysterious and sinister political associations. Carwin, who in addition to using the art of ventriloqy to trick Wieland, is also under the tutelage of Ludloe, a member of the Illuminati who moulds Carwin's radical politics. Ormond too, is a dissembler and a dangerous illuminatus. According to Brown, those who believe in the Illuminati conspiracy assume that all the disastrous consequences were produced by certain individuals and were 'forseen and intended'. To avoid such simple-minded beliefs, wrote Brown, we must be 'conscious of the uncertainty of history' and recognize that 'actions and motives cannot be truly described'.[44] Brown's fiction, therefore, provides a warning against the determinism of cause and effect, probing instead Wordsworth's aphorism: 'The study of human nature suggests this awful truth, that, as in the trials to which life subjects us, sin and crime are apt to start from their very opposite qualities.'[45] The Gothic's concern with conspiracy and deception, then, is not the result of an irrational or paranoiac frame of mind but engages directly with what Shelley called 'the master theme of the epoch in which we live': the awful realization that the actions of liberal, enlightened and well-intentioned individuals could produce such horror, terror and chaos.[46] Whether receptive to revolutionary ideas or fanning the embers of orthodox discontent, American Gothic's impulse towards deception, dissimulation and hidden design is deeply rooted in its historical moment, and thrives on the Enlightenment encounter between deception and truth.

Conspiracy and causality in the twentieth century

In cold war America, the spectre of hidden malevolent design still functioned as a potent explanatory structure in the public imagination. As Weinstein observes, '[b]asic to all conspiracy theories of Cold War America has been the image of some covert, rational scheme to undermine the republic, some smoothly-functioning, well-oiled attempt to interfere with and "control" the ordinary course of events'.[47] An extreme example of this mode of thought is J. Edgar Hoover's *Masters of Deceit*. Hoover's account of communist infiltration reflects the grandiose and paranoid character Hofstadter identifies. Like Senator Joseph McCarthy, Hoover views communism as an 'arm of revolution' and a powerful system organized by a 'dedicated conspiratorial group'.[48] More dangerous than individual agents are the thought-control mechanisms of the party: communism is an 'infection', a 'poison' and a 'spell' duping unsuspecting citizens through the party's invisible 'transmission belt' which infiltrates legitimate groups, clubs and organizations that constitute a democratic society.[49] And like the Illuminati, the ultimate aim of the communist conspiracy is the complete destruction of America's religious, political and social institutions. Particularly frightening is the realization that the majority of individuals are unaware that they are being plotted against and therefore are at risk of being duped by Moscow's agents and fellow travellers. The introduction of loyalty oaths, Congressional hearings, blacklists, surveillance technology, union-busting legislation and immigration restrictions are, for cold warriors such as Hoover, all justified reactions in the face of public acquiesence and apathy. Similarly, in the 1960s, the conspiracy theories surrounding the assassinations of John F. Kennedy, Robert Kennedy and Martin Luther King confirmed the propensity to view unexplainable events as a form of deliberate design. The widespread belief that Oswald did not act alone, for example, is what social scientists call 'cabalism' whereby behaviour which is spontaneous and situational is seen as having been well planned in advance as part of some sort of conspiratorial plot: 'Rather than indicating widespread paranoia and demonstrating the consequences of extremist propaganda . . . in many cases cabalism provides the most easily understandable and acceptable explanation'.[50] Cabalism, in other words, removes the irrationality, incomprehensibility and unpredictability from the event.

These contemporary conspiracy theories speak to the continuing belief in a systemic operation of hidden design, a belief that supports a traditional moral order that relies on causation as the primary explanation of events. Most memorably characterized by the rise of McCarthyism, it was this belief in a fundamental and homogeneous relationship between cause and effect that governed many of the high-profile security cases of the Truman–Eisenhower period. The Alger Hiss case, the Rosenberg trial and the Oppenheimer hearing, for example, each publicly dramatized not only the power of conspiratorial fears, but also the operation of a moral order whereby action is the direct consequence of individual intention. In each of these dramas, the central players were characterized either as 'principals in [a] diabolical conspiracy to destroy a God-fearing nation' or the innocent scapegoats of an anti-communist witch-hunt.[51] However, the final judgements in these cases also rested on the presupposition that the individuals involved were morally accountable for their actions. In his analysis of the Alger Hiss case, Richard Nixon framed the 'real and present danger to the security of the nation' in moral terms. Hiss did not join the Communist Party for money, power or because he was duped; according to Nixon, he joined because:

> he deeply believed in Communist theory, Communist principles, and the Communist 'vision' of the ideal society . . . His morality could be reduced to one perverted rule: anything that advances the goals of

Communism is good. Hiss followed his beliefs deliberately and consciously to the utmost logical extreme, and ended up in the area of espionage.[52]

A similar moral intention is advanced in the Rosenberg case. In his sentencing statement, Judge Irving Kaufman declared:

> I believe your conduct in putting into the hands of the Russians the A-Bomb . . . has already caused, in my opinion, the Communist aggression in Korea, with the resultant casualties exceeding 50,000 and who knows but what millions more of innocent people may pay the price of your treason. Indeed, by your betrayal you undoubtedly have altered the course of history to the disadvantage of our country . . . In the light of this, I can only conclude that the defendants entered into this most serious conspiracy against their country with full realization of its implications.[53]

Like many individuals caught up in the red scare of the 1950s, Alger Hiss and the Rosenbergs were not judged as dupes of an insidious design, but willing and morally responsible participants. Although unwary people could be deceived, in the fight against communism, individual intention still mattered.

As the writings of the generation's cold warriors reveal, the discourse of conspiracy restates for a modern liberal era, the threat of dissimulation, hypocrisy and tyranny that so terrified the revolutionary generation. That this approach is, in many ways, heir to the conservative moral order espoused by Morse and Burke reveals the reactionary turn of cold war culture. In the age of consensus and containment, the radicalism of Mandeville's 'private vices, public benefits' or Brown's 'unanticipated consequences of behaviour' is effaced for the determinism and moral absolutism of cause and effect. In twentieth-century Gothic fiction, these themes often take a diabolical turn. Situated in the aftermath of the Kennedy assassination, and at the beginning of the Vietnam War, Ira Levin's *Rosemary's Baby* explores the interaction between motives and intentions, hypocrisy and authenticity in the post-war era.[54] What is truly hazardous to modern civilization, the novel suggests, is not the worldwide diabolical conspiracy against society and religion, but the rise of self-deception in a world where individual consciousness, free will and morality itself are overwhelmed by the effects of consumer and media culture.

Conspiracy and hypocrisy in Rosemary's Baby

> Self-deceit is the veiled image of unknown evil.
> Percy Bysshe Shelley, 'A defense of poetry'[55]

Rosemary's Baby tells the story of a newly-wed couple who move to a Victorian apartment building in the theatre district of New York. Reputed to be popular with actors, the Bramford also harbours a sinister history of murder, suicide and witchcraft. Unfazed by the rumours, Rosemary and Guy Woodhouse take up residence in the building where they soon befriend Minnie and Roman Castevet, an elderly, seemingly benevolent couple who occupy the apartment next to theirs. Shortly after they arrive, Guy's acting career takes off and Rosemary becomes pregnant. However, as the pregnancy progresses, Rosemary begins to suspect that her neighbours are not what they appear; that they are in fact, members of a coven of witches who plan to use her child in their cult rituals. The plot against her is confirmed when Rosemary discovers that, with the help of her husband, she has been drugged, raped and impregnated by the devil and subsequently delivers a demon child.

As members of a secret coven of witches, the Castevets reflect the popular image of a communist conspiracy conveyed in post-war propaganda. The global reach of their plot, their techniques of manipulation and their false benevolence dupe the unsuspecting couple into participating in a diabolical conspiracy against society and religion. Equally, their depiction as Satanic figures exploit the reader's knowledge of demonology lore while at the same time engaging with the popular anti-communist metaphor of witchcraft. From this perspective, *Rosemary's Baby* can be interpreted as yet another post-war cautionary tale warning against apathy and promoting vigilance. However, reading *Rosemary's Baby* as a simple battle between good and evil diminishes the moral complexity of the novel. Integral to the narrative of cultural and moral decline is the depiction of a materialistic world drained of spirituality and virtue; a world where appearances are mistaken for substance, and where hypocrisy and self-deception replace reality.

The novel opens with a small deception that sets in motion the series of diabolical events. Guy lies in order to get out of a previous lease agreement and secure the apartment in the Bramford. While Rosemary does not participate directly in the deception, she goads Guy with flattery and 'mock anguish' (p. 9): 'See how you can think of things . . . You're a *marvellous* liar' (p. 10). To Rosemary, Guy's ability to '[spin] a story' is an appealing quality because she, too, is not above lying to get what she wants: 'Sure he was vain and self-centred; he was an actor, wasn't he . . . And yes he might lie now and then; wasn't that exactly what had attracted her and still did?' (p. 87). Knowing Guy's wish to postpone having children until his career is established, Rosemary's plan is to 'get pregnant by accident': 'Indulgently he studied the calendar and avoided the "dangerous days", and she said "No, it's safe today, darling; I'm sure it is"' (p. 59). Although seemingly innocuous, these small deceptions ominously presage future events. Guy's story foreshadows the theatrical role he is offered when a rival actor goes blind at the hands of the coven, and Rosemary's plan to get pregnant by accident foreshadows her unconscious rape and impregnation by the devil. These initial lies also reveal Rosemary and Guy's capacity for deceit. Rather than mere dupes of a diabolical plot, they are exposed from the onset as morally culpable actors in their own downfall. The impetus of the plot is Rosemary's gradual awareness that all is not what it seems at the Bramford. Innocent, idealistic and painfully traditional, her task is to decode and unmask evil intention in a world of fluid and indiscriminate identity. Assisting her process of awareness is her older friend Edward Hutchins who functions as an irritant to the coven's aims. It is the British-born 'Hutch' who introduces Rosemary and Guy to the Bramford's diabolical history and eventually to the presence of witchcraft. Representing the rational approach to the concept of evil, Hutch's explanation for the Bramford's 'high incidence of unpleasant happenings' (p. 21) is causal: 'eventually a house becomes a – a kind of rallying place for people who are more prone than others to certain types of behaviour. Or perhaps there are things we don't know yet – about magnetic fields or electrons or whatever – ways in which a place can quite literally be malign' (p. 20). Hutch's analysis reflects the deterministic operation of cause and effect. The presence of evil is explained by individual intention or rational science. Only individuals predisposed to evil will gravitate toward its epicentre or are drawn by some unknown natural phenomena. This explanation directly contradicts Guy's preference for an uncertain world: 'I don't see why the Bramford is any more of a "danger zone" than any other house in the city. You can flip a coin and get five heads in a row; that doesn't mean that the coin is any different from any other coin. It's coincidence, that's all' (p. 22). For Guy, events are governed by fortune or chance and the manifestation of evil, if it exists at all, is merely the luck of the draw. Given the choice, Rosemary opts for Guy's world view, and even though signs of evil are still present at the Bramford, she wilfully ignores Hutch's warning. 'Partial ignorance, she decided, was partial bliss. *Damn Hutch and his good intentions!*' (p. 28). Hutch's good intentions backfire, because both Rosemary and Guy opt for false illusions and their own self-interests. For Rosemary, in particular, ignorance is preferred over awareness; fantasy over reality.

Foregrounding the themes of pretence and deception is the novel's focus on naming and renaming. Rosemary and Guy's world is the world of the theatre, of role playing and imposture, a world where no one is exactly whom they seem and where characters deliberately don masks and assume false identities. Hutch writes 'adventure stories for boys' under three different pseudonyms, the name Roman Castevet is really an acronym for Steven Marcato, and before he changed it to Guy Woodhouse, Guy's real name was Sherman Peden. For Guy, in particular, a marketable name is crucial to his success as an actor; after losing a coveted role to a 'grotesquely named' (p. 47) rival, his reaction is 'what kind of a name is *Donald Baumgart?*' (p. 33). While the novel's play on names betrays the mass of duplicity at the core of Rosemary and Guy's world, naming also links to wider historical themes. As the arch conspirator and primary agent of decline, Roman provides an allusion to the historical downfall of the ancient republic. As an allegorical figure, he represents the historical correlation between corruption and national dissolution, a theme raised later in the novel when, during her pregnancy, Rosemary starts 'finally' on *The Decline and Fall of the Roman Empire* (p. 102). Why Rosemary reads Gibbon is unexplained but the adjective 'finally' implies a didactic function. Gibbon's reputation is largely that of a man warning his country of the need to throw off the restraints of superstition. In the eighteenth century, Gibbon's text functioned as a call to rationality as well as a warning against the encroachment of corruption and tyranny, and its inclusion on Rosemary's reading list highlights the continuing relevance of this warning in modern American culture.

If Roman represents a worldwide conspiracy reminiscent of Illuminati or Jacobin plotting, in the rogues' gallery of demonology, Guy is the prototypical hypocrite, a figure, which in every age, every form of literature and every public stage, has been held up for contempt and ridicule.[56] As Mandeville claimed: 'No Habit or Quality is more easily acquired than Hypocrisy, nor any thing sooner learn'd than to deny the Sentiments of our Hearts and the Principle we Act from: But the Seeds of every Passion are innate to us, and nobody comes into the World without them.' If hypocrisy commonly explained villainous and corrupt behaviour in the eighteenth century, in the mid twentieth century it was still the one quality that inspired scorn, as Hannah Arendt noted in 1963:

> What makes it so plausible to assume that hypocrisy is the vice of vices is that integrity can indeed exist under the cover of all other vices except this one. Only crime and the criminal, it is true, confront us with the perplexity of radical evil; but only the hypocrite is really rotten to the core.[57]

Originally, a hypocrite meant an actor on the stage, a pretender or dissembler. Hypocrisy is also defined as assuming a false appearance of virtue or goodness, with dissimulation of real character or inclination. While this definition readily applies to the Castevets, as an actor schooled in the affectations of sincerity, Guy is ostensibly the novel's primary object of contempt. Even his name positions him as a figure of derision. In the American noun form, 'guy' denotes simply a man or a fellow. In this usage, Guy is a stand-in for Everyman, a representative of the upwardly mobile, middle-class male. However, in theatrical slang, the verb 'guy' also means to subject to ridicule or mockery. In this context, as an actor, Guy represents the universally detested figure of the dissembler. Evil coalesces around the Bramford because it attracts individuals like Guy who are prone to hypocrisy and corruption. He is open to what Mandeville called 'the witchcraft of flattery' because he chooses to be and because he is willing to abdicate moral responsibility for his own gain; motivated by self-interest, he manipulates sincerity to further his own career.[58] That Guy's hypocrisy is conscious and active is evident in his interaction with others. Despite finding Hutch 'a bit boring', he suffers his company because Hutch has theatrical connections, and connections 'often proved crucial in the theatre, Guy knew, even connections at second-hand' (p. 19). His initial reluctance to befriend the Castevets also quickly turns to enthusiasm once exposed to Roman's flattery and name-dropping. It is only after Rosemary discovers the truth about his participation in the conspiracy, that he experiences a momentary pang of conscience but then appeases his own guilt by arguing for their mutual self-interest: 'They promised me you wouldn't be hurt . . . and you haven't been, really. I mean, suppose you'd had a baby and lost it; wouldn't it be the same? And we're getting so much in return Ro' (p. 201). Guy's reward for facilitating Rosemary's rape by the devil is an important acting part that ironically exemplifies his duplicity: 'It's a very difficult part, a crippled boy who *pretends* that he's adjusted to his crippled-ness' (p. 84). The double pretence of playing the role of a character playing a role mirrors Guy's real life pretence of acting the part of a sincere husband. The eventual triumph of the coven, then, is not due solely to their supernatural power, but to a 'united mental force . . . a concentrated battery of malevolent wills' (p. 163). The conspiracy, in other words, could never have succeeded without Guy's wilful participation. In *Rosemary's Baby*, evil is not the result of random forces, but the rational consequence of deceit masquerading as sincerity.

Guy's role as the novel's villain, however, is somewhat of a red herring. Too predictable and orthodox to be horrifying, his character provides no moral lesson on the nature of hypocrisy. Like the Castevets, his sins do not start from opposite qualities, nor is he undone by his actions. In *Rosemary's Baby*, the moral complexity of evil is more clearly manifest in the character of Rosemary who is the novel's more dangerous impostor. Amidst the cultural convulsions that roused the 1960s, Rosemary is an anachronism, an uneasy reminder of the previous decade's repressive gender and social politics. Despite her positioning in a decade that included the civil rights and women's movements, the beat generation, student uprisings and the

Vietnam War, Rosemary embraces the traditional role of wife and mother. Ensconced in her Victorian apartment, she trades the harsh realities of modern times for the mock-Victorian vision of the happy family. Whereas Guy views the Bramford as a good place for 'becoming [a] star' (p. 21), Rosemary sees it as a house 'where people keep falling in love, and getting married and having babies' (p. 21). Easily swayed by experts, television advertisements and soap heroines, she lives in a fantasy world in which media images market happiness as a purchasable commodity, a theme magnified by the frequent references to brand names, designer labels and media celebrities. Rosemary, we learn, reads *Time*, *Life* and *The New Yorker*; she clips ads from *House Beautiful* and watches soap operas and television commercials. Flush with residuals from Guy's Anacin adverts, Rosemary consults 'a folder of decorating schemes' (p. 23) to guide her renovation of the apartment. When Minnie Castevet compliments Rosemary on her decorating skills, she responds, 'it was in a magazine' (p. 44). For Rosemary, the post-war 'good life' is played out in the idea of home and family, and through the display and consumption of consumer goods. Rosemary's reliance on adverts and media experts reflects the mood of moral apathy in a consumer culture completely detached from political awareness. As Aldous Huxley warned in *Brave New World Revisited* (1958), 'a society, most of whose members spend a great deal of their time . . . in the irrelevant other worlds of sport and soap opera . . . will find it hard to resist the encroachments of those who would manipulate and control it'.[59] American society, argued Herbert Marcuse, was inert, manipulable and mass-consuming. Americans were passive consumers who defined themselves through the purchase of consumer goods that had reduced civilization to the 'tinsel tawdriness of Hollywood fan magazines and titillating advertisements'.[60] Rosemary exemplifies this modern condition: rendered pliant and inattentive by television, shopping and other distractions of post-war prosperity, she is blind to the realities of the outside world. Underlying the moral conflict of the novel is the persistent tension between her awareness and wilful blindness.

However, for Rosemary, the dulling effects of consumerism eventually manifests in a compendium of debilitating symptoms: her domesticating impulse requires her to adhere to the standardized gender rules that existed between the sexes. She must exhibit obedience, dependence and a complete lack of personal identity. That this is not Rosemary's natural inclination is evident in her response to a disagreement with Guy. Deciding that he is 'vain, self-centred, shallow and deceitful', she decides that if he does not change, 'she would go back to work and get again that sense of independence and self-sufficiency she had been so eager to get rid of'. (p. 86). This ultimatum suggests that Rosemary has been living a lie: in marrying Guy, she has sacrificed her individuality for what Betty Friedan called the 'feminine mystique', the female practice of seeking personal fulfilment and identity in the home and family.[61] Believing in the 'female principle' of nurturance, it is only after becoming pregnant that Rosemary achieves a personal sense of identity: 'Now she was alive; was doing, was being, was at last herself and complete' (p. 99). It is this false sense of identity that leaves her vulnerable to the coven's influence. She is targeted because she is identified as an individual with no sense of self or moral core. As Minnie Castevet reveals, the chosen woman could be anybody as long, as 'she's young, and healthy and not a virgin' (p. 42). 'Anybody' in the depreciatory form is a person of any sort, an ordinary person, as opposed to 'a somebody', or an individual. It is the act of surrendering her identity that allows for the incredible abuse of power enacted by Guy and the Castevets.

Rosemary's lack of identity and self-imposed exclusion from the real world is evident in her ignorance concerning broader political events. In *Rosemary's Baby*, the subject of Vietnam is never far from the surface. Temporally, the action of the novel takes place between 3 August 1965 and 1 August 1966. This timeline hints at the national turmoil gathering in the periphery of the novel. On 3 August, the day Rosemary and Guy view the apartment at the Bramford, images of the atrocities committed by American soldiers in Vietnam are broadcast for the first time on television, galvanizing the anti-war movement. In the same month, the Voters' Rights Act is passed, affirmative action is introduced and the Watts Riots begin. Juxtaposed to this national disorder is Rosemary's apathy and denial: 'She looked at newspapers and tried to be interested in students burning draft cards and the threat of a city-wide transit strike, but she couldn't: this was news from a world of fantasy' (p. 120). While Rosemary's friends discuss Thomas Altizer's famous 1966 essay in *Time Magazine* entitled 'Is God Dead?', she ignores the article and turns instead to the show business section. This lack of engagement is observed by the Castevets who broach the subject of conspiracy by discussing the Warren Report on the Kennedy assassination:

> Rosemary . . . felt oddly out of things, as if the Castevets were old friends of Guy's to whom she had just been introduced. 'Do *you* think it could have been a plot of some kind?' Mr Castevet asked her, and she answered awkwardly, aware that a considerate host was drawing a left-out guest into conversation (p. 56).

Rosemary's awkwardness reveals two facts to the coven: first, she is uninterested and therefore not prone to suspicion; and secondly, she is politically uninformed, a condition that will prevent her from recognizing any signs of duplicity and manipulation. Their predictions are eventually proven accurate when, during her pregnancy, Roman makes an ominous toast, '"To 1966, The Year One", – that puzzled Rosemary, although everyone else seemed to understand and approve of it. She felt as if she had missed some literary or political reference – not that she really cared' (p. 121). Even when Rosemary does demonstrate an interest in current events, it is shallow and ineffective. During the Pope's visit to New York, Rosemary does not go to see him in person, choosing instead to stay in and watch him on television. 'His speech at the UN moved her . . . "War never again," he said; wouldn't his words give pause to even the most hardheaded statesman?' (p. 69). Despite her claim that 'the sharing of the event made people more open and communicative than they ordinarily were' (p. 69), Rosemary substitutes genuine participation with a media sound bite, 'War never again', which she repeats to Guy who promptly ignores her (p. 72). For Rosemary, real life is merely a composite of media images fuelled by an unwillingness to distinguish fantasy and reality.

As a substitute for genuine political and social awareness, Rosemary simulates understanding through acts of repetition. Relying on others to express her own subjectivity, she merely parrots what she hears. When asked what acting work Guy has done, Rosemary offers a standardized answer: 'He was in *Luther* and *Nobody Loves an Albatross* and a lot of television plays and television commercials' (p. 10). Mimicking

Conspiracy and Hypocrisy in Rosemary's Baby

Guy's role as an actor reciting his lines, Rosemary's automatic and frequent reiteration of Guy's résumé signifies the superficial nature of her awareness. Over the course of her pregnancy, this pattern of thoughtless repetition and lack of engagement has serious consequences on her physical well-being. On the advice of Minnie and Roman, Rosemary changes her obstetrician to Dr Sapirstein, another coven member. Initially reluctant to quit Dr Hill, who 'looked a little bit like Dr Kildare on television' (p. 90), she agrees to the change when she learns that Dr Sapirstein 'delivers all the Society babies' and that he 'was on *Open End*' (p. 94). Even after enduring months of excruciating pain under Sapirstein's care, she justifies his continued involvement by parroting Guy's words: 'he's well known. He was on *Open End*' (p. 131). When Sapirstein advises Rosemary that is it perfectly normal to lose weight and that her pain is due to an expansion of the hips, she does not question his authority but merely repeats his words: 'Stiff pelvic joints … It's fairly common and it'll probably stop any day now … and it's perfectly normal to lose a little during the first few months. Later on I'll be gaining' (p. 105). Eventually, the dehumanizing effects of her lack of self-awareness are pushed to Gothic extremes. As Guy's star rises, Rosemary herself becomes unrecognizable: isolated in the apartment she sleeps during the day and eats only raw meat. Rosemary puts her sickly appearance down to being pregnant, but Hutch detects a more ominous reality: '"That's ridiculous," he said. "Pregnant women *gain* weight, they don't lose it. And they look *healthy* not—"' (104). Rosemary, Hutch claims, looks like she has been 'drained by a vampire' (p. 105), accentuating the enervating effects of media and consumer culture: Rosemary's vitality, along with her identity, is sapped by the effects of acquisitiveness and self-deception.

Rosemary's mindless faith in Dr Sapirstein also reflects the postwar veneration of experts and media personalities. With the advent of television, in particular, scientists, medical doctors, government officials and advertisers had access to a visual medium in which to promote ideas, educate the public and sell products. The general belief was that if individuals appeared on television, they were reliable and sincere.[62] Television also allowed for the unmasking of real-life villains and hypocrites. The televised congressional hearings into organized crime or the denouement of anti-communist demagogues exposed the corruption of individuals who had initially professed their sincerity to the television audience. After his televised 'Checkers' speech, where he defended himself against charges of corruption, Richard Nixon claimed that 'sincerity is the quality that comes through on television' and in the first televised debates in the 1960 Kennedy–Nixon campaign, Nixon's performance would ultimately cost him the election.[63] Kennedy's success, on the other hand, is also attributed to his on-screen performance. In his inaugural speech, Kennedy noted, 'sincerity is always subject to proof' and during his candidacy he repeatedly emphasized that action not words were the determinants of intention.[64] In the 1960s, the concept of sincerity as an index of political citizenship was repeatedly played out on the burgeoning medium of television and *Rosemary's Baby* reflects the growing power of this new medium to influence and deceive. Besotted with media images, Rosemary can only gauge sincerity and expertise through the appearances and performances of celebrities and experts. Television, and the messages it offers, reinforces Rosemary's sense of self and confirms her belief in the honesty and integrity of individuals such as Guy and Dr Sapirstein; this propensity to trust images is carefully exploited by Guy and the Castevets. While probing Rosemary and Guy for signs of malleability, they introduce the topic of performance in religion. When Roman claims, 'No Pope ever visits a city when the newspapers are on strike', Guy's responds, 'Well . . . that's show biz' (p. 52); agreeing, Roman says, 'It *is*, you know! That's *just* what it is; show biz! . . . The costumes, the rituals . . . every religion, not only Catholicism. Pageants for the ignorant' (p. 52). Despite being a professed agnostic, Rosemary expresses some discomfort at the concept of religion as spectacle: 'Well he *is* the Pope . . . I guess I've been conditioned to have respect for him and I still do, even if I don't think he's holy any more' (p. 52). Conditioned by television, Rosemary's impulse is to trust the performance of sincerity for which she is denounced by Roman as hypocritical: 'If you don't think he's holy . . . you should have no respect for him at *all*, because he's going around deceiving people and pretending he *is* holy' (p. 52).

Ultimately, it is Rosemary's inability to distinguish words from deeds and intentions from actions that prevents her from uncovering Guy's betrayal. Initially, his self-declared good intentions have the opposite effect: his sudden interest in having a child coupled with his ability to spin a story breeds suspicion and distrust, and for the first time she begins to question the apparent discrepancy between his motives and actions: 'Now, looking back over the past weeks and months, she felt a disturbing presence of overlooked signals . . . of a disparity between what he said and what he felt' (p. 82).

Being prone to deception herself, Rosemary recognizes a similar quality in Guy along with a growing awareness that motives and actions do not always agree. But just as Rosemary begins to strip away the layers of pretence, Guy deflects her concerns by accusing her of paranoia and, despite evidence to the contrary, she accepts Guy's depiction of her as irrational and emotional:

> In the apartment, in the blessedly-cool shaded apartment, she tried to tell herself that she was mad. *You're going to have your baby in four days, Idiot Girl. Maybe even less. So you're all tense and nutty and you've built up a whole lunatic persecution thing out of a bunch of completely unrelated coincidences. There are no real witches. There are no real spells. Hutch died a natural death, even if the doctors couldn't give a name to it . . . See, Idiot Girl? It all falls apart when you pick at it.* (p. 165)

Isolated from the reality of the outside world, Rosemary ignores the warning signs because she cannot bear evidence that would shake her trust in Guy and in her own self-delusion. When he lies to her about his inattention after the rape, she once again misreads his words: 'It was awkward and charming and sincere, like his playing of the cowboy in *Bus Stop*' (p. 83). Yet, in the end, neither the superstitious world of chance nor the rationality of cause and effect are reliable determinants in judging Guy's responsibility for the unexplained events. Both positions simply result in a permanent state of confusion: 'She didn't know if she was going mad or going sane . . . if Guy was her loving husband or the treacherous enemy of the baby and herself' (p. 166). Her decision to rely on the performance of sincerity is what leaves her vulnerable to the coven's influence. As Minnie Castevet reminds her: 'He chose you out of all the world, Rosemary. Out of all the women in the world, He chose you . . . 'cause he wanted you to be the mother of his only living Son' (pp. 198–9).

Despite being depleted both physically and psychologically during her pregnancy, with the birth of her demon child, Rosemary's vitality returns and she begins the process of humanizing the monstrous: 'Even if he was half Satan, wasn't he half *her* as well, half decent, ordinary, sensible, human being? If she worked *against* them, exerted a good influence to counteract their bad one ...' (p. 204). Although the ellipsis suggests a flicker of self-doubt, Rosemary once again quells her misgiving and assumes her maternal role and in a rare display of independence, insists on naming her baby. However, this final act of defiance is not directed against the authority of the conspirators: naming her corrupt child is simply another occasion for resisting reality and perpetuating the illusion of normative motherhood: 'His name is Andrew John. He's my child, not yours, and this is one point that I'm not even going to argue about' (p. 205). Although the novel ends with the palpable image of the Antichrist, it is not the presence of a demon child that ultimately proves horrifying. In *Rosemary's Baby*, the representative of the modern crisis is Rosemary. Unaware, and with a false sense of self, Rosemary's self-deception is more insidious because it remains hidden. Her propensity for deceit and her inability to distinguish words from actions has unleashed a new form of domination, a corrupt embodiment of moral blindness and self-interest: a newborn symbol of oppression and tyranny. Just as Guy is rewarded by the coven for his efforts, Rosemary too, is honoured for her final repudiation of reality: 'Hail Rosemary, mother of Andrew ... Hail Satan' (p. 205).

In *Rosemary's Baby*, the Gothic themes of conspiracy and dissimulation do not articulate the period's paranoia regarding communism; rather, the novel affirms an intellectual and moral model for the belief in hidden design that furnish contemporary liberal society with a model of self-criticism. *Rosemary's Baby* exposes a world where the consequences of behaviour are often unplanned and unforeseen and where motives often prove unreliable in judging moral responsibility. While the worldwide conspiracy of witches provides a familiar structure to the era's communist paranoia, in *Rosemary's Baby*, it is hypocrisy and self-deception that are the taproots of modern evil.

Notes

[1] John Playfair, 'Biographical account of the late John Robison, LL.D, F.R.S. Edin. and professor of natural philosophy in the University of Edinburgh', in

Conspiracy and Hypocrisy in Rosemary's Baby

1.   *Transactions of the Royal Society of Edinburgh*, vol. 7 (Edinburgh: Archibald Constable, 1814) pp. 495–531.
2.   Michael Rogin, 'Kiss me deadly: communism, motherhood, and cold war movies', *Representations*, 6 (1984), 1–36 (1).
3.   Ibid., 2, 3.
4.   Richard Hofstadter, 'The paranoid style in American politics', in *The Paranoid Style in American Politics and other Essays* (New York: Vintage, 1965), pp. 3, iv.
5.   Ibid., p. 4.
6.   Ibid., pp. 35, 31, 32, 39.
7.   Ibid., p. viii.
8.   David Punter and Glennis Byron, *The Gothic* (Blackwell: Oxford, 2004), p. 273.
9.   Eric Savoy, 'The Rise of American Gothic', in Jerrold E. Hogle (ed.), *The Cambridge Companion to Gothic Fiction* (Cambridge: Cambridge University Press, 2002), p. 175.
10. Gordon S. Wood, *The Radicalism of the American Revolution* (New York: A. A. Knopf, 1992) pp. 60–1.
11. Thomas Jefferson, *Summary View of the Rights of British America* (1774), The Avalon Project at Yale Law School, http://www.yale.edu/lawweb/Avalon/jeffsumm.htm (accessed 14 January 2004).
12. James Madison, 'The Federalist, no. 10', in Nina Baym et al. (eds), *Norton Anthology of American Literature*, vol. 1 (4th edn; New York: W. W. Norton, 1994), pp. 759–63 (p. 762).
13. Thomas Jefferson, *A Declaration by the Representatives of the United States of America, in General Congress Assembled*, in ibid., pp. 729–33 (p. 730).
14. King George III, 'Address to Parliament', 27 October 1775, Library of Congress, http://memory.loc.gov/learn/features/timeline/amrev/shots/address.html (accessed 21 March 2005).
15. Edmund Burke, 'Thoughts on the cause of the present discontents', in *The Works of The Right Honourable Edmund Burke, Vol. 1* (London: Henry G. Bohn, 1854), pp. 308, 320, 339, 316, 323, 324.
16. Gordon S. Wood, 'Conspiracy and the paranoid style: causality and deceit in the eighteenth century', *William and Mary Quarterly*, 39, 3 (1982), 401–41 (408). The following section is indebted to Wood's article.
17. Ibid., 401.
18. Ibid., 411.
19. Ibid., 413.
20. Ibid., 416.
21. See Bernard Mandeville, *The Fable of the Bees: Or, Private Vices, Publick Benefits*, ed. F. G. Kaye (Oxford: Clarendon Press, 1924).
22. Thomas Jefferson to James Madison (15 November 1795), Jefferson Digital Archive, University of Virginia Library, http://etext.lib.virginia.edu/jefferson/ (accessed 7 March 2006).
23. Wood, 'Conspiracy', 420; Wood, *The Creation of the American Republic, 1776–1787* (Williamsburg: University of North Carolina Press, 1969), p. 41.
24. Playfair, 'Biographical account', p. 495.

25 Quoted in Vernon Stauffer, *New England and the Bavarian Illuminati* (New York: Columbia University Press, 1918), p. 110.
26 Ibid., p. 107.
27 George Washington, 'Sixth annual message' (19 November 1794), The Avalon Project at Yale Law School, *http://www.yale.edu/lawweb/Avalon/presiden/sou/wash06.htm* (accessed 18 December 2003).
28 Quoted in Stauffer, *Bavarian Illuminati*, p. 108.
29 Robert S. Levine, *Conspiracy and Romance: Studies in Brockden Brown, Cooper, Hawthorne, and Melville* (Cambridge: Cambridge University Press, 1989), p. 18.
30 Jedidiah Morse, 'A SERMON, Delivered at the New North Church in Boston, in the Morning, and In the Afternoon at Charlestown, May 9th, 1798, Being the Day Recommended by JOHN ADAMS, President of the United States of America, for Solemn Humiliation, Fasting and Prayer', *Early American Imprints, Series I*, Evan's Document Display, *http://infoweb.newsbank.com/iw-search/we/Evans* (accessed 6 March 2006).
31 Ibid.
32 Ibid.
33 Quoted in Stauffer, *Bavarian Illuminati*, p. 244.
34 Quoted in Ibid., pp. 250–1.
35 Edmund Burke, 'Letter to the Abbé Barruél, May 1, 1797', in R. B. McDowell and John A. Wood (eds), *The Correspondence of Edmund Burke, Vol. IX* (Chicago: Chicago University Press, 1970), pp. 319–20.
36 Quoted in Stauffer, *Bavarian Illuminati*, p. 312.
37 Bernard N. Schilling, 'The English case against Voltaire: 1789–1800', *Journal of the History of Ideas*, 4, 2 (1943), 193–216 (193).
38 Larry E. Tise, *The American Counterrevolution: A Retreat from Liberty, 1783–1800* (Mechanicsburg, PA: Stackpole, 1998), p. 357.
39 Quoted in Robert A. Ferguson, *Reading the Early Republic* (Cambridge, Mass.: Harvard University Press, 2004), p. 147.
40 Ibid., p. 123.
41 Quoted in Robert Miles, 'Introduction', Anne Radcliffe, *The Italian*, ed. Robert Miles (London: Penguin, 2000), p. xxiii.
42 Jay Fliegelman, 'Introduction', in Charles Brockden Brown, *Wieland; Or the Transformation: An American Tale*, ed. Jay Fliegelman (New York: Penguin, 1991), p. xii.
43 Charles Brockden Brown, *Wieland; Or the Transformation: An American Tale* (Kent, Ohio: Kent State University Press, 1977), pp. 215–16. Subsequent quotes will appear in parenthesis in the text.
44 Quoted in Wood, 'Conspiracy', 430.
45 William Wordsworth, *The Borderers*, ed. Robert Osborn (London: Cornell University Press, 1982), p. 813.
46 Quoted in Wood, 'Conspiracy', 431.
47 Allen Weinstein, 'The symbolism of subversion: notes on some cold war icons', *Journal of American Studies*, 6, 2 (1972), 165–79, (178).
48 J. Edgar Hoover, *Masters of Deceit: The Story of Communism in America* (London: Dent and Sons, 1958), p. vi.

49   Ibid., pp. 81, 82, viii, vii.
50   P. B. Sheatsley and J. S. Feldman, 'A national survey of public reactions and behaviour', in Bradley S. Greenberg and Edwin B. Parker (eds), *The Kennedy Assassination and the American Public: Social Communication in Crisis* (Stanford: Stanford University Press, 1965), p. 174.
51   Irving Kaufman, 'Judge Kaufman's statement upon sentencing the Rosenbergs', *Famous Trials*, University of Missouri-Kansas City, http://www.law.umkc.edu/faculty/projects/ftrials/rosenb/ROS_SENT.HTM (accessed 25 March 2006).
52   Richard Nixon, '"What was the Hiss Case?" An answer for Trisha' (1962), *Famous Trials*, University of Missouri-Kansas City, http://www.law.umkc.edu/faculty/projects/ftrials/hiss/nixononhisscase.html (accessed 2 April 2006).
53   Kaufman, *Famous Trials*.
54   Ira Levin, *Rosemary's Baby* (1967; London: Pan, 1968). Further references will appear in parenthesis in the text; emphasis throughout is author's.
55   Percy Bysshe Shelley, 'A defense of poetry', in M. H. Abrams et al. (eds), *The Norton Anthology of English Literature*, vol. 2 (New York: W. W. Norton, 1962), p. 478.
56   Judith Shklar, 'Let us not be hypocritical', *DÆDALUS: Journal of the American Academy of Arts and Sciences*, 108, 3 (1979), 1–25 (1).
57   Mandeville, *The Fable of the Bees*, p. 281; Hannah Arendt, *On Revolution* (1963; Middlesex: Penguin, 1973), p. 103.
58   Mandeville, *Fable of the Bees*, p. 51.
59   Aldous Huxley, *Brave New World Revisited* (New York: Harper and Row, 1965), p. 4.
60   Quoted in Jackson Lears, 'A matter of taste: corporate cultural hegemony in a mass-consumption society', in Lary May (ed.), *Recasting America: Culture and Politics in the Age of Cold War* (Chicago: Chicago University Press, 1989), pp. 38–57 (p. 47).
61   Betty Friedan, *The Feminine Mystique* (New York: Penguin, 1963). In a speech given at the University of California at Berkeley in 1964, Friedan posed the question central to her thesis: 'If girls today still have no image of themselves as individual human beings, if they think their only road to status, to identity, in society is to grab that man—according to all the images of marriage, from the ads, the television commercials, the movies, the situation comedies, and all the experts who counsel them—and if therefore they think they must catch him at nineteen and begin to have babies and that split-level dream house so soon that they never have time to make other choices, to make other active moves in society, to risk themselves in trial-and-error efforts, are they, are we, really free and equal?' Quoted in Stuart A. Kallen (ed.), *Sixties Counterculture* (San Diego: Greenhaven Press, 2001), p. 51.
62   Douglas T. Miller and Marion Nowak, *The Fifties: The Way We Really Were* (New York: Double Day, 1975), p. 343.
63   Ibid., p. 354.
64   John F. Kennedy, 'Inaugural address' (20 January 1961), The Avalon Project at Yale Law School, http://www.yale.edu/lawweb/avalon/presiden/inaug/kennedy.htm (accessed 10 April 2006).

5

Virtue and Corruption in Truman Capote's In Cold Blood

> Americanism means the virtues of courage, honor, justice, truth, sincerity, and hardihood— the virtues that made America. The things that will destroy America are prosperity-at-any-price, peace-at-any-price, safety-first instead of duty first, the love of soft living and the get-rich-quick theory of life.
>
> Theodore Roosevelt (1917)[1]

Originally published in four instalments in *The New Yorker*, Truman Capote's *In Cold Blood* established a new genre of creative non-fiction which he called the 'non-fiction novel'. Since its initial success, the form has spawned a host of practitioners, the most celebrated being Norman Mailer's *The Executioner's Song* (1979), Gabriel Garcia Márquez's *Chronicle of a Death Foretold* (1981), and John Berendt's *Midnight in the Garden of Good and Evil* (1994). While each tells the story of killers and their crimes, *In Cold Blood* holds a unique position in American literary history. It was the first conscious attempt to blur journalism with novelistic devices to create a new literary art form. It was also the first to exploit the conventions and motifs of the Gothic to tell a '*True Account of a Multiple Murder and its Consequences*'. In an interview with *The Saturday Review*, Capote claimed to have had no particular interest in crime per se but that once he had settled on the subject for his project, he would 'half-consciously, when looking through the papers, always notice any item that had a reference to a crime'.[2] The headline that ultimately captured his imagination appeared in the *New York Times* on 16 November

Virtue and Corruption in Truman Capote's In Cold Blood

1959: 'Wealthy Farmer, 3 of Family Slain'. According to Capote, when he saw the title, it was 'sort of as though one had been sitting for a long time watching for a certain bird—if you were a bird watcher—come into view, and there it was'.[3] Despite his claim of unconscious inspiration, for many critics, Capote's framing of the narrative around this particular tragedy attests to the continuing identification of the farmer and the 'myth of the garden' in American literature. As one reviewer noted, it was a case of 'instant symbolism on which the imagination of a sensitive novelist would have seized'.[4] While reviews of *In Cold Blood* were mixed, the contention that the narrative employs myth as its organizing mode is a common feature of the criticism devoted to Capote's work. The method is largely ahistorical privileging symbol, image and psychological interiority. Capote's work is seen as either Oedipal, narcissistic in nature or representative of a mythical American experience with no grounding in history or reality. Tony Tanner, for example, notes that Capote continues 'an old American tradition when he tries to get at the "mythic" significance of the facts', which, in the case of *In Cold Blood*, was to 'extract a black fable from contemporary reality'. Capote contributes to this tradition, he claims, by producing 'a stark image of the deep doubleness of American Life'.[5] Melvin Friedman, too, sees Capote

> entering a more authentically American tradition of story-telling than any revealed in his earlier work . . . We can now begin using such literary catchphrases as 'Adamic myth' to explain Capote, just as we've used them up to now to explain the 'great tradition' in American fiction from Cooper to Hawthorne through William Styron.[6]

The critical practice of mythologizing Capote's narrative of the Clutter family murder relies on a particular interpretation of agrarian ideology; although critics acknowledge the potency of the image of the farmer, analysis is often devoid of historical nuance beyond the mythical garden or 'frontier hypothesis'.

Tracing the pastoral myth back to the eighteenth-century concept of agrarian virtue provides an alternate approach to Capote's text. In republican discourse, the farm and farmer are interdependent with and reinforce concepts of citizenship and democracy. Narratives of the invaded pastoral, therefore, function to dramatize the tension between virtuous liberty and corrupt self-interest; between country and city, and tradition and progress that have characterized the American experience since the founding. *In Cold Blood* is first and foremost an invasion narrative, an attack on the pastoral and therefore on America's sense of identity and security, and Capote's 'true account' exploits the conventions of the Gothic to depict this terrifying encounter between agrarian virtue and the monstrous embodiments of industrialized culture.

Eighteenth-century agrarianism

Since the founding of America, images of the farm and the farmer have furnished history and literature with an enduring symbol of freedom and independence, and while the relevance of agrarianism has undergone numerous valuations, these images are still among the most potent incitements to nationalism available to American authors.[7] Commonly associated with Jeffersonian democracy, the importance of agrarianism as a model for American citizenship appears throughout eighteenth-century poetry, novels, political pamphlets and private correspondence.[8] In the early colonial period through to the mid eighteenth century, agrarianism was still English in conception and pastoral in tradition. Farmers were idealized as 'jolly ploughmen', 'happy swains' or 'happy rustic clown[s]', and ownership of land was linked to Britain's hierarchical social structure:

> The Yeomanry or Farmers are the boast of our nation; they have always been, and continue to be, of great consequence and use to us, and a very necessary link in the chain of government, as having an immediate connection with the gentleman on the one side, and the labourer on the other.[9]

In an attempt to entice settlers to the colonies, early agrarianism fixed national identity on two factors: first, on the difference between the farmer, the land and the conditions of farming in America and in the Old World; and secondly, on the advantages of the New World compared with the Old. While there was no concerted intention of creating an independent American state, agriculture promoted the special quality of American life.[10] John Holme's 'A true relation of the flourishing state of Pennsylvania' (1698), for example, crystallized the common sentiment of America's abundance:

> Come, then, you that would well bestow your money,
> View this good land which flows with milk and honey.[11]

Initially such advertisements served to encourage emigration and commerce, but under the stress of revolution, agrarianism and the national sentiment it fostered underwent considerable transformation. In an attempt to establish difference and superiority, American writers began to emphasize the interdependence between democracy and agrarianism, and during the revolutionary years, nationalistic expression found its most powerful vehicle in what Eisinger calls the 'freehold concept', a model that 'adapted all the imported democratic ideas to the conditions of American life and thus guaranteed the economic, political, and moral well-being of the individual citizens'.[12] In the republican mind, every man possessed a natural right to productive landed property, and ownership provided economic and political independence in addition to contributing to each man's physical and moral health. 'America', wrote Richard Price, 'consisted of only a body of yeomanry supported by agriculture, and all independent, and nearly upon a level'. England, in contrast, was old and withered: 'inflated and irreligious; enervated by luxury; encumbered by debts; and hanging by a thread'.[13]

Identifying Europe as the centre of corruption was an established convention in American literature that emphasized the differences between America and Britain and the superiority of the new republic. In 'American farmer', an anonymous poem published in *The American Museum* in 1790, the advantages of American agrarianism are contrasted with the decadence of Europe:

> And where so blest, as here, the farmer's lot—
> Sole owner of his independent cot?
> He sees no palace rear its tow'ring head,
> In guilty splendour, near his humble shed:
> But heav'n-born Freedom, like the lamp of day,
> O'er all, alike, extends her genial ray.[14]

Two comparisons animate this stanza. The first contrasts the 'heav'n-born Freedom' and 'independen[ce]' of America with the 'tow'ring head' of Europe, which, by implication, derives its power from a less divine source. Secondly, national pride is founded on the agrarian simplicity of the 'humble shed' compared with the corrupt and 'guilty splendour' of the palace. Providence, it infers, had selected them to be 'a chosen people, in the New World, separate and removed far from the regions and wretched Politics of the old One'.[15] The numerous imitations of Oliver Goldsmith's English pastoral *The Deserted Village* (1770) published in the new republic reinforced this view. Timothy Dwight's *Greenfield Hill* (1787–94) distinguishes American equality and independence from monarchical tyranny through a depiction of the farm:

> In these contrasted climes, how chang'd the scene,
> Where happiness expands, in living green!
> Through the whole realm, behold convenient farms
> Fed by small herds, and gay with cultur'd charms;
> To sons, in equal portions, handed down,
> The sire's bold spirit kindling in the son;
> No tyrant riding o'er th' indignant plain;
> A prince, a king, each independent swain;
> No servile thought, no vile submission, known;
> No rent to lords, nor homage to a throne;
> But sense to know, and virtue to extend,
> And nerves to feel the bliss, and bravery to defend![16]

In a similar imitation, Philip Freneau's *The Rising Glory of America* (1771) sees America escaping the fate of Europe, Rome and Carthage by virtue of her political, economic and moral superiority which is similarly rooted in the vision of the 'rustic reign':

> Paradise anew
> Shall flourish, by no second Adam lost.
> No dangerous tree with deadly fruit shall grow;
> No tempting serpent to allure the soul
> From native innocence.—A *Canaan* here,
> Another Canaan shall excel the old . . . Such days the world,

Virtue and Corruption in Truman Capote's In Cold Blood

> And such, AMERICA, thou first shalt have,
> When ages, yet to come have run their round,
> And future years of bliss remain.[17]

In these and many other eighteenth-century works, the values of pastoralism and republicanism often overlapped and mutually reinforced each other to define the essence of citizenship. Even individuals not identified with the revolution promoted American agrarianism as the essence of republican virtue. Hector de Crèvecoeur begins *Letters from an American Farmer* with a utopian vision of the farm and, more importantly, the political freedom implicit in the rural way of life:

> We are a people of cultivators, scattered over an immense territory, communicating with each other by means of good roads and navigable rivers, united by the silken bands of mild government, all respecting the laws, without dreading their power, because they are equitable ... farmer is the only appellation of the rural inhabitants of our country ... We have no princes, for whom we toil, starve, and bleed: we are the most perfect society now existing in the world.[18]

While no supporter of Jeffersonian democracy, Crèvecoeur nonetheless contrasts the virtues of the New World with the corruption of the Old. The nation's literary pastorialism, therefore, functioned not solely as a polemical device: even individuals with opposing political views propounded an image of national happiness as intrinsically linked with the agrarian landscape and the revolutionary themes of virtue and freedom from tyranny, primogeniture and hereditary aristocracy. Virtue, in particular, was 'the soul of republican freedom.'[19] Used synonymously with 'nature', 'essence' or 'essential characteristic', or as the practice of an ethical code, virtue signified a devotion to the public good, 'the activity and equality of ruling and being ruled', and the 'independence from any relation which could make him corrupt'.[20] The willingness to surrender private interests to the good of the community not only signalled an individual's patriotism, but also revealed their private virtues. America could preserve its liberties only as long as its citizenry remained virtuous; as long as agriculture was the principal occupation of the new republic, virtue would last.

If property and benevolent disinterestedness were the qualifications for political participation and an index of the moral health of the republic, corruption was the term used to denote the degeneration of these principles. Corruption was located in the passion for distinction, in the various forms of emulation, ambition, jealousy, envy and vanity. It was, according to John Adams, the struggle between 'the cause of liberty, truth, virtue, and humanity' on the one hand, and 'ignorance, misery, and despotism on the other'.[21] A republic was a particularly delicate system because it demanded an extraordinary moral character and not all Americans believed that their new society could be completely free of the vices of the Old World. In the years leading up to the revolution, it became apparent that a drastic and frightening transformation was underway, and with it, signs of regression: 'To increase in numbers, in wealth, in elegance and refinements, and at the same time to increase in luxury, profaneness, impiety, and a disesteem of things sacred, is to go backward and not forward.' While Americans had denounced rising wealth and luxury in the past, never before had they been so 'carried away by the stream of prosperity'.[22] 'Will you tell me', asked Adams, 'how to prevent riches from becoming the effects of temperance and industry? Will you tell me how to prevent riches from producing luxury? Will you tell me how to prevent luxury from producing effeminacy, intoxication, extravagance, vice and folly?'[23] 'Ambition and avarice', wrote Mercy Otis Warren, 'are *the leading* springs which generally actuate a restless mind. From these *primary sources of corruption* have arisen all the rapine and confusion, the depredation and ruin, that have spread distress over the face of the earth.'[24] It was the aristocratic passions of avarice and ambition or, as Benjamin Franklin termed it, 'the Love of Power and the Love of Money' that seemed to pose the greatest threat to the survival of the republic.[25]

While many writers affirmed the durability of virtue in a democracy, the dialectic of virtue and corruption often revealed an ambivalent and contradictory conception at the heart of the agrarian republic. Even Jefferson, who apotheosized the farmer, understood the inherent inconsistencies in this philosophy:

> Those who labour in the earth are the chosen people of God, if ever he had a chosen people, whose breasts he has made his peculiar deposit

for substantial and genuine virtue . . . Corruption of morals in the mass of cultivators is a phenomenon of which no age nor nation has furnished an example. It is the mark set on those who, not looking up to heaven, to their own soil and industry, as does the husbandman, for their subsistence, depend for it on the casualties and caprice of customers. Dependence begets subservience and venality, suffocates the germ of virtue, and prepares fit tools for the designs of ambition. This, the natural progress and consequence of the arts, has sometimes perhaps been retarded by accidental circumstance: but, generally speaking, the proportion which the aggregate of the other classes of citizens bears in any state to that of its husbandmen is the proportion of its unsound to its healthy parts, and is a good-enough barometer whereby to measure its degree of corruption.

That 'natural progress' is sometimes hampered by 'accidental circumstance', or that men continue to be influenced by 'casualties and caprice' suggests, as Pocock points out, the operation of commerce and *fortuna*, or 'fortune and fantasy'. Though committed to the idea of virtue, Jefferson, like many of his contemporaries, also doubted whether it could be preserved indefinitely: 'the spirit of the times may alter, will alter. Our rulers will become corrupt, our people careless'.[26]

While the corruption of morals evinced by the rise of commerce and individual self-interest was widely viewed as a serious social and political sickness, the virtuous agrarian republic was particularly vulnerable to infection by progress and the growth of cities:

> The mobs of great cities add just so much to the support of pure government, as sores do to the strength of the human body. It is the manners and spirit of a people which preserve a republic in vigour. A degeneracy in these is a canker which soon eats to the heart of its constitution.[27]

Cities are cankerous sores on the healthy republican body, consuming her vitality and virtue. For Jefferson, the expansion of cities and the rising influence of progress perverts the self and leads to the degeneration of society:

> I think our governments will remain virtuous for many centuries; as long as they are chiefly agricultural; and this will be as long as there shall be vacant lands in any part of America. When they get piled upon one another in large cities, as in Europe, they will become corrupt as in Europe.[28]

As the writings of Jefferson and others attest, implicit in the principle of an agrarian republic is the fear of the city, of progress and the future. Despite Victor Sage's suggestion that 'the paradigm of the horror-plot is the journey from the capital to the provinces', in American culture, it is the narrative of the invaded pastoral that nourishes fear in the historical and contemporary imagination.

Agrarianism in the mid twentieth century

In the mid twentieth century, agrarianism remained a dominant feature of cultural and national identity. During the post-war period, in particular, the importance of agrarianism to the nation's literature and culture became a primary feature of the burgeoning American studies curriculum, which gave the agrarian setting a central position in national mythology. Between 1950 and 1957 alone, seven books were devoted to the subject, a trend that continued into the mid 1960s.[29] Most of these investigations were largely dismissive of eighteenth-century intellectual history as either irrelevant, ideological or a form of false consciousness. Instead, analysis focused on nineteenth-century texts and set about refuting the evolutionary approaches that had dominated analysis until the early part of the century. The first of these was Herbert Baxter Adams's 'germ theory' which contended that American democracy lay in the Gothic councils 'out of which evolved the parliamentary system, religious reformation and popular revolution' and it was these ideas that 'formed Germany, England and the *United States*'. For Adams, the rhetoric of the farmer or of America as a new Gothic empire was commonsensical. 'It is just as improbable', he wrote, 'that free local institutions should spring up without a germ along American shores as that English Wheat should have grown here without planting.'[30] This interpretation implied a shared heritage, a transmission of ideas from the Old World to the New, which in the mid twentieth century became increasingly unpopular. More palatable to the liberal mind was Frederick Jackson Turner's late nineteenth-century theory of the new frontier. In 1893, Turner rejected Adams's idealist theory of American institutions as an outgrowth of English or Teutonic germs in favour of what he termed the 'frontier hypothesis'. Turner contended that it was the 'existence of an area of free land, its continuous recession, and the advance of American Settlement westward' that explained American development'.[31] Turner did not believe that development occurred because of any ideological theories or transplanted germs but because of the encounter between the American and the noble savage. For Turner, American social development was 'continually beginning over again on the frontier. This perennial rebirth, this fluidity of American life, this expansion westward with its new opportunities, its continuous touch with the simplicity of primitive society, furnish the forces dominating American character.' Moreover, America was not the fifth and last act of history; rather the exhaustion of land was only the beginning of America's development: 'And now, four centuries from the discovery of America, at the end of a hundred years of life under the Constitution, the frontier has gone, and with its going has closed the first period of American history.'[32]

Turner's theory of westward expansion perpetuated the 'myth of the West' that dominated analysis until the 1930s when Progressive historians began to interpret American history as a series of conflicts between rival interests groups. Eschewing the determinism of the evolutionary school, early American history was viewed as a battle between Jefferson and Hamilton, agrarianism and capitalism, the propertied and the unpropertied. For the Progressives, it was these perpetual struggles that fuelled America's reforms and contributed to her development. In the post-war years, Turner's 'myth of the West' was no longer seen as a useful symbol to explain American development, and historians and literary critics alike set out to trace the declining meaning of agrarianism in public life. Henry Nash Smith's *Virgin Land: The American West as Symbol and Myth* argued that despite economic and technological changes in America, the myth persisted into the nineteenth century:

With the passage of time this symbol, like that of the Wild West, became in its turn a less and less accurate description of a society transformed by commerce and industry ... But the image of an agricultural paradise in the West, embodying group memories of an earlier, a simpler and, it was believed, a happier state of society, long survived as a force in American thought and politics. So powerful and vivid was the image that down to the very end of the nineteenth century it continued to seem a representation, in Whitman's words, of the core of the nation, 'the real genuine America'.[33]

For Smith, this myth is naive and utopian, and in *Virgin Land* he differentiates three separate myths of America. The myth of the 'noble savage' or 'deerslayer' of the wild west is contrasted with the agrarian west of nineteenth-century utopianism and the myth of the American farmer. Rather than promoting any single myth as the essential one, Smith discusses the logical conflicts of American mythology, emphasizing that neither the noble savage nor the American farmer fit with the 'modern myth of America as a new industrial civilization and the colossus of the Western world'.[34] For Smith, the persistence of the old frontier ideal in modern industrial America is illogical. Yet, in a later essay, he notes the tenacity of the pastoral image in his own time, linking it to cold war anxieties of communist invasion. In 'The west as an image of the American past' (1951), he analyses a contemporary political cartoon depicting an aggressive Soviet soldier rising over a dark horizon. In the forefront is a snow-covered log cabin billowing smoke which spells out the word 'freedom'. A man, fist clenched and rolling up his sleeve, returns the stare of his aggressor. Although the man's clothing identifies him as an urban office worker, Smith claims 'his roots are not defined by the skyline of a city or the smokestacks of a factory but by the conventional symbol of the agricultural frontier'. The cartoonist, Smith argues, proposes 'that the meaning of our society is implicit in the cabin, or, in other words, that the essence of our institutions and our way of life is the frontier experience'.[35] R. W. B. Lewis, in contrast, advanced the single myth of 'the American Adam' before the fall as a way of unifying the diverging elements of American mythology that Smith articulated. A combination of frontiersman and homesteader, this new figure lived 'hopeful and innocent in the peaceful nineteenth-century'.[36]

Lewis addresses Adam's confrontation with evil emphasizing the dichotomy between the agrarian America of a century ago and the present industrialized state. Adam's 'fall' has been partly fortunate. He is a wiser, more mature Adam, with a clear understanding of the ironies of experience. For Lewis, the concept of pastoral innocence equals a distrust of this experience and, like Smith, links it with cold war anxieties: 'Ours is an age of containment ... we huddle together and shore up defences; both our literature and our public conduct suggest that exposure to experience is certain to be fatal.'[37]

In *The Machine in the Garden*, Leo Marx traces the emergence of the pastoral ideal as a 'distinctively American theory of society' and its subsequent transformation under the impact of industrialization. Like his predecessors, Marx believes that pastoralism has defined the meaning of America since the age of discovery:

> Since Jefferson's time, the cardinal image of American aspirations was a rural landscape, a well-ordered green garden magnified to continental size. Although it probably shows a farmhouse or a neat white village, the scene usually is dominated by natural objects: in the foreground a pasture, a twisting brook with cattle grazing nearby, then a clump of elms on a rise in the middle distance and beyond that, way off on the western horizon, a line of dark hills. This is the countryside of the old Republic, a chaste, uncomplicated land of rural virtue.[38]

Why this ancient ideal should still be relevant in the modern world is, according to Marx, what requires explanation. He begins by differentiating what he sees as two kinds of pastoralism: the popular or sentimental, and the imaginative and complex. The sentimental is an expression 'less of thought than of feeling', and is expressed in contemporary longings for a more 'natural' environment, in the 'wilderness cult' and in what he calls 'the lower plane of our collective fantasy', that is, bucolic images in the mass media. For Marx it is the psychic desire for a simple life close to nature that explains the appeal of the pastoral: 'the soft veil of nostalgia that hangs over our urbanized landscape is largely a vestige of the once dominant image of an undefiled, green republic, a quiet land of forests, villages, and farms dedicated to the pursuit of happiness'.[39] For these post-war historians 'agrarianism', 'rural values', the 'old Republican idyll' or 'myth of the

Garden' not only impedes clarity of thought and social progress, it is also a 'reactionary or false ideology', masking 'the real problems of an industrial civilization'.[40] While Marx concurs with his contemporaries in viewing sentimental pastoralism as 'diffuse nostalgia' and 'infantile wish-fulfilment', he claims that the pastoral impulse defines a larger body of meanings and seeks to demonstrate that there exists in literature an imaginative and complex form of pastoralism. This divergence in consciousness, the point where the pastoral ideal moves from an impediment to clarity of thought to one that enriches and clarifies experience occurs when writers draw upon the symbolic property of the pastoral. 'What the writer discovers', writes Marx, 'is a metaphor; he seizes upon the symbolic property or meaning in the event itself— its capacity to express much of what he thinks and feels about his situation.'[41] Marx acknowledges that since Jefferson's time, industrialization's encounter with the pastoral has fuelled the nation's literature, and in the nineteenth century this encounter took the form of machine technology. However, the trope of the 'interrupted idyll' does not direct attention to the world 'out there', the world of politics or institutional change. For Marx, like most of his contemporaries, the chief concern is the landscape of the mind.[42]

Concomitant with the intellectual search for a single myth to explain American character and history, popular culture dramatized the mythic garden as either a site of security or vulnerability. Cartoons, comic books and films each found imaginative currency in the depiction of the agrarian landscape as the entry point of enemy infiltration and invasion. These popular-cultural fantasies conventionally linked with cold war anxieties of communist takeover or the dehumanizing effects of social conformity. In this context, the agrarian setting functions as a synecdoche for the United States and the scenario of the invaded pastoral becomes a metaphor for the rivalry between the Soviet Union and the United States, or democracy and totalitarianism. From a politically conservative perspective, the rural landscape is suffused with nostalgia for the past, for the pre-industrial world of simpler, purer values and the individual lighting out for the frontier. For anti-communist liberals, however, the pastoral suggested an unsophisticated target, easily penetrated by superior technologies or political subversives. An escape to the nostalgia of the past, they suggested, was putting the country at risk; as long as Adam remains wilfully ignorant in the prelapsarian garden, America was vulnerable to the serpentine wiles of communist subversives.

Gothic agrarianism

'It is, of course,' writes Ihab Hassan, 'as a Southern and Gothic writer that we insist on knowing Capote.'[43] It was Hassan who famously divided Capote's *oeuvre* into two distinct modes: the supernatural dread of the 'nocturnal' style, and the humour and reality of the 'daylight' style. Firmly linked to the southern Gothic tradition, critical analysis repeatedly points to the numerous echoes of Edgar Allan Poe, Eudora Welty, William Faulkner, Flannery O'Connor and Carson McCullers.[44] In *Tree of Night* (1949) for example, Eisinger claims that 'one feels the presence of Poe everywhere in this volume, in the ubiquitous threat of death and in the easy familiarity with madness, in the exploitation of the abnormal, in the calculated striving for effect'.[45] Frank Baldanza claims that in the case of Truman Capote and Carson McCullers, the resemblances are pervasive and unique: 'What these two authors share, along with Eudora Welty . . . is a nearly morbid preoccupation with sublunar imperfection. They most typically treat characters whose spiritual loneliness is paralleled by some form of physical defect.'[46] For others, Capote was simply an 'ephebic purveyor of Gothic extravaganzas, the fashionable opportunist of a mid-century madness'.[47] When John Aldridge first observed the Gothic impulse in Capote's early fiction, he dismissed it as 'narcissistic and insular, mere concoction rather than synthesis'. The short stories, he claimed, 'carry no symbolic weight', and are 'little more than the images of grotesquerie and horror upon which they depend'.[48] While none of these critics had the opportunity to consider *In Cold Blood* in their analysis, subsequent commentators forged a connection between Capote's earlier Gothic work and his new 'non-fiction novel' and largely dismissed *In Cold Blood* as true-crime trussed up in modern Gothic machinery. Stanley Kaufmann's review in *The New Republic* derides Capote's claim to have founded a new form of literature and links it instead to his earlier writing: 'What it all amounts to is the puffery of an artistically unsuccessful writer of fiction pursuing his love of the Gothic . . . into real life.'

Tony Tanner claimed that 'behind the mask of the dispassionate reporter we can begin to make out the excited stare of the Southern Gothic novelist with his furbile delight in weird settings and lurid details', while Sol Yurick labelled *In Cold Blood* 'a form of sob-sisterism married to Southern Gothic prose'. Others questioned Capote's claim to objective reportage in light of the preoccupations of his early work, in particular, 'its nostalgia for states of innocence together with its fascination with deformed or precocious or odd-ball types of human creepiness'.[49]

Certainly, real life events supplied Capote with the necessary material with which to construct a traditional Gothic narrative: an isolated setting, a modern American castle invaded by invisible and unpredictable monsters, an authoritarian father, an absent mother and a virginal daughter threatened with rape. And while these real events are seemingly beyond his control, Capote exploits the Gothic potential of the material through his careful selection, arrangement and manipulation of the 'facts'. First, Capote establishes a Gothic atmosphere in the initial description of the landscape. As his biographer Gerald Clarke observes, 'Another writer might have laid emphasis on Holcomb's small-town closeness and the warmth and good-heartedness of its citizens. Truman chooses instead to pick up a thread from his fiction and dwell on its isolation':[50] 'The village of Holcomb stands on the high wheat plains of western Kansas, a lonesome area that other Kansans call "out there"'.[51] Located very near to the geographical centre of the United States, Holcomb is 'flat, and the views are awesomely extensive . . . a white cluster of grain elevators rising as gracefully as Greek temples are visible long before a traveller reaches them' (p. 1). Described as 'haphazard' (p. 1), 'falling-apart' (p. 2) and 'melancholy' (p. 2), Capote's depiction is emblematic of Gothic decay:

> At one end of the town stands a stark old stucco structure, the roof of which supports an electric sign—DANCE—but the dancing has ceased and the advertisement has been dark for several years. Near by is another building with an irrelevant sign, this one in flaking gold on a dirty window—HOLCOMB BANK. The bank failed in 1933, and its former counting rooms have been converted into apartments. (p. 1)

Virtue and Corruption in Truman Capote's In Cold Blood

Despite his claim to objectivity, Capote intensifies the Gothic mood by assigning mysterious dimensions to the unfolding events. Prior to the murders, a sense of foreboding is created in the unnatural cowardice of the Clutter dog: '[t]hough he was a good sentry, alert, ever ready to raise Cain, his valour had one flaw: let him glimpse a gun ... and his head dropped, his tail turned in' (p. 9). Equally ominous is the persistent smell of cigarette smoke in the Clutter's abstentious household. On the morning of the murders, Nancy Clutter asks, '*Why* do I keep smelling smoke? Honestly, I think I'm losing my mind ... it's as though somebody had just been there, smoking a cigarette' (p. 16). The selection and arrangement of these otherwise irrelevant details accentuates the eeriness of the story and points to Capote's conscious engagement with Gothic motifs.

In addition to eliciting a Gothic atmosphere of menace, Capote's narrative employs a traditional plot structure of female entrapment and male transgression. The description of the 'sensible and sedate' (p. 6) Clutter home, for example, is undercut by the revelation that Herb Clutter's invalid wife is 'strange' (p. 19). Obliquely described as 'nervous' (p. 4) and plagued by 'little spells' (p. 4), Bonnie Clutter is, in her own estimation, a 'kind of ghost' (p. 23) with no sense of adequacy or usefulness: 'All my children are very efficient. They don't need me' (p. 19). In Capote's hands, Bonnie Clutter becomes the modern embodiment of the Gothic 'mad woman in the attic', a community misfit isolated in an austere upstairs bedroom, 'to think that she was Nancy's mother! An aunt—that seemed possible; a visiting spinster aunt, slightly odd, but *nice*' (p. 19). In the traditional Gothic plot, it is often the young heroine who steps in to provide familial stability in the absence of the mother; *In Cold Blood* reproduces this pattern in the representation of the youngest daughter Nancy Clutter, 'a pretty and virginal girl' (p. 67), memorialized for her virtue and industriousness: 'Where she found the time, and still managed to "practically run that big house" ... was an enigma the community pondered, and solved by saying, "She's got *character*. Gets it from her old man"' (p. 13). Yet, beneath the surface of private virtue and industry lurks the problem of parental authority. While Bonnie Clutter is rendered invisible, Nancy's life is dominated by domestic and communal obligation: 'Each moment was assigned; she knew precisely, at any hour, what she would be doing, how long it would require'

(p. 13). Not only is every moment of her life controlled, Nancy's personal relationships are monitored and proscribed. Herb Clutter's 'laws were laws' (p. 5); he opposes her infatuation with Bobby Rupp who is Roman Catholic, 'a fact that should in itself be sufficient to terminate whatever fancies she and this boy might have of some day marrying' (p. 5). Maintaining a conventional sense of duty, Nancy agrees to 'begin a gradual breaking off with Bobby' (p. 5): 'I just want to be his daughter and do as he wishes' (p. 16).

Ultimately, *In Cold Blood* fulfils the salient Gothic plot of the female protagonist trapped and pursued by a transgressive male. While both Bonnie and Nancy are murdered, Dick Hickock's confession reveals that Nancy is the specific target and main reason for his participation in the crime:

> Before I ever went to their house I knew there would be a girl there. I think the main reason I went there was not to rob them but to rape the girl. Because I thought a lot about it. That is one reason why I never wanted to turn back when we started to. Even when I saw there was no safe. I did make some advances towards the Clutter girl when I was there. But Perry never gave me a chance. (p. 229)

In Cold Blood plays on the traditional Gothic revelation that the domestic sphere is dangerous to women, whether from the threat of rape from without or from authority within.

Mid-century critics largely ignored Capote's arrangement of the factual material around a conventional Gothic plot, focusing instead on the characterization of the murderers. For many, it was Dick and Perry's physical deformities that linked them to Capote's earlier characters and to the southern Gothic tradition where everyone is 'a cripple, a physical or emotional or mental defective'.[52] Echoes of Capote's earlier characters do permeate *In Cold Blood*: the pygmy figure Jesus Fever and Miss Wisteria in *Other Voices, Other Rooms* (1948), and the nameless old woman in *Tree of Night* (1949), are each, like Perry Smith, freakishly out of proportion. Capote continues this tradition by accentuating the physical deformities of the murderers. Describing Perry Smith, Capote writes:

His tiny feet, encased in short black boots with steel buckles, would have neatly fitted into a delicate lady's dancing slippers; when he stood up, he was no taller than a twelve-year old child, and suddenly looked, strutting on stunted legs that seemed grotesquely inadequate to the grown-up bulk they supported, not like a well-built truck driver but like a retired jockey, overblown and muscle-bound. (p. 11)

While not an 'undersized, overmuscled half-breed' (p. 36) like Perry, Dick, too, is superficially malformed, disfigured by an 'inky gallery' of elaborate tattoos, many of them 'self-designed and self-executed' (p. 24). More disturbing are his crooked facial features which hint at a deeper corruption:

It was as though his head had been halved like an apple, then put together a fraction off centre . . . the left side rather lower than the right, with the results that the lips were slightly aslant, the nose askew, and his eyes not only situated at uneven levels but of uneven size, the left eye being truly serpentine, with a venomous, sickly-blue squint that although it was involuntarily acquired, seemed nevertheless to warn of bitter sediment at the bottom of his nature. (pp. 24–5)

Some reviewers even detected shades of nineteenth-century physiognomy in the description of Perry and Dick's deformities, and objected to the deterministic connotations these seemingly atavistic qualities implied. Norman Mailer, for example, considered that 'Truman decided too quickly this is all heredity, that in their genes his killers were doomed and directed to act in this fashion.'[53] Capote's focus on Perry's racial characteristics in particular, suggests this deterministic tilt:

His mother had been a full-blooded Cherokee; it was from her that he had inherited his colouring—the iodine skin, the dark, moist eyes, the black hair . . . His mother's donation was apparent; that of his father, a freckled, ginger-haired Irishman, was less so. It was as though the Indian blood had routed every trace of the Celtic strain. (p. 12)

What fuelled the ire of other commentators was Capote's apparent refusal to dehumanise Perry and Dick, deriding what they saw as

Capote's focus on the social causes of Perry and Dick's behaviour; rather than heredity, the narrative seemed to point to a systemic or societal cause. In a later interview with George Plimpton, Capote confirms this view:

> Perry wasn't an evil person. If he'd had any chance in life, things would have been different. But every illusion he'd ever had, well, they all evaporated, so that on that night he was so full of self-hatred and self-pity that I think he would have killed somebody.[54]

In her review of Capote's *Other Voices, Other Rooms*, Diana Trilling objected to the causal explanations for Joel's homosexuality and the urging that he be judged as a 'passive victim of his early circumstances'. 'Is no member of society', she asks, 'to be held accountable for himself, not even Hitler?' She was even less inclined to pity Perry and Dick in her subsequent review of *In Cold Blood*. Abandoning her usual objections to capital punishment, Trilling remarks, 'But in this case, if ever, the death sentence was warranted — wanton, brutal killers and I didn't feel any sympathy for them which was what Truman was calling for.'[55] For most critics, Perry's racial ancestry coupled with his tragic upbringing represented either a sociohistorical reality or a link in a chain of necessity. The counterpoint to the racial and social causes of Perry's criminality is the absence of similar factors in Dick's history. Beyond rural poverty, Capote provides no explanation for Dick's paedophilia or violence. He is described as an 'American-style "good kid" with an outgrown crew cut, sane enough but not too bright' (p. 25). In stark contrast to Perry's circumstances, Dick's home life was 'normal':

> My school years went quite the same as most other boys my own age... We were always what you would call semi-poor. Never down and out, but several times on the verge of it. My dad was a hard worker and did his best to provide for us. My mother also was always a hard worker. Her house was always neat, and we had clean clothes aplenty... In high-school I did real well, made above average grades the first year or two... While in school I participated in all the sports, and received 9 letters in all. (p. 228)

Dick's history confounds attempts to ascribe the killings to familial dysfunction, heredity or the system, but by highlighting his apparent 'normality', Capote creates a profoundly sinister character: Dick is the Gothic's ubiquitous stranger, the marauding rapist and, even more frightening, the boy next door.

While Capote's depiction of Perry and Dick as physically deformed does suggest an affinity with his earlier fictional characters, their moral ambiguity is equally reminiscent of traditional Gothic villains. Like many literary rogues before him, Perry Smith has a leading part in the narrative. His early life is described as a Gothic saga of familial dysfunction, violence and suicide, 'an ugly and lonely progress towards one mirage and then another' (p. 203). Characterized as a 'deeply frustrated man striving to project his individuality against a backdrop of rigid conformity' (p. 35), Perry lives in a 'half-world suspended ... between self-expression and self-destruction' (p. 35). Part 'corrupt gipsy', part 'gentle romantic' (p. 11), he is a 'disappointed *poète maudit*' and a 'heroic, poetic villain ... capable of evoking considerable sympathy'.[56] The depiction of Perry as a Gothic hero-villain blurs the moral distinction between the Clutters and their killers, differences obscured not only in the descriptions of Perry but in the very structure of the text. From the onset, the reader knows who the killers are, but why they committed the crime is intentionally deferred allowing the reader to experience events as they unfold. Capote employs a contrapuntal technique, a cinematic device whereby the narrative constantly switches between the family and the killers until the moment of encounter. Chapter sections begin and end at precise moments of convergence between the victims and their killers as if to hint at deeper parallels. At the end of one section, for example, Dick honks a car horn for Perry and in the first line of the next section Nancy calls 'I hear you' to her brother Kenyon (p. 13). Implicit in this structure is the notion of a shared humanity between the killers and their victims. This is particularly evident in the mutual alienation of Bonnie Clutter and Perry Smith. In the narrative Bonnie is reported to have bemoaned how Herb travels a great deal. 'Oh, he's always headed somewhere. Washington and Chicago and Oklahoma and Kansas City—sometimes it seems like he's never home' (p. 21). Perry, too, we learn, is a traveller and a 'conceiver of voyages': 'Ink-circled name populated the map.

COZUMEL, an island off the coast of Yucatán, where, so he had read in a men's magazine, you could "shed your clothes, put on a relaxed grin, [and] live like a Raja!"' (pp. 10–11). Bonnie Clutter also claims that wherever Herb goes he brings her a small souvenir: 'he remembers how I dote on tiny things... little things really belong to you...They don't have to be left behind. You can carry them in a shoebox... wherever you go' (p. 21). 'Or,' she adds, 'you might never go home. And—it's important always to have with you something of your own. That's really yours' (p. 22). Bonnie's imaginary box of treasured memories and trinkets mirrors Perry's actual boxes of 'books and maps, yellowing letters, song lyrics, poems, and unusual souvenirs' (p. 102) that he carries wherever he goes, and which ultimately yields the evidence for his conviction. Bonnie Clutter and Perry Smith, both outcasts in their respective worlds, share a need for belonging and recognition. Perry's situation, his life story emphasizes, is easy to understand, but the inclusion of Bonnie Clutter's thoughts suggest that beneath the surface of the agrarian 'good life' lurks a similar sense of loss and alienation. While Perry laments the inability to realize his fantasy of becoming a nightclub singer, Bonnie regrets not completing her nursing diploma 'just to prove... that I once succeeded at something' (p. 20). This mutual dissatisfaction reflects the tenor of the era: for Bonnie, the post-war ennui characterized by a life of abundance and rigid gender roles, and for Perry, the false promise of social mobility.

While *In Cold Blood* attends to traditional Gothic structures and characterization, the text also explicitly draws on republican agrarian ideology. Early republican writers expressed the political and moral superiority of the New World through the dialectics of virtue and corruption, city and country, tradition and progress, and these oppositions come under scrutiny in Capote's narrative. Foregrounding these antitheses is the character of Mrs Archibald William Warren-Browne, whose presence in the novel functions to contrast the innocent rural values of Kansas and the corrupt values of Europe. Described as 'a peacock trapped in a turkey pen' (p. 93), the British Mrs Warren-Browne explains in an 'accent almost incoherently upper-class' (p. 93) why she and her husband abandoned the 'family estates in the North of England' for a farmhouse in western Kansas:

Taxes, my dear. Death duties. *Enor*mous, *crim*inal death duties. That's what drove us out of England. Yes, we left a year ago. Without regrets. None. We love it here ... Though, of course, it's very *different* from our other life. The life we've always known. Paris and Rome. Monte. London. I do—oc*cas*ionally—think of London. Oh, I don't *really* miss it—the frenzy, and never a cab, and always worrying how one looks. Positively not. We love it here ... *la vraie chose.* (p. 94)

For Mrs Warren-Browne, the special quality of American life is located not only in the rural landscape, but also in the freedom from the corruption of big cities, and Capote's mockery of her aristocratic affectations hinges on this perennial polarity between city and country and, by extension, between the virtuous New World and the corrupt but sophisticated Old World. That rural identity is founded on this ancient opposition is evident in the attitudes of the local citizens who emphasize the interdependence between democracy and agrarianism: 'No, sir. Nothing like that here. All equal, regardless of wealth, colour, or creed. Everything the way it ought to be in a democracy; that's us' (p. 27). For the residents of Holcomb, Kansas, rural life is free from the social hierarchies of the Old World and promotes an ethical code founded on community, simplicity and decency: 'there's no better place to raise kids than right here ... Good neighbours, people who care about each other, that's what counts. And everything else a decent man needs' (pp. 26–7). The country/city divide is also reflected in Perry Smith's world view. Perry, his father claims, prefers the 'company of decent type[s]—outdoors people' (p. 105); his subsequent criminality, it is suggested, was not due to any inherent defect, but traced to his city upbringing: 'We lived in the country. We are all truly outdoor people ... [the trouble] all started when my wife wanted to go to the City and live a wild life' (p. 105). As the site of progress and industrialization, the city breeds social sickness and degeneracy. Perry's mother dies an alcoholic prostitute, two of his siblings commit suicide and Perry spends his youth in and out of gaol. In Capote's arrangement of the details of the Clutter murders, the narrative articulates themes and images that have been at the heart of republican ideology since the eighteenth century: the opposition between the virtuous New World and the corrupt Old World, and between the country and the city.

Approaching Capote's text through the dialectic of virtue and corruption also requires an alternative reading of the landscape. While Gerald Clarke interprets the expansiveness of the setting as an isolated Gothic space, from the aperture of republicanism, the Clutter farm becomes the land of milk and honey proselytized in eighteenth-century agrarian discourse. Before the murders, River Valley Farm is an organic utopia, a historical republic replete with metaphorical 'Greek temples' (p. 1). With its bursting silos of Westland sorghum and milo grain, its 'lion-coloured' fields 'luminously golden with after-harvest stubble' (p. 9), and the orchard of 'fruit-bearing trees growing by the river' (p. 9), Herb Clutter's 800 acres is 'a patch of paradise, [a] green, apple-scented Eden' (p. 9). Equally, the farm's isolation and obscurity from the highway suggests a pre-industrial oasis, unassailable by foreign intruders. Apart from the occasional hunters who came to down the 'grain-fattened birds' (p. 10), there were no trespassers: 'a mile and a half from the highway, and arrived at by obscure roads', River Valley Farm 'was not a place strangers came upon by chance' (p. 9). Untransformed by the impact of industrialization, the Clutter farm avoids the encounter with machine technology and the problems of industrial civilization: 'like the motorists on the highway, and like the yellow trains streaking down the Santa Fe tracks, drama, in the shape of exceptional happenings, had never stopped there' (p. 2). Implicit in this setting are the identification of happiness and independence with an agrarian existence free of urban problems and the corrupting forces of modernity.

The alliance between republican virtue and agrarianism is also embodied in Capote's characterization of the victims. The Clutters represent historical agrarian stability, a foundational identity in an era of unbridled progress. Their destruction is more than an end to innocence, but the death of a national ancestral icon.

> Feeling wouldn't run half so high if this had happened to anyone *except* the Clutters. Anyone *less* admired. Prosperous. Secure. But that family represented everything people hereabouts really value and respect, and that such a thing could happen to them—well, it's like being told there is no God. (p. 71)

Herb Clutter, in particular, is singled out as the model of virtue. As one critic noted:

Virtue and Corruption in Truman Capote's In Cold Blood

Clutter was the embodiment of the self-made man, as well as the exemplar of the White Anglo-Saxon Protestant values with which that favourite of all American myths is conventionally associated ... The Clutters remind us of the reinforcing reality which rests behind America's dream of herself—an intelligent, public-spirited family, who lead a simple, unpretentious life.[57]

Yet, Herb Clutter is more than an archetypal pattern. His 'plain virtue' (p. 64) does not originate in the nineteenth-century 'frontier hypothesis' but is rooted in the eighteenth-century theory of agrarian citizenship. As Pocock argues, republicanism represents a paradigmatic language that embodies a collection of values, ideas and principles that in the eighteenth century were taken for granted; because it was so powerfully authoritative, its conventions and vocabulary still resonate in the twentieth century. Structured around the oppositions of liberty versus power, public good versus self-interest, virtue versus corruption, self-discipline versus appetite, the language of republicanism serves to perpetuate early modern values in the contemporary world. In early agrarian ideology, man was pictured in classical terms struggling between these forces.

> Rural life was celebrated not for its wild or natural beauty but for its simplicity and repose to which in Horatian fashion virtuous men could retire after a lifetime of devotion to duty and country. The traits of character most praised were the classical ones—restraint, temperance, fortitude, dignity, and independence.[58]

Herb Clutter exemplifies these values. As Capote notes, he preferred 'Spartan breakfasts', he touched 'neither coffee nor tea ... The truth was he opposed all stimulants, however gentle. He did not smoke, and of course he did not drink; indeed, he had never tasted spirits, and was inclined to avoid people who had' (p. 6). Never known to 'act the Squire', Herb Clutter was not a member of the country club, and 'never sought to associate with the reigning coterie'. He had no use for 'card games, golf, cocktails, or buffet suppers ... or, indeed, for any pastime that he felt did not "accomplish something"' (p. 27). In addition to his stoicism, Herb Clutter's civic virtue is exemplified by his public activism: a 'die-hard community booster',

Herb Clutter was a 'joiner' and 'born leader' (p. 21). As a member of the local 4H Club whose goal is to help those living in rural areas 'develop practical abilities and moral character' (p. 27), his actions follow 'a public route, a march of satisfying conquests' (p. 21). If Clutter's devotion to the public good signals his civic virtue, his outright ownership of the farm and his independence from the vagaries of debt denote his political freedom within the republic. The republican view of the political economy was that virtue was also achieved through land ownership which guaranteed personal independence and autonomy which, in turn, provided the material conditions for an orderly society governed by reason and self-restraint.[59] This independence of property ownership, coupled with private and civic virtue position Herb Clutter as the iconic republican citizen as identified in eighteenth-century agrarian ideology.

If Herb Clutter signalled active citizenship, land ownership and private morality, Perry and Dick represent the degeneracy of these principles and manners. Both embody qualities that denote corruption and a threat to the republic: self-interest, appetite, avarice, envy and effeminacy. As Capote's central character, Perry's corruption is most fully developed. His vanity and passion for distinction is evident in his childish fantasies of becoming a Las Vegas nightclub singer and in his incessant quest for buried treasure: a quest which is manifest in Perry's recurring dream of being in a jungle with diamond-encrusted trees. As he attempts to pick one of the diamonds, he is confronted by a snake. However, just as Perry is about to be devoured by the snake, a bird, a 'yellow sort of parrot' (p. 75) lifts him off to an Edenic garden: 'A real place. Like out of a movie. Maybe that's were I *did* see it—remembered it from a movie. Because where else would I have seen a garden like that?' (p. 76). For Perry, the Hollywood image of Eden is not a place of spiritual redemption; rather it offers only material and social rewards. In one version of the dream, the ascension is 'merely "a feeling", a sense of power, of unassailable superiority' (p. 76). In another, the garden is replete with unlimited food. 'And listen—it's every bit *free*. I mean, I don't have to be afraid to touch it, and it won't cost a cent' (p. 76). Stripped of the moral supports of virtue, the imagined Eden is a place of unlimited riches and power. Perry's quest is not for the simple life, but represents only those desires which foreshadow corruption.

Virtue and Corruption in Truman Capote's In Cold Blood

If virtue is also an inherently masculine trait denoting civic activism, courage and political autonomy, in gendered terms, its opposite is weak and self-indulgent, traits repeatedly emphasized in the portrayal of the killers. Perry and Dick's 'effeminacy' is located not only in their passion for distinction and pursuit of wealth, but is represented metaphorically in their sexual deviation. Dick, admired by Perry for being 'authentically tough, invulnerable, [and] "totally masculine"' (p. 12) is in fact a paedophile, while Perry's sexual orientation is ambiguous. Together, they embody the marginal countertype of rural masculinity. Perry's effeminacy, in particular, is displayed anatomically through his 'tiny' feet, 'pink' lips, 'perky' nose and 'prim' and 'soft' voice (p. 18), in stark contrast to Clutter's broad shoulders, square jaw and unstained teeth 'strong enough to shatter walnuts' (p. 2). Herb Clutter, Capote emphasizes, 'cut a man's-man figure' (p. 92). Yet, if the gendered contours of virtue provide a semantic matrix for Perry and Dick's corruption, its effects are complicated by the instabilities of virtue in the modern world. Herb Clutter's masculinity, his 'fearless self-assurance' (p. 29) and perceived ability to talk his way out of any situation in the end does not protect him or his family; confronted by intruders, he is stupefied into passivity. Untouched by progress, the Clutters go to their deaths quietly because they are innocent to the realities of the outside world. The moral imperatives of agrarian virtue, the narrative suggests, are no defence against the unseen, violent forces of modernity.

In *The Machine in the Garden*, Leo Marx argues that progress in the form of machine technology has been the chief threat to the bucolic image of America since the eighteenth century:

> Anti-pastoral forces at work in our literature seem indeed to become increasingly violent as we approach our own time. For it is industrialization, represented by images of machine technology that provides the counterforce in the American archetype of the pastoral design.[60]

Although the 'eight non-stop trains [that] hurry through Holcomb every twenty-four hours' (p. 54) echo Marx's theme of the 'interrupted idyll', in Capote's narrative, the modern 'machine in the garden' is Perry and Dick's car, the quintessential symbol of progress and freedom repeatedly mythologized in the American imagination. Structurally,

Perry and Dick's 10,000-mile road trip to and away from the Clutter farm functions as a guide into and through the narrative. Interposed between the activities of the Clutter family and the police manhunt, the reader follows the movements of the killers up to the moment of the crime and their subsequent escape to Mexico and back again until their capture. Perry's confession takes place 'on an Arizona highway', in 'sage-brush country—the mesa country of hawks and rattlesnakes and towering red rocks' (p. 190). Handcuffed in the back of a car, the police, along with the reader, hear for the first time Perry's version of the Clutter family murder.

More significantly, as an icon of social mobility, the automobile represents the American values of democracy, equality and self-determination. Mobility is associated with the open road, with limitlessness and escape. It signals lighting out for the frontier and access to a new life, an ethos represented in Perry's early years with his prospector father and their travels in a 'house car' (p. 104). Like early pioneers, Perry and his father fashioned themselves as adventurers and individualists free from the constraints of government and societal rules, and it was his father's dream of striking it rich in the Alaskan frontier that fuelled Perry's romanticized images of a golden life: 'Tex taught his son to dream of gold, to hunt for it in the sandy beds of snow-water streams, and there, too, Perry learned to use a gun, skin a bear, track wolves and deer' (p. 109). Perry and Dick's road trip to Mexico is reminiscent of these earlier experiences; their aimless odyssey of escape and random experience stimulated by fantasies of buried treasure is realizable only by hitting the open road. Capote draws this connection between mobility and independence in his description of Perry's imaginary quest for gold:

> The dream of drifting downward through strange waters, of plunging towards a green sea-dusk, sliding past the scaly, savage-eyed protectors of a ship's hulk that loomed ahead, a Spanish galleon—a drowned cargo of diamonds and pearls, heaping caskets of gold. A car honked. At last—Dick (pp. 12–13).

Dick's arrival signals the promise of a journey and freedom 'against social, economic, and political pressure' (p. 11). Yet, for all their mobility, Perry and Dick's American dream remains illusive. Perry's frontier schemes fail, and his quest for gold is reduced to a pathetic treasure hunt for empty bottles discarded along America's network of highways. The journey towards independence and self-determination inevitably leads back to the city where Perry's efforts lead to near starvation; in the city he must steal, cheat and forage for his basic subsistence: 'He was still (and wasn't it incredible, a person of his intelligence, his talents?) an urchin dependent, so to say, on stolen coins' (p. 158).

The dark side of this emblem of the future and of America's technological superiority is suggested in Perry and Dick's physical corruption. As one critic noted, in the 1950s 'the greatest single factor in subverting the virtues of both city and countryside was the automobile . . . General Motors triumphed over commonsense and the result was smog . . . decaying cities, divided freeways, despoiled landscapes, and very often early death'.[61] Unlike Capote's previous characters, Perry and Dick's disfigurements are not inherently grotesque or the result of congenital defects; as Capote points out, their injuries are 'involuntarily acquired' (p. 24), the result of motor vehicle accidents. Both maimed and scarred, their physical damage reflects more than a preoccupation with imperfection and spiritual loneliness; rather their injuries register the impact of progress on both the moral and physical self.

Juxtaposed to the stability of the Clutter family, the perpetual motion of the killers renders them anonymous and invisible. Inside their car, they become dangerous marauders, free to commit their crimes with relative impunity. The symbol of modern progress becomes, in effect, a material accomplice in the murders. As chapter sections begin and end, the two are seen either driving or getting in or out of their car. When the reader is first introduced to Perry, he is waiting for Dick to arrive in his 'black 1949 Chevrolet sedan' (p. 17). From this moment, the car becomes a central character in the narrative, facilitating their movements and protecting their anonymity. At times, the killers themselves recede from view inside the prowling machine: 'By mid-afternoon the black Chevrolet had reached Emporia, Kansas' (p. 29); 'The black Chevrolet was again parked, this time in front of a Catholic hospital on the outskirts of Emporia' (p. 33); 'The old Chevrolet left Kansas city November 21, Saturday night' (p. 86). Anthropomorphisms highlight the effect: prior to the murders, the killers spend the morning repairing the vehicle because 'the aged Chevrolet' is expected 'to perform punishing feats' (p. 18). As they arrive at the Clutter farm, it is not the killers, but the black sedan that silently 'crept forward' (p. 47).

With the death of the Clutter family, the Edenic garden, too, transmogrifies from a pastoral ideal into a decaying Gothic space: 'The cider-tart odour of spoiling apples ... now that it was deprived of the late owner's dedicated attention, the first threads of decay's cobweb were being spun. A grave rake lay rusting in the driveway; the lawn was parched and shabby ... though the weather was glittering, the Clutter place seemed shadowed, and hushed, and motionless'(p. 169). Once invaded by strangers, the peaceful agrarian vista that once attracted Mrs Warren-Browne suddenly takes an eerie turn: 'after dark, when the wind commences, that *hateful* prairie wind, one hears the most a*ppalli*ng moans ... Dear God! That poor family!' (p. 94).

In Capote's 'non-fiction novel', the tension between virtue and corruption is enacted in the encounter between the Clutters and their killers. Consciously or unconsciously, Capote asserts the values of eighteenth-century agrarianism through the depiction of the Clutter family, while at the same time registering the implicit vulnerability of this ideology when in confrontation with the unforeseen forces that progress itself has unleashed. The image of the new son of Adam is unsupportable in modern capitalist culture, however, this is not due to the beneficence of progress: far from shaking off the sins of the Old World, modern culture has engendered a form of rampant individualism whereby the logical extreme is social exclusion and violence. Leo Marx's 'interrupted idyll' has indeed moved from the nineteenth-century intrusion of train whistles or steamboats to violent invasions by the modern symbol of freedom and industrialization. Post-war prosperity and progress have not led to unfettered liberty, but to the perpetual confrontation between virtue and corruption. Capote's 'true story' re-enacts the terror of this encounter through the Gothic themes of invasion, degeneration and decline.

Notes

[1] Theodore Roosevelt, *Proceedings of the Congress of Constructive Patriotism*, Washington DC (NewYork: National Security League, 25–7 January 1917), p. 172.

Virtue and Corruption in Truman Capote's In Cold Blood

2   Haskel Frankel, 'An interview with Truman Capote', *Saturday Review*, vol. XLIX (1966), 36–7 (37).
3   Ibid., 37.
4   David Galloway, 'Why the chickens came home to roost in Holcomb, Kansas: Truman Capote's *In Cold Blood*', in I. Malin (ed.), *Truman Capote's* In Cold Blood: *A Critical Handbook* (Belmont, CA: Wadsworth, 1968), pp. 154–62 (p. 155).
5   Tony Tanner, 'Death in Kansas', in I. Malin (ed.), *Truman Capote's* In Cold Blood: *A Critical Handbook* (Belmont, CA.: Wadsworth, 1968), pp. 98–102 (p. 99).
6   Melvin J. Friedman, 'Towards an aesthetic: Truman Capote's other voices', in I. Malin (ed.), *Truman Capote's* In Cold Blood: *A Critical Handbook* (Belmont, CA: Wadsworth, 1968), pp. 163–76 (p. 165).
7   Chester E. Eisinger, 'Land and loyalty: literary expressions of agrarian nationalism in the seventeenth and eighteenth centuries', *American Literature*, 21, 2 (1947), 160–78 (160).
8   See for example the poetry of the Connecticut Wits, Philip Freneau's 'The Bergen planter' (1790), and 'The American village', in ed. Fred Lewis Pattee, *The Poems of Philip Freneau, Vol. 3* (New York: Russell & Russell, 1963); Enos Hitchcock's novel *The Farmer's Friend* (1793); George Logan's *Letters Addressed to the Yeomanry of the United States* (1791).
9   Quoted in Richard Bridgman, 'Jefferson's farmer before Jefferson', *American Quarterly*, 14, 4 (1962) 567–77 (570).
10 Eisinger, 'Land and loyalty', 160–1. See also, Chester E. Eisinger, 'The freehold concept in eighteenth-century American letters', *William and Mary Quarterly*, IV, 1 (1947), 42–59.
11 Quoted in Eisinger, 'Land and loyalty', 162.
12 Ibid., 165.
13 Quoted in Gordon S. Wood, *The Creation of the American Republic, 1776–1787* (Williamsburg: University of North Carolina Press, 1969), p. 99.
14 Quoted in Eisinger, 'Land and loyalty', 166.
15 Quoted in Wood, *Creation of the American Republic*, p. 101.
16 Quoted in Eisinger, 'Land and loyalty', 171.
17 Philip Freneau, 'The rising glory of America', in ed. Fred Lewis Pattee, *The Poems of Philip Freneau, Vol. 1* (New York: Russell & Russell, 1963) pp. 49–84, (pp. 71, 82).
18 Hector St Jean de Crèvecoeur, *Letters from an American Farmer*, in Nina Baym et al. (eds), *The Norton Anthology of American Literature, Vol. 1* (4th edn; New York: W. W. Norton, 1994), pp. 657–8.
19 Quoted in Stow Persons, 'The cyclical theory of history in eighteenth-century America', *American Quarterly*, 6, 2 (1954), 153.
20 J. G. A. Pocock, *Virtue, Commerce, and History: Essays on Political Thought and History, Chiefly in the Eighteenth Century* (New York: Cambridge University Press, 1985), pp. 41, 48.
21 Quoted in Persons, 'Cyclical theory of history', 154.
22 Quoted in Wood, *Creation of the American Republic*, p. 108.
23 Quoted in Persons, 'Cyclical theory of history', 154.

24 Quoted in Wood, 'Conspiracy and the paranoid style: causality and deceit in the eighteenth century', *William and Mary Quarterly*, 39, 3 (1982), 417, original emphasis.
25 Quoted in Wood, *The Radicalism of the American Revolution* (New York: A. A. Knopf, 1992), p. 108.
26 Jefferson, *Notes on the State of Virginia*, The Avalon Project, Yale Law School, http://www.yale.edu/lawweb/Avalon/jevifram.htm (accessed 2 February 2005); Pocock, *The Machiavellian Moment: Florentine Republican Thought and the Atlantic Republican Tradition* (Princeton: Princeton University Press, 1975), pp. 545, 533.
27 Jefferson, *Notes on the State of Virginia*.
28 Thomas Jefferson to James Madison (20 December 1787), Jefferson Digital Archive, University of Virginia Library, http://etext.lib.virginia.edu/jefferson (accessed 2 February 2005).
29 Jon Lance Bacon, *Flannery O'Connor and Cold War Culture* (Cambridge: Cambridge University Press, 1993), p. 14. For example, Henry Nash Smith, *Virgin Land: The American West as Symbol and Myth* (Cambridge, Mass.: Harvard University Press, 1950); R. W. B. Lewis, *The American Adam: Innocence, Tragedy and Tradition in the Nineteenth Century* (Chicago: Chicago University Press, 1955); Leslie A. Fiedler, *An End to Innocence* (Boston: Beacon Press, 1955); Robert E. Spiller, *The Cycle of American Literature* (New York: Macmillan, 1955); Frederic I. Carpenter, *American Literature and the Dream* (New York: Philosophical Library, 1955); Kenneth S. Lynn, *The Dream of Success* (Boston: Little Brown, 1955); Max Lerner, *America as a Civilization* (New York: Simon & Schuster, 1957); Leo Marx, *The Machine in the Garden: Technology and the Pastoral Ideal in America* (London: Oxford University Press, 1964).
30 Quoted in John Barker, 'Changing frontiers', *Wilson Quarterly*, VII, 1 (1983) 88–99 (93).
31 Frederick Jackson Turner, *The Frontier in American History* (New York: Henry Holt, 1947), p. 1.
32 Ibid., pp. 3–4.
33 Smith, *Virgin Land*, pp. 124, 159.
34 Frederick Carpenter, 'The American myth: paradise (to be) regained', *PMLA*, 74 (1959), 599–606 (599).
35 Quoted in Bacon, *Flannery O'Connor*, p. 16.
36 Lewis, *The American Adam*, p. 4.
37 Ibid., p. 196.
38 Marx, *Machine in the Garden*, p. 3.
39 Ibid., p. 6.
40 Ibid., p. 7. See also, Richard Hofstadter, *The Age of Reform: From Byran to F.D.R.* (New York: A. A. Knopf, 1955); Marvin Meyers, *The Jacksonian Persuasion: Politics and Belief* (Palo Alto, CA: Stanford University Press, 1960).
41 Marx, *Machine in the Garden*, p. 11.
42 Ibid., p. 28.
43 Ihab Hassan, 'The daydream and nightmare of Narcissus', *Wisconsin Studies in Contemporary Literature*, 1, 2 (1960), 5–21 (5).

44 For examples, see Mark Schorer, 'McCullers and Capote: basic patterns', in Nona Balakian and Charles Simmons (eds), *The Creative Present: Notes on Contemporary American Fiction* (Garden City, NY: Doubleday, 1963), pp. 79–107; Paul Levine, 'Truman Capote: the revelation of the broken image', *Virginia Quarterly Review*, XXXIV, (1958), 600–17.
45 Chester E. Eisinger, *Fiction of the Forties* (Chicago: Chicago University Press, 1963), p. 240.
46 Frank Baldanza, 'Plato in Dixie', *Georgia Review*, XII (1958), 151–67 (151).
47 Hassan, 'Daydream and nightmare of Narcissus', 5.
48 John W. Aldridge, 'The metaphorical world of Truman Capote', in Joseph J. Waldmeir and John C. Waldmeir (eds), *The Critical Response to Truman Capote* (1951; Westport, Conn.: Greenwood Press, 1999), pp. 32–48 (pp. 5–6).
49 Stanley Kaufman, 'Capote in Kansas', in I. Malin (ed.), *Truman Capote's In Cold Blood: A Critical Handbook* (Belmont, CA: Wadsworth, 1968), p. 63; Tanner, 'Death in Kansas', p. 101; Sol Yurick, 'Sob-sister Gothic', in I. Malin (ed.), *Truman Capote's In Cold Blood: A Critical Handbook* (Belmont, CA: Wadsworth, 1968), p. 77; F. W. Dupee, 'Truman Capote's score', in I. Malin (ed.), *Truman Capote's In Cold Blood: A Critical Handbook* (Belmont, CA: Wadsworth, 1968), p. 71.
50 Gerald Clarke, *Capote: A Biography* (London: Ballantine, 1989), pp. 357–8.
51 Truman Capote, *In Cold Blood: A True Account of a Multiple Murder and its Consequences* (1965; Bristol: The Reprint Society, 1967), p. 1. Further references will appear in parantheses in the text; emphasis throughout is author's.
52 Eisinger, *Fiction of the Forties*, p. 239.
53 Quoted in Nick Rance, '"Truly Serpentine": "New Journalism", *In Cold Blood* and the Vietnam war', *Literature and History*, 11, 2 (2002), 78–100 (82).
54 George Plimpton, *Truman Capote* (London: Anchor Books, 1998), p. 79.
55 Quoted in Rance, '"Truly Serpentine"', 82.
56 Dupee, 'Truman Capote's score', p. 72; Phillip K. Tompkins, 'In cold fact', in I. Malin (ed.), *Truman Capote's In Cold Blood: A Critical Handbook* (Belmont, CA: Wadsworth, 1968), p. 56.
57 Galloway, 'Why the chickens came home to roost', pp. 157–8.
58 Wood, *Creation of the American Republic*, p. 50.
59 Cathy Matson, 'Toward a republican empire: interest and ideology in revolutionary America', *American Quarterly*, 37, 4 (1985), 496–531 (498).
60 Marx, *Machine in the Garden*, p. 26.
61 Douglas T. Miller and Marion Nowak, *The Fifties: The Way We Really Were* (New York: Double Day, 1975), pp. 136–7.

Afterword

༄

It is by our image of the past and present and future, rather than from our confidence in the uniqueness of our crisis, that the character of our apocalypse must be known.

Frank Kermode (1967)[1]

In *Fear: A Cultural History*, historian Joanna Bourke writes that in the wake of the terrorist attacks on New York and Washington, the world seems a more terrifying place: 'Death and disaster; nightmares and phobias; new killing techniques and dangerous technologies; treacherous bodies—a seemingly endless range of terrifying trials and tribulations seem to face people in the twentieth century.'

For Bourke, this fear manifests in modern surveillance systems, in persecution of immigrants and in the spectre of the terrorist. It is, she notes, a 'fear *of* something that may befall us, rather than fear *for* others'.[2] In a subsequent article, Bourke comments on the politicization of fear in the wake of the terrorist attack on London. The bombings, she claims, generated an 'apocalyptic mood' that the authorities manage by introducing repressive legislation that acts to criminalize dissent. In twenty-first-century America, the Patriot Act functions to contain a culture engrossed by fear. Yet, we keep up appearances, she claims, with the rhetoric of democracy, freedom, fundamentalism and terrorism. Bourke then calls for a 'new paradigm of resistance', a new form

Afterword

of political activism that ensures government does not undermine the very values they are defending.[3]

In a similar observation, Frank Furedi notes how apocalyptic visions keep society in a permanent state of anxiety: 'Fear today has a free-floating dynamic that can attach itself to a variety of phenomena ... terrorist violence, global warming, flu pandemics and technological catastrophes ... reinforce[ing] fear about our existence.' The terrorist attacks, he argues, have left humanity with no common system of meaning through which to make sense of tragedy:

> The tendency to engage with uncertainty through the prism of fear and therefore anticipate destructive outcomes is a crisis in our understanding of cause and effect ... Increasingly, the questions of what to fear and whom to blame become subjects of acrimonious debate. In such an atmosphere, conspiracy theories flourish ... transform[ing] our anxieties about causation into tangible fears.

It is the adoption of what he calls an 'apocalyptic vocabulary' that fuels the mood of vulnerability, powerlessness and fear.[4]

This book set out to consider whether republicanism, as defined by American post-war historians, is useful as a hermeneutical device. The question arose when, in the aftermath of 9/11 and the beginning of the war in Iraq, a lexicon of fear dominated public discourse: terrorism, torture, conspiracy and nuclear war appeared as buzzwords in almost every speech and media broadcast. As Susan Faludi remarked, with 9/11, the old 'terror-dream' was once again forced to the surface of national consciousness.[5] I shared with these commentators a desire to understand the rhetoric of fear and apocalypse that pervades our contemporary politics and culture, but I also knew that these jeremiads were not new, that the discourse constructing the contemporary 'war on terror' has a long echo, and that what critics writing on the current crisis uncovered was a mode of discourse that has articulated the Western world's sense of vulnerability and peril since the Enlightenment. The anticipation of tyranny, the fear of lost liberty and national degeneration reverberates in the revolutionary language of the American founders, in the English country Whigs and in the classical texts that informed both their politics and their fears. Politicians, then as now, frame national crisis as a conflict between national security and individual liberty; liberal and conservative; virtue and corruption.

I have argued that one way of historicizing and hopefully making sense of this oppositional discourse is through the concept of republicanism which, in an American context, offers an ideological structure to the nation's values and its fears. I also argued that in both its motifs and themes, American Gothic takes the conceptual language of republicanism to nightmarish extremes. Engaging the political lexicon of corruption, tyranny and degeneration, it recounts for each American generation a new apocalyptic mood, a new 'terror dream'. It remains to be seen how future American writers of Gothic fiction will dramatize the contemporary conflict, whether the conceptual language of the early republic will inform their narratives, and whether, unconsciously or not, the anticipation of tyranny and lost liberty will incite Gothic terror in the twenty-first century.

Notes

[1] Frank Kermode, *Sense of an Ending: Studies in the Theory of Fiction* (Oxford: Oxford University Press, 2000), p. 96.
[2] Joanna Bourke, *Fear: A Cultural History* (London: Virago, 2005), pp. viv, x (original emphasis).
[3] Bourke, 'The politics of fear are blinding us to the humanity of others', *The Guardian* (Saturday, 1 October 2005), 28.
[4] Frank Furedi, 'When fear leaves us paralysed', *The Observer* (5 September 2005), 27.
[5] Susan Faludi, *The Terror Dream: What 9/11 Revealed About America* (New York: Atlantic Books, 2008).

Bibliography

Aldridge, John W., 'The metaphorical world of Truman Capote', in Joseph J. Waldmeir and John C. Waldmeir (eds), *The Critical Response to Truman Capote* (1951; Westport, Conn.: Greenwood Press, 1999), pp. 32–48.
Appleby, Joyce, 'Republicanism and ideology', *American Quarterly*, 37, 4 (1985), 461–73.
Arendt, Hannah, *On Revolution* (1963; Middlesex: Penguin, 1973).
Bacon, Jon Lance, *Flannery O'Connor and Cold War Culture* (Cambridge: Cambridge University Press, 1993).
Bailyn, Bernard, *Pamphlets of the American Revolution: 1750–1776, Vol. 1* (Cambridge, Mass.: Harvard University Press, 1965).
Baker, Brian, 'Gothic masculinities', in Catherine Spooner and Emma McEvoy (eds), *The Routledge Companion to Gothic* (London: Routledge, 2007), pp. 164–73.
Baldanza, Frank, 'Plato in Dixie', *Georgia Review*, XII (1958), 151–67.
Baldick, Chris and Robert Mighall, 'Gothic criticism', in David Punter (ed.), *A Companion to the Gothic* (Oxford: Blackwell, 2000), pp. 209–28.
Barker, John, 'Changing frontiers', *Wilson Quarterly*, VII, 1 (1983), 88–99.
Barruél, Augustin, *Mémoires pour servir à l'histoire du Jacobinisme* (London: E. Booker, 1797).
Beard, Charles A., *An Economic Interpretation of the Constitution of the United States* (1913; New York: Macmillan, rev. edn 1935).
—— and Mary R. Beard, *The Rise of American Civilization*, vol. 1 and 2 (New York: Macmillan, n.d.).
Beaumont, Charles, 'Place of meeting', in Alan Ryan (ed.), *The Penguin Book of Vampire Stories* (London: Penguin, 1987), pp. 371–5.

Bell, Daniel, *The End of Ideology* (New York: Collier Books, 1961).
Bercovitch, Sacvan, *The Rites of Assent: Transformations in the Symbolic Construction of America* (New York: Routledge, 1993).
Biskind, Peter, *Seeing is Believing: Or How Hollywood Taught Us to Stop Worrying and Love the 50s* (1983; London: Bloomsbury, 2000).
Bloch, Ruth H., 'The gendered meanings of virtue in republican America', *Signs: Journal of Women in Culture and Society*, 13, 1 (1987), 37–58.
Botting, Fred, *Gothic* (London: Routledge, 1996).
——, 'In Gothic darkly: heterotopia, history, culture', in David Punter (ed.), *A Companion to the Gothic* (Oxford: Blackwell, 2000), pp. 3–14.
——, 'Preface', in Fred Botting (ed.), *The Gothic, Essays and Studies*, 54 (Cambridge: D. S. Brewer, 2001), 1–6.
Bourdieu, Pierre, *In Other Words: Essays Towards a Reflective Sociology* (Stanford: Stanford University Press, 1990).
Bourke, Joanna, *Fear: A Cultural History* (London: Virago, 2005).
——, 'The politics of fear are blinding us to the humanity of others', *The Guardian* (Saturday, 1 October 2005), 28.
Bridgman, Richard, 'Jefferson's farmer before Jefferson', *American Quarterly*, 14, 4 (1962), 567–77.
Brockden Brown, Charles, *Wieland; Or the Transformation: An American Tale* (Kent, Ohio: Kent State University Press, 1977).
——, *Ormond: Or the Secret Witness* (Kent, Ohio: Kent State University Press, 1982).
——, *Edgar Huntly, Or Memoirs of a Sleep-Walker* (New York: Penguin, 1988).
——, *Wieland; Or the Transformation: An American Tale*, ed. Jay Fliegelman (New York: Penguin, 1991).
Burke, Edmund, 'Reflections on the revolution in France and on the proceedings in certain societies in London relative to that event', in *The Works of the Right Honourable Edmund Burke, Vol. II* (London: Henry G. Bohn, 1854), pp. 277–518.
——, 'Thoughts on the cause of the present discontents', in *The Works of The Right Honourable Edmund Burke, Vol. 1* (London: Henry G. Bohn, 1854), 306–81.
——, 'Letter to the Abbé Barruél, May 1, 1797', in R. B. McDowell and John A. Wood (eds), *The Correspondence of Edmund Burke, Vol. IX* (Chicago: Chicago University Press, 1970), 319–20.
Butler, Marilyn, 'Introduction', in Marilyn Butler (ed.), *Burke, Paine, Godwin, and the Revolution Controversy* (New York: Cambridge University Press, 1984), pp. 1–17.

Bibliography

Capote, Truman, *In Cold Blood: A True Account of a Multiple Murder and its Consequences* (1965; Bristol: The Reprint Society, 1967).

——, 'Ghosts in sunlight: the filming of *In Cold Blood*', in *Truman Capote, A Capote Reader* (London: Penguin, 2002), pp. 621–7.

Carpenter, Frederick, 'The American myth: paradise (to be) regained', *PMLA*, 74 (1959), 599–606.

Carmichael, Virginia, *Framing History: The Rosenberg Story and the Cold War* (Minneapolis: University of Minnesota Press, 1993).

Chase, Richard, *The American Novel and its Tradition* (London: G. Bell and Sons, 1957).

Chomsky, Noam, *Deterring Democracy* (London: Vintage, 1992).

Clarke, Gerald, *Capote: A Biography* (London: Ballantine, 1989).

Clery, E. J. and Robert Miles (eds), *Gothic Documents: A Sourcebook, 1700–1820* (Manchester: Manchester University Press, 2000).

Cohen, Lester H., 'Explaining the revolution: ideology and ethics in Mercy Otis Warren's historical theory', *William and Mary Quarterly*, 37, 2 (1980), 200–18.

Colbourn, Trevor H., 'Thomas Jefferson's use of the past', *William and Mary Quarterly*, 15, 1 (1958), 56–70.

Cuordileone, K. A., '"Politics in an Age of Anxiety": cold war political culture and the crisis in American masculinity, 1949–1960', *The Journal of American History*, 87, 2 (2000), 1–25.

Davenport-Hines, Richard, *Gothic: 400 Years of Excess, Horror, Evil and Ruin* (London: Fourth Estate, 1998).

Davidson, Cathy N., *Revolution and the Word: The Rise of the Novel in America* (Oxford: Oxford University Press, expanded edn 2004).

de Crèvecoeur, J. Hector St Jean, *Letters from an American Farmer*, in Nina Baym et al. (eds), *The Norton Anthology of American Literature, Vol. 1* (4th edn; New York: W. W. Norton, 1994), pp. 657–81.

Dean, Robert D., 'Masculinity as ideology: John F. Kennedy and the domestic politics of foreign policy', *Diplomatic History*, 22, 1 (1998), 29–62.

Deane, Seamus, *The French Revolution and Enlightenment in England, 1789–1832* (Cambridge, Mass.: Harvard University Press, 1988).

Dupee, F. W., 'Truman Capote's score', in I. Malin (ed.), *Truman Capote's In Cold Blood: A Critical Handbook* (Belmont, CA: Wadsworth, 1968), pp. 68–76.

Dutcher, George M., 'The rise of republican government in the United States', *Political Science Quarterly*, LV, 2 (1940), 199–216.

Edwards, Justin D., *Gothic Passages: Racial Ambiguity and the American Gothic* (Iowa City: University of Iowa Press, 2003).

Eisenhower, Dwight D., 'First inaugural address' (20 January 1953), The Dwight D. Eisenhower Library, http://www.eisenhower.archives.gov/1stinaug. htm (accessed 19 July 2004).

——, 'Farewell address' (17 January 1961), The Dwight D. Eisenhower Library, http://www.eisenhower.archives.gov/farewell.htm (accessed 19 June 2004).

Eisinger, Chester E., 'The freehold concept in eighteenth-century American letters', *William and Mary Quarterly*, IV, 1 (1947), 42–59.

——, 'Land and loyalty: literary expressions of agrarian nationalism in the seventeenth and eighteenth Centuries', *American Literature*, 21, 2 (1947), 160–78.

——, *Fiction of the Forties* (Chicago: Chicago University Press, 1963).

Ely, David, *Seconds* (London: Four Square, 1963).

Faludi, Susan, *The Terror Dream: What 9/11 Revealed About America* (New York: Atlantic Books, 2008).

Fiedler, Leslie, *Love and Death in the American Novel* (2nd edn; New York: Dell, 1966).

Ferguson, Robert A., *Reading the Early Republic* (Cambridge, Mass.: Harvard University Press, 2004).

Frankel, Haskel, 'An interview with Truman Capote', *Saturday Review*, vol. XLIX (1966), 36–7.

Friedan, Betty, *The Feminine Mystique* (New York: Penguin, 1963).

Friedman, Melvin J., 'Towards an aesthetic: Truman Capote's other voices', in I. Malin (ed.), *Truman Capote's* In Cold Blood: *A Critical Handbook* (Belmont, CA: Wadsworth, 1968), pp. 163–76.

Freneau, Philip, 'The American village', in ed. Fred Lewis Pattee, *The Poems of Philip Freneau, Vol. 3* (New York: Russell & Russell, 1963), pp. 381–393.

——, 'The rising glory of America', in ed. Fred Lewis Pattee, *The Poems of Philip Freneau, Vol. 1* (New York: Russell & Russell, 1963), pp. 49–84.

Furedi, Frank, 'When fear leaves us paralysed', *The Observer* (5 September 2005), 27.

Galloway, David, 'Why the chickens came home to roost in Holcomb, Kansas: Truman Capote's *In Cold Blood*', in I. Malin (ed.), *Truman Capote's* In Cold Blood: *A Critical Handbook* (Belmont, CA: Wadsworth, 1968), pp. 154–62.

Geertz, Clifford, 'Ideology as a cultural system', *The Interpretation of Cultures* (New York: Basic Books, 1973).

George III's 'Address to Parliament' (27 October 1775), Library of Congress, http://memory.loc.gov/learn/features/timeline/amrev/shots/address.html (accessed 21 March 2005).

Bibliography

Gibbon, Edward, *The Decline and Fall of the Roman Empire* (Middlesex: Penguin, 1966).
Goddu, Teresa, *Gothic America: Narrative, History, and Nation* (New York: Columbia University Press, 1997).
Gribbin, William, 'Rollin's histories and American republicanism', *William and Mary Quarterly*, 29, 4 (1972), 611–22.
Hartz, Louis, *The Liberal Tradition in America: An Interpretation of American Political Thought since the Revolution* (New York: Harcourt Brace, 1955).
Hassan, Ihab, 'The daydream and nightmare of Narcissus', *Wisconsin Studies in Contemporary Literature*, 1, 2 (1960), 5–21.
——, *Radical Innocence: Studies in the Contemporary American Novel* (Princeton: Princeton University Press, 1961).
Hedges, William L., 'The myth of the republic and the theory of American literature', *Prospects*, 4 (1974), 101–20.
Hicks, Jack, '"Fire, Fire, Fire Flowing Like a River, River, River": history and postmodernism in Truman Capote's *Handcarved Coffins*', in Joseph J. Waldmeir and John C. Walmeir (eds), *The Critical Response to Truman Capote* (Westport: Greenwood Press, 1999), pp. 167–77.
Hoffmeister, Gerhart, 'From Goethe's *Wilhelm Meister* to anti-*Meister* novels: the Romantic novel between Tieck's *William Lovell* and Hoffman's *Kater Murr*', in Dennis F. Mahoney (ed.), *The Literature of German Romanticism*, Vol. 8 (New York: Camden House, 2004), pp. 79–100.
Hofstadter, Richard, 'The paranoid style in American politics', in *The Paranoid Style in American Politics and other Essays* (New York: Vintage, 1965), pp. 3–40.
——, *The Progressive Historians: Turner, Beard, Parrington* (New York: A.A. Knopf, 1968).
Hogle, Jerrold E. (ed.), *The Cambridge Companion to Gothic Fiction* (Cambridge: Cambridge University Press, 2002).
Hoover, J. Edgar, *Masters of Deceit: The Story of Communism in America* (London: Dent and Sons, 1958).
Howe, Irving, 'This age of conformity', in Philip Rahv and William Phillips (eds), *The Partisan Review Anthology* (1954; London: Macmillan, 1962), pp. 145–64.
Howe, Jr., John R., 'Republican thought and the political violence of the 1790s', *American Quarterly*, 19, 1 (1967), 147–65.
Hughes, William, 'Vampire', in Marie Mulvey-Roberts (ed.), *The Handbook to Gothic Literature* (New York: New York University Press, 1998), pp. 240–5.

Hunter, James Davison, 'The modern malaise', in James Davison Hunter and Stephen C. Ainlay (eds), *Making Sense of Modern Times* (London: Routledge & Kegan Paul, 1986), pp. 76–100.

Hurley, Kelly, *The Gothic Body: Sexuality, Materialism, and Degeneration at the Fin de Siècle* (Cambridge: Cambridge University Press, 1996).

——, 'British Gothic fiction, 1835–1930', in Jerrold E. Hogle (ed.), *The Cambridge Companion to Gothic Fiction* (Cambridge: Cambridge University Press, 2002), pp. 189–208.

Huxley, Aldous, *Brave New World Revisited* (New York: Harper and Row, 1965).

Ingebretsen, Edward J., *At Stake: Monsters and the Rhetoric of Fear in Public Culture* (Chicago: Chicago University Press, 2001).

Jefferson, Thomas, *A Summary View of the Rights of British America* (1774), The Avalon Project at Yale Law School, http://www.yale.edu/lawweb/avalon/jeffsumm.htm (accessed 14 January 2004).

——, 'Declaration of independence', in Robert Birley (ed.), *Speeches and Documents in American History: Vol. 1: 1776–1815* (London: Oxford University Press, n.d.), pp. 1–5.

——, *A Declaration by the Representatives of the United States of America, in General Congress Assembled*, in Nina Baym et al. (eds), *The Norton Anthology of American Literature*, vol. 1 (4th edn; New York: W. W. Norton, 1994), 729–33.

——, *Notes on the State of Virginia*, The Avalon Project, Yale Law School, http://www.yale.edu/lawweb/Avalon/jefffram.htm (accessed 14 January 2004).

——, to James Madison (20 December 1787), Jefferson Digital Archive, University of Virginia Library, http://etext.lib.virginia.edu/jefferson/ (accessed 2 February 2005).

——, to James Madison (15 November 1795), Jefferson Digital Archive, University of Virginia Library, http://etext.lib.virginia.edu/jefferson/ (accessed 7 March 2006).

——, 'First inaugural address', in Robert Birley (ed.), *Speeches and Documents in American History: Vol. 1: 1776–1815* (London: Oxford University Press, n.d.), pp. 251–6.

——, to John Norwell (14 June 1807), Jefferson Digital Archive, University of Virginia Library, http://etext.lib.virginia.edu (accessed 3 March 2005).

Kaid, Lynda Lee, 'Political processes and television', *The Museum of Broadcast Communications*, http://www.museum.tv/archives/etv/P/html.

Kallen, Stuart A. (ed.), *Sixties Counterculture* (San Diego: Greenhaven Press, 2001).

Bibliography

Kaufman, Irving, 'Judge Kaufman's statement upon sentencing the Rosenbergs', *Famous Trials*, University of Missouri-Kansas City, http://law.umkc.edu/faculty/projects/ftrials/rosenb/ROS_SENT.HTM (accessed 25 March 2006).

Kaufman, Stanley, 'Capote in Kansas', in I. Malin (ed.), *Truman Capote's In Cold Blood: A Critical Handbook* (Belmont, CA: Wadsworth, 1968), pp. 60–4.

Kennan, George, *Memoirs: 1925–1950* (London: Hutchinson, 1967).

Kennedy, John F., 'Are we up to the task?', *The Strategy of Peace* (New York: Harper Collins, 1960).

——, 'The presidency in 1960', address by Senator John F. Kennedy, National Press Club, Washington DC (14 January 1960), John F. Kennedy Library and Museum, http://www.jfklibrary.org/Historical+Resources/Archives/Reference+Desk/speeches/JFK/JFK+Pre-Pres/1960/The+Presidency+in+1960.htm.

——, Address of Senator Robert F. Kennedy accepting the Democratic Party nomination for the presidency of the United States' (15 July 1960), John F. Kennedy Library and Museum, http://www.jfklibrary.org/Asset+Tree/Asset+Viewers/Audio+Video+Asset+Viewer.htm?guid=%7BB9D9721F-64AB-4624-800D-C38EFE69241B%7D&type=Audio/.

——, 'Inaugural address' (20 January 1961), The Avalon Project at Yale Law School, http://www.yale.edu/lawweb/avalon/presiden/inaug/kennedy.htm (accessed 10 April 2006).

Kerber, Linda, 'Republican ideology of the revolutionary generation', *American Quarterly*, 37, 4 (1985), 474–95.

Kermode, Frank, *Sense of an Ending: Studies in the Theory of Fiction* (Oxford: Oxford University Press, 2000), p. 96.

Kilgour, Maggie, *The Rise of the Gothic Novel* (London: Routledge, 1995).

King, Stephen, *Salem's Lot* (1975; New York: Simon & Schuster, 1999).

Kliger, Samuel, 'Emerson and the usable Anglo-Saxon past', *Journal of the History of Ideas*, 16, 4 (1955), 476–93.

Kloppenberg, James T., 'The virtues of liberalism: Christianity, republicanism, and ethics in early American political discourse', *The Journal of American History*, 74, 1 (1987), 9–33.

Lawson-Peebles, Robert, *American Literature before 1880* (Harlow: Pearson Longman, 2003).

Lears, Jackson, 'A matter of taste: corporate cultural hegemony in a mass-consumption society', in Lary May (ed.), *Recasting America: Culture and Politics in the Age of Cold War* (Chicago: Chicago University Press, 1989), pp. 38–57.

Leiber, Fritz, 'The girl with the hungry eyes', in Alan Ryan (ed.), *The Penguin Book of Vampire Stories* (New York: Penguin, 1987), p. 335
Levin, Ira, *Rosemary's Baby* (1967; London: Pan, 1968).
Levine, Robert S., *Conspiracy and Romance: Studies in Brockden Brown, Cooper, Hawthorne, and Melville* (Cambridge: Cambridge University Press, 1989).
Lewis, R. W. B., *The American Adam: Innocence, Tragedy and Tradition in the Nineteenth Century* (Chicago: Chicago University Press, 1955).
MacDonald, Dwight, 'A theory of mass culture', in Bernard Rosenberg and David Manning White (eds), *Mass Culture: The Popular Arts in America* (Glencoe, Ill.: Free Press, 1957), pp. 59–73.
McLay, Wilfred A., 'The hipster and the organization man', *First Things*, 43 (1994), 23–30.
McWilliams, Carey, *Witch Hunt: The Revival of Heresy* (Westport, CT: Greenwood Press, 1950).
Madison, James, 'The Federalist, no. 10', in Nina Baym et al. (eds), *Norton Anthology of American Literature*, vol. 1 (4th edn; New York: W. W. Norton, 1994).
Malin, Irving, *New American Gothic* (Illinois: Southern Illinois University Press, 1962).
Mandeville, Bernard, *The Fable of the Bees: Or, Private Vices, Publick Benefits*, ed. F. G. Kaye (Oxford: Clarendon Press, 1924).
Martin, Robert K. and Eric Savoy (eds), *American Gothic: New Interventions in a National Narrative* (Iowa City: University of Iowa Press, 1998).
Marx, Leo, *The Machine in the Garden: Technology and the Pastoral Ideal in America* (London: Oxford University Press, 1964).
Matheson, Richard, *I Am Legend* (New York: Orb, 1995).
Matson, Cathy, 'Toward a republican empire: interest and ideology in revolutionary America', *American Quarterly*, 37, 4 (1985), 496–531 (498).
May, Ernest (ed.), *American Cold War Strategy: Interpreting NSC68* (Boston: Bedford Books, 1993).
May, Lary, 'Introduction', in Lary May (ed.), *Recasting America: Culture and Politics in the Age of Cold War* (Chicago: Chicago University Press, 1989), pp. 1–16.
Mazzeo, Joseph Anthony, 'Some interpretations of the history of ideas', *Journal of the History of Ideas*, 33, 3 (1972), 379–94 (389).
Melton, Gordon J. (ed.), *The Vampire Book: The Encyclopedia of the Undead* (Farmington Hills, MI: Visible Ink Press, 1999).
Miles, Robert, '"Tranced Griefs": Melville's *Pierre* and the origins of the Gothic', *ELH*, 66, 1 (1999), 157–77.

Bibliography

———, 'Introduction', in Anne Radcliffe, *The Italian*, ed.Robert Miles (London: Penguin, 2000), pp. vii–xxxiii.

———, *Gothic Writing, 1750–1820: A Genealogy* (Manchester: Manchester University Press, 2002).

Miller, Douglas T. and Marion Nowak, *The Fifties: The Way We Really Were* (New York: Double Day, 1975).

Mills, C. Wright, *White Collar: The American Middle Classes* (New York: Oxford University Press, 1951).

Morse, Jedidiah, 'A SERMON, Delivered at the New North Church in Boston, in the Morning, and In the Afternoon at Charleston, May 9th, 1798, Being the Day Recommended by JOHN ADAMS, President of the United States of America, for Solemn Humiliation, Fasting and Prayer', *Early American Imprints, Series I*, Evan's Document Display, http://infoweb.newsbank.com/iw-search/we/Evans (accessed 6 March 2006).

Mulvey-Roberts, Marie (ed.), *The Handbook to Gothic Literature* (New York: New York University Press, 1998).

Navasky, Victor, S., *Naming Names* (New York: Viking Press, 1980).

Nixon, Richard, '"What was the Hiss Case?" An answer for Trisha' (1962), *Famous Trials*, University of Missouri-Kansas City, http://www.law.umkc.edu/faculty/projects/ftrials/hiss/nixononhisscase.html (accessed 2 April 2006).

Packard, Vance, *The Hidden Persuaders* (1957; London: Penguin, 1981).

Paine, Thomas, *Common Sense* (London: Penguin, rev. edn 2004).

———, *Rights of Man*, ed. Gregory Claey (Indianapolis: Hackett, 1992).

Paulin, Tom, *Crusoe's Secret: The Aesthetics of Dissent* (London: Faber, 2005).

Payson, Edward, *Memoir and Selected Thoughts*, vol. 1, http://pbministries.org/articles/payson/the_works_vol_1/payson_vol_1.htm (accessed 14 June 2006).

Persons, Stow, 'The cyclical theory of history in eighteenth-century America', *American Quarterly*, 6, 2 (1954), 147–63.

Pitt, William (Earl of Chatham), 'Speech to the House of Lords' (2 November 1770), *The Speeches of Lord Chatham*, http://classicpersuasion.org/cbo/chatham/chat11.htm (accessed 12 August 2006).

Playfair, John, 'Biographical account of the late John Robison, LL.D, F.R.S. Edin. and professor of natural philosophy in the University of Edinburgh', in *Transactions of the Royal Society of Edinburgh*, vol. 7 (Edinburgh: Archibald Constable, 1814), 495–531.

Plimpton, George, 'The story behind a nonfiction novel', *New York Times Review of Books* (16 January 1966), 2–3.

———, *Truman Capote* (London: Anchor Books, 1998).

Pocock, J. G. A., *The Machiavellian Moment: Florentine Republican Thought and the Atlantic Republican Tradition* (Princeton: Princeton University Press, 1975).

———, 'Gibbon's decline and fall and the world view of the late Enlightenment', *Eighteenth Century Studies*, 10, 3 (1977), 287–303.

———, *Virtue, Commerce, and History: Essays on Political Thought and History, Chiefly in the Eighteenth Century* (New York: Cambridge University Press, 1985).

———, 'Between Gog and Magog: the republican thesis and the ideologia Americana', *Journal of the History of Ideas*, 48, 2 (1987), 325–46.

Punter, David, *The Literature of Terror: Volume 1, The Gothic Tradition* (New York: Longman, 1996).

———, and Glennis Byron, *The Gothic* (Blackwell: Oxford, 2004).

Rahv, Philip, 'Our country and our culture', *Partisan Review*, 19 (1952), 283–326.

———, 'Fiction and the criticism of fiction', *Kenyon Review*, 18 (1956), 276–99.

Rance, Nick, '"Truly Serpentine": "New Journalism", *In Cold Blood* and the Vietnam war', *Literature and History*, 11, 2 (2002), 78–100.

Reising, Russell. J., *The Unusable Past: Theory and the Study of American Literature* (New York: Methuen, 1986).

Riesman, David, Nathan Glazer and Reuel Denney, *The Lonely Crowd: A Study of the Changing American Character* (1950; New Haven: Yale University Press, 1961).

Robbins, Caroline, 'Algernon Sidney's *Discourses Concerning Government*: Textbook for revolution', *William and Mary Quarterly*, 4, 3 (1947), 267–96.

———, 'The strenuous Whig: Thomas Hollis of Lincoln's Inn', *William and Mary Quarterly*, 7, 3 (1950), 406–53.

Roberts, J. M., *The Mythology of the Secret Societies* (London: Secker and Warburg, 1972).

Robison, John, *Proofs of a Conspiracy against all the Religions and Governments of Europe* (London: T. Cadell and W. Davies, 1797).

Rogers, Daniel T., 'Republicanism: the career of a concept', *The Journal of American History*, 79, 1 (1992), 11–38.

Rogin, Michael, 'Kiss me deadly: communism, motherhood, and cold war movies', *Representations*, 6 (1984), 1–36.

Roosevelt, Theodore, *Proceedings of the Congress of Constructive Patriotism*, Washington DC (New York: National Security League, 25–7 January 1917), p. 172.

Bibliography

Rossiter, Clinton, L., 'Nationalism and American identity in the early republic', in Sean Wilentz (ed.), *Major Problems in the Early Republic: 1787–1848* (Lexington: D. C. Heath, 1992), pp. 14–23.

Rotundo, Anthony E., *American Manhood: Transformations in Masculinity from the Revolution to the Modern Era* (NewYork: Basic Books, 1993).

Rumsfeld, Donald 'Speech' (Tuesday, 27 May 2003), *The Guardian Unlimited http://www.guardian.co.uk/* (accessed 3 December 2007).

Savoy, Eric, 'The rise of American Gothic', in Jerrold E. Hogle (ed.), *The Cambridge Companion to Gothic Fiction* (Cambridge: Cambridge University Press, 2002), pp. 167–88.

Schilling, Bernard N., 'The English case against Voltaire: 1789–1800', *Journal of the History of Ideas*, 4, 2 (1943), 193–216.

Schlesinger, Jr., Arthur M., *The Vital Center: The Politics of Freedom* (Cambridge, Mass.: Riverside Press, 1949).

——, *The Politics of Hope* (London: Eyre and Spottiswoode, 1964).

Sekora, John, *Luxury: The Concept in Western Thought, Eden to Smollett* (Baltimore: John Hopkins University Press, 1977).

Shalhope, Robert E., 'Toward a republican synthesis: the emergence of an understanding of republicanism in American historiography', *William and Mary Quarterly*, 29, 1 (1972), 49–80.

Sheatsley, P. B., and J. S. Feldman, 'A national survey of public reactions and behaviour', in Bradley S. Greenberg and Edwin B. Parker (eds), *The Kennedy Assassination and the American Public: Social Communication in Crisis* (Stanford: Stanford University Press, 1965).

Shelley, Percy Bysshe, 'A defense of Poetry', in M. H. Abrams et al.(eds), *The Norton Anthology of English Literature*, vol. 2 (NewYork:W.W. Norton, 1962).

Sherwood, Samuel, 'The church's flight into the wilderness: an address on the times', *Political Sermons of the American Founding Era, 1730–1895* (1 April 1776), ed. Ellis Sandoz, part II: 1774–81, *http://oll.libertyfund.org/Texts/LFBooks* (accessed 3 June 2006).

Shklar, Judith, 'Let us not be hypocritical', *DÆDALUS: Journal of the American Academy of Arts and Sciences*, 108, 3 (1979), 1–25.

Smith, Henry Nash, *Virgin Land: The American West as Symbol and Myth* (Cambridge, Mass., Harvard University Press, 1950).

Smith-Rosenburg, Carroll, 'Dis-covering the subject of the "Great Constitutional Discussion", 1786–1789', *The Journal of American History*, 79, 3 (1992), 841–73.

——, 'The republican gentleman: the race to rhetorical stability in the new United States', in Stefan Dudink, Karen Hagemann and John Tosh (eds), *Masculinities in Politics and War: Gendering Modern History* (Manchester: Manchester University Press, 2004), pp. 61–76.
Sontag, Susan, *Against Interpretation* (New York: Dell Publishing, 1967).
Stauffer, Vernon, *New England and the Bavarian Illuminati* (New York: Columbia University Press, 1918).
Stevenson, Robert Louis, *Dr Jekyll and Mr Hyde* (1886; London: Penguin, 1994).
Suchoff, David, 'New historicism and containment: towards a post-cold war cultural theory', *Arizona Quarterly*, 48 (1992), 137–61.
Tanner, Tony, 'Death in Kansas', in I. Malin (ed.), *Truman Capote's In Cold Blood: A Critical Handbook* (Belmont, CA: Wadsworth, 1968), pp. 98–102.
Tise, Larry E., *The American Counterrevolution: A Retreat from Liberty, 1783–1800* (Mechanicsburg, PA: Stackpole, 1998).
Tompkins, Phillip K., 'In Cold Fact', in I. Malin (ed.), *Truman Capote's In Cold Blood: A Critical Handbook* (Belmont, CA: Wadsworth, 1968), pp. 44–58.
——, *The Liberal Imagination* (New York: Viking Press, 1950).
——, *Beyond Culture: Essays on Literature and Learning* (Middlesex: Penguin, 1963).
Turner, Frederick Jackson, *The Frontier in American History* (New York: Henry Holt, 1947).
Tyler, Moses Coit, *The Literary History of the American Revolution, 1763–1783* (New York: n.p., 1897).
Walpole, Horace, *The Castle of Otranto* (2nd edn; London: Oxford University Press, 1982).
Warner, Michael, *The Letters of the Republic: Publication and the Public Sphere in Eighteenth-Century America* (Cambridge, Mass.: Harvard University Press, 1990).
Warren, Charles, 'Samuel Adams and the Sans Souci Club in 1785', *Massachusetts Historical Society Proceedings*, 60 (1927), 318–44.
Washington, George, 'Sixth annual message', The Avalon Project at Yale Law School, http://www.yale.edu/lawweb/Avalon/presiden/sou/wash06.htm (accessed 18 December 2003).
Weinstein, Allen, 'The symbolism of subversion: notes on some cold war icons', *Journal of American Studies*, 6, 2 (1972), 165–79.
Whyte, Jr., William H., *The Organization Man* (New York: Anchor, 1956).
Wilson, Katharina M., 'The history of the word "Vampire"', *Journal of the History of Ideas*, 46, 4 (1985), 577–83.

Wood, Gordon S.,'Rhetoric and reality', *William and Mary Quarterly*, 23, 1 (1966), 3–32.

——, *The Creation of the American Republic, 1776–1787* (Williamsburg: University of North Carolina Press, 1969).

——, 'Conspiracy and the paranoid style: causality and deceit in the eighteenth century', *William and Mary Quarterly*, 39, 3 (1982), 401–41.

——, *The Radicalism of the American Revolution* (New York: A. A. Knopf, 1992).

Wordsworth, William, *The Borderers*, ed. Robert Osborn (London: Cornell University Press, 1982).

Yurick, Sol, 'Sob-sister Gothic', in I. Malin (ed.), *Truman Capote's In Cold Blood: A Critical Handbook* (Belmont, CA: Wadsworth, 1968), pp. 76–80.

Index

abhuman 81
Adams, Herbert Baxter 150, 151
Adams, John 22, 37, 41, 61, 83, 85, 91, 148
Adams, John Quincy 82
Adams, Samuel 83, 85
Administration of Justice Act 41
affirmative action 133
agrarianism 25, 144, 145, 147, 150, 151, 153, 155, 163, 164, 170
Aldridge, John 155
Alien and Sedition Acts 120
Alien Registration Act 4
Altizer, Thomas 133
American Bill of Rights 35
American renaissance 3, 6, 11
American Revolution 17, 21, 23, 24, 25, 27, 31, 32, 33, 35, 38–40, 60, 85, 110
ancien régime 85
Anglo-Saxon 20, 21, 23, 71, 165
anti-Catholicism 16, 108
  see also Catholicism
anti-Communism 67, 68, 69, 89, 108, 125, 127, 135, 154

  see also Communism
anti-Enlightenment 119, 123, 124, 175
  see also Enlightenment
anti-Federalist 36, 85, 86
  see also Federalist
antiquity 42, 43, 45, 59
apocalypse 58, 109, 121, 174, 175, 176
Arendt, Hannah 130
aristocracy 10, 12, 13, 16, 17, 37, 38, 43, 63, 114, 147, 148, 163
Arnold, Benedict 121
authenticity 36, 110, 126

Bailyn, Bernard 24, 35, 39–42, 44, 110
Baldick, Chris 15–16
barbarism 20, 22, 24, 60, 61, 66, 67, 72
Barruél, Augustin 118, 119, 120
  Mémoires 118
Beard, Charles 31, 32, 33
Beaumont, Charles 54
Bell, Daniel 3

Ben Hur (1959) 22
Bercovitch, Sacvan 7
Berendt, John
    Midnight in the Garden of Good
    and Evil 142
Biskind, Peter 68
Bolingbroke, Henry St John 55, 58
Boorstin, Daniel, J. 31, 32
Boston Tea Party 41
Botting, Fred 1, 8
Bourke, Joanna 174
Brocken Brown, Charles 6, 13,
    14, 16, 109, 122
    Edgar Huntly 6, 13, 122
    Ormond: Or, the Secret Witness
    122, 123
    Wieland; or the Transformation
    122–3
Burke, Edmund 17, 20, 111, 119,
    126
Butler, Marilyn 17, 19

cabalism 125
Calmet, Augustin 61
capitalism 3, 10, 23, 47, 48, 68,
    94, 151
Catholicism 16, 17, 108, 136,
    158, 169
    see also anti-Catholicism
Cato's Letters 39
causality 25, 110, 113, 114, 116,
    122, 124, 128, 160, 175
    see also determinism
Chase, Richard 5–6
Chomsky, Noam 47
Cicero 59
civic humanism 44, 88
Clarke, Gerald 156, 164
cold war 9, 23, 24, 25, 36, 47, 54,
    63, 64, 68, 71, 76, 82, 89–91,
    102, 103, 105, 107, 108, 124–6

common good 42, 60, 86, 87, 88
commonwealth 33, 34, 35, 42, 43,
    86
Communism 4, 24, 47, 54, 67–9,
    71, 78, 107, 108,124–7, 138–
    40, 152, 138, 152, 154, 155
    see also anti-communism; red
    scare
conformity 9, 22, 23, 25, 27, 81,
    82, 88, 90, 91, 98, 102, 154,
    161
conspiracy
    cold war 107, 115, 124–7, 129,
    130–1, 134, 138
    eighteenth-century 13, 19, 23,
    25, 34, 40, 41, 48, 107, 108–13,
    116, 117–20, 123–4
    post 9/11 175
consumerism 87, 88, 91, 110,
    132
containment 11, 67, 126, 153
Craftsman, The 62

Davidson, Cathy 10
de Crèvecoeur, Hector 14, 147
de Rapin, Paul 21
degeneration 23, 24, 43, 47, 48,
    53, 54, 55, 61, 63, 66, 67, 70,
    74, 75, 81, 84, 87, 99, 144, 170,
    176
    moral 121, 148
    national 10, 12, 24, 39, 53, 54,
    55, 57, 67, 77, 82, 175
determinism 76, 122, 123, 126,
    128, 151, 159
Dracula 70
Dwight, Timothy 118, 146
dystopia 69, 70, 82, 102

effeminacy 24, 25, 52, 81, 85, 87,
    88, 92, 103, 148, 166, 167

Index

Eisenhower, Dwight D. 46, 63–8, 77, 125
Eisinger, Chester E. 5, 145, 155
English Civil War 40
  see also Glorious Revolution
Enlightenment 8, 10, 16, 18, 19, 20, 25, 37, 39, 59, 81, 83, 85, 104, 112, 113, 115

Fall of the Roman Empire, The 22
Faludi, Susan 175
Faulkner, William 155
Federalist 36, 43, 44, 46, 85, 111, 114, 116, 117, 120
  see also anti-Federalist
Federalist, The 37
Fiedler, Leslie 2–3, 11–12
fin de siècle 81
Franklin, Benjamin 34, 118, 148
Freemasons 18, 108
French Revolution 8, 20, 85, 115, 117, 118, 119, 120
Freneau, Philip 146
Freud, Sigmund 31
Friedan, Betty 133, 141 n. 61
frontier, new 12, 46, 91–3, 98, 143, 151–2, 154, 165, 168
Furedi, Frank 175

Geertz, Clifford 44, 51 n. 43
George III, King 32, 110, 111
Gibbon, Edward 18, 129, 130
  The Decline and Fall of the Roman Empire 59, 80, 129
Glorious Revolution 19, 22
  see also English Civil War
Goddu, Teresa 2, 6
Godwin, William 6, 16, 120
  The Adventures of Caleb Williams 109, 122
Goldsmith, Oliver 146

Gordon, Thomas 35, 40
Goth, myth of 19–22
Great Awakening 55

Hamilton, Alexander 37, 151
Harrington, James 34, 35, 45
Hartz, Louis 31, 33
Hassan, Ihab 7, 155
Hawthorne, Nathaniel 7, 143
Hiss, Alger 125–6
Hoadly, Benjamin 40
Hofstadter, Richard 31, 32, 33, 108–9, 124
Hogg, James
  The Private Memoirs and Confessions of a Justified Sinner 109
Hollis, Thomas 17, 34, 35, 50 n. 18
Holme, John 145
Hoover, J. Edgar 67, 68, 75, 124, 125
Howe, Irving 7
Hurley, Kelly 80, 81
Huxley, Aldous 132
hypocrisy 25, 107, 109–10, 114, 121, 127, 128, 130–1, 138

Illuminati 12, 13, 108, 117–20, 123–4, 130

Jackson, Andrew 46
Jacobin plot 33, 115, 116–21, 130
James, Henry 12
Jefferson, Thomas 10, 11, 21, 32, 37, 57, 58, 60, 61, 65, 87
  agrarianism 46, 88, 144, 147, 148, 149, 150, 151, 153, 154
  conspiracy 110, 111, 114, 115, 119, 120
jeremiad 45, 83, 86, 175

Johnson, Samuel 34
Julius Caesar 22

Kaufman, Irving 126
Kaufmann, Stanley 155
Kennan, George 67, 68
Kennedy, John F. 48, 81, 89,
   91–3, 98, 125, 126, 134,
   136
Kennedy, Robert 125
Kenyon, Cecilia 23
Kerber, Linda 47
Kermode, Frank 174
King, Martin Luther 125
King, Stephen, 52–4
Kliger, Samuel 21, 26 n. 3

Leiber, Fritz 69
Lewis, Matthew 6, 16
   The Monk 122
Lewis, R. W. B. 152–3
liberalism 4–5, 7, 9, 18, 43, 44,
   46, 49 n. 3, 66, 90
   liberal ideology 3, 10, 15
   liberal historiography 8, 33,
      36, 109
Linder, Robert
   Must you Conform? 90
Locke, John 32–4, 39, 40, 44–6
loyalist 86, 110
Ludlow, Edmund 34, 35
luxury
   cold war 89, 91, 93, 109
   eighteenth-century 18, 24,
      25, 38, 41, 43, 48, 52, 58, 59–
      60, 62, 63, 66, 81, 83–5, 87,
      145, 148

McCarran Internal Security Act 4
McCarthy, Joseph 124, 125
McCullers, Carson 7, 155

Machiavelli, Niccolò 44, 45, 58,
   59, 86, 112
Madison, James 37, 111, 119
Mailer, Norman 98, 159
   The Executioner's Song 142
Malin, Irving 6–7
Mandeville, Bernard 114, 126,
   130
Marcuse, Herbert 132
Márquez, Gabriel Garcia,
   Chronicle of a Death Foretold 142
Martin, Robert K. 3
Marvell, Andrew 18, 34, 35
Marx, Leo 153–4, 167, 170
Marxism 3, 4, 31, 34
masculine virtue 25, 86, 87, 88,
   167
masculinity, crisis of 81, 82, 87,
   88, 92, 97, 98
mass culture 9, 22, 23, 90, 110,
   153
Massachusetts Government Act
   41
Mather, Moses 82
Maturin, Charles Robert,
   Melmoth the Wanderer 109
melodrama 6
Melville, Herman 7
Mighall, Robert 15–16
Miles, Robert 2, 20
military-industrial complex 46,
   66, 77
Mills, C. Wright 81, 93
   White Collar 90
Milton, John 17, 18, 34, 35, 40
modernity, fear of 10, 18, 45, 46,
   67, 69, 81, 164, 167
Molesworth, Robert 35, 40
monstrosity 7, 25, 32, 48, 68, 69,
   121, 138, 144, 156
Montesquieu 39, 40

Index

Morse, Jedidiah 117–19, 120, 126
nature versus culture 54, 71, 72, 74, 75, 76
Navasky, Victor 68
Nedham, Marchamont 35
New Critics 3
Newton, Isaac 113
Nixon, Richard 125, 136

O'Connor, Flannery 7, 155
Oppenheimer, Robert J. 68, 125
Organization man 5, 89, 90, 94, 95
  see also conformity; masculinity, crisis of
Oswald, Lee Harvey 125

Packard, Vance 96
Paine, Thomas 17, 37, 40, 56, 115, 119
paranoia 108–10, 112, 124, 125, 137–8
Parsons, Theophilous 86
pastoral 25, 58, 143, 146, 147, 150–4, 167, 170
Patriot Act 174
Paul, Arnold 61, 62
Paulin, Tom 48
Payson, Edward 63
Pennsylvania Packet 121
Persons, Stow 55, 61
Playfair, John 107, 115
Plimpton, George 160
pluralism 3, 6, 7, 46–7, 67–9, 74, 89, 90, 100, 102, 109
Plutarch 59
Pocock, J. G. A. 12, 18, 24, 35, 44–6, 48, 58, 149, 165
Poe, Edgar Allan 155
Presbyterianism 41

Price, Richard 39, 40, 119, 120, 145
Priestly, Joseph 39, 40, 119, 120
progress 4, 5, 10, 17, 18, 24, 36, 48, 53–61, 65, 67, 69, 70, 76, 92, 144, 150, 154, 162, 163, 164, 167, 169, 170
progressive historiography 31–2, 34, 36, 48–9, 53, 57, 65–6, 151
progressive ideology 3–5, 9, 23, 25, 68–9, 74, 89
propaganda 39, 40, 41, 42, 108, 125, 127
Providence 11, 55, 113, 114, 115, 146
psychological interpretations 2, 3, 6, 7, 15, 28 n. 51, 108, 110, 112, 143
public good 37, 43, 44, 81, 93, 147, 165, 166
  see also common good
Punter, David 11
puritanism 2, 9, 90

Quartering Act 41
Quebec Act 41
Quo Vadis? 22

Radcliffe, Anne 6, 16
  The Italian 122
Rahv, Philip 4, 5
red scare 68, 107, 108, 126
  see also Communism
Reising, Russell 4
Riesman, David
  The Lonely Crowd 90
Robbins, Caroline 23, 24, 33–5, 49 n. 17, 50 n. 18
Robison, John 120
  Proofs of a Conspiracy 118

195

Rogin, Michael 107–8
Rollin, Charles 56, 57, 59, 84
romance 5, 6, 17
romantic 5, 15–16, 80, 161, 168
Rosenberg, Emily 47
Rosenberg Trial 125, 126
Roosevelt, Theodore 48, 142
Rousseau, Jean-Jacques 40, 118
Rush, Benjamin 86

Sage, Victor 150
Sallust 59
Sans Souci Club 84, 85, 87
Savoy, Eric 3, 10, 109
Schlesinger, Jr., Arthur 5, 68, 89–91, 92, 93, 98
Second World War 4, 9, 31, 32, 68
secret societies 12, 100, 115, 116
secularism 9, 39, 45, 56–7, 61, 115, 121
Sekora, John 84, 87
Selective Service Act 4
self-deception 127, 128, 135, 138
self-interest 9, 10, 25, 32, 43, 62, 81, 84, 87, 88, 93, 103, 129, 131, 144, 149, 165, 166
Shelley, Percy Bysshe 124, 127
Sidney, Algernon 18, 33–5
sincerity 25, 37, 38, 121, 122, 123, 130, 131, 135, 136, 137, 142
slavery 2, 19, 40, 47, 59, 111
Smith, Henry Nash 151–2
Smith-Rosenburg, Carroll 86
Sontag, Susan 54
Soviet Union 5, 68, 108, 152, 154
Sparticus 22
Stamp Act 41
Stauffer, Vernon 116

Stevenson, Robert Louis
    Dr Jekyll and Mr Hyde 93
surveillance 70, 100, 124, 174

Tacitus 21, 59
Tanner, Tony 143, 156
Tappan, David 58, 59, 65, 118
terrorism 174, 175
Tory 17, 19, 34, 111
Townsend Duties 41
Trenchard, John 35, 40
Trilling, Diana 160
Trilling, Lionel 3–4
Truman, Harry 63, 125
Turner, Frederick Jackson 151
Tyler, Moses Coit 10, 11

un-American 4, 47
Un-American Activities Committee 4
utopia 5, 42, 57, 58, 69, 76, 95, 101, 102, 103, 147, 152, 164

Vietnam War 52, 126, 132, 133
virtue
    civic 17, 37, 38, 43, 82, 84, 86, 91, 93, 165, 166
    masculine 86–7
    private 38, 86, 147, 157
Volney, C. F.
    The Ruins 59
Voltaire 17, 39, 40, 63, 115, 118, 120
Voter's Rights Act 133

Walpole, Horace 17, 19
    The Castle of Otranto 17
Walpole, Robert 19
Warner, Michael 14, 15
Warren, Mercy Otis 52, 60, 82, 85, 148

Index

Warren Report 134
Washington, George 13, 63, 64,
  116, 118, 121
Watts Riots 133
Welty, Eudora 155
Weishaupt, Adam 118, 119
Whigs 12, 16, 17, 18, 19, 22, 26 n. 3,
  34, 38, 42, 43, 45, 110, 111, 115
  neo-Whigs 23, 24, 36, 46
  old (radical) Whigs 17, 18, 19,
  20, 21, 34, 35, 59, 115, 175

Whiskey Rebellion 116
Whyte, Jr., William H.
  The Organization Man 90, 94, 100
witchcraft 34, 127, 128, 130
Wood, Gordon S. 24, 35, 42–4, 46,
  59, 112, 115
Wordsworth, William 123
Wylie, Philip
  A Generation of Vipers 90

Yurick, Sol 156